A New Partnership in Education

From Consultation to Legislation in the Nineties

John Walshe

IPA

INSTITUTE OF PUBLIC
ADMINISTRATION

First published 1999
by the Institute of Public Administration
57-61 Lansdowne Road
Dublin 4

ISBN 1 902448 10 3

British Library Cataloguing in Publication Data
A catalogue record of this book is available from the
British Library

Cover design by Butler Claffey Design
Typeset in Garamond 10/11.5
by Wendy A. Commins, The Curragh
Printed by Criterion Press Limited

Contents

Acknowledgements

As a journalist, it has been my privilege to get to know the people who helped shape Irish educational policy for over a quarter of a century. Sometimes they influenced policy and practice in a planned way, sometimes in a political way, but always, it must be said, they did so with the best interests of the system and the students at heart.

I am indebted to a great number of people for their encouragement with this publication. The work began as an MEd thesis under the supervision of Professor Áine Hyland of the National University of Ireland, Cork, to whom I am especially grateful. It is unfair to mention some and not others but I must thank in particular Professor John Coolahan, Dr Tom Mitchell, Pat Keating, Ray Kennedy, Bro. Declan Duffy, Senator Joe O'Toole, Dave Gordan, Dr Séamus Ó Buachalla, George O'Callaghan, Fionnuala Kilfeather, John Hayden, Tom Turley and Tony McNamara. The Minister for Education and Science, Micheál Martin, his predecessors, officials and in particular the staff in the information section of the department were most helpful at all times, as were the teacher unions, church bodies, managerial and parental organisations as well as colleagues at Independent House.

There are many people who assisted me in this work but who must remain anonymous. Journalists have to protect sources and many who have helped me over the years also gave me invaluable support and information for this publication. I want to thank them all. It would, of course, have been impossible to write this book without the understanding and assistance of my family and I am forever thankful to Deirdre, Conor, Maria and Bryan for their forebearance and tolerance while I spent many hours monopolising the home computer.

Irish parents have long recognised what economists are increasingly able to measure – namely the 'payback' to spending on education. In a society which until recently could not have been described as wealthy, parents instinctively saw education as a form of 'cultural investment' and acted accordingly. They may not have had much material wealth to pass on to their children but they were very determined to give them the best opportunity in life and saw education as a means of doing just that. This book is dedicated to them and in particular to my parents – my mother Betty and my late father 'Capt. Jack', whom I proudly number among such selfless educators.

Abbreviations

ACS: Association of Community and Comprehensive Schools
AMCSS: Association of Management of Catholic Secondary Schools
ASTI: Association of Secondary Teachers Ireland
CERT: State Tourism Training Industry
CMRS: Conference of Major Religious Superiors
CORI: Conference of Religious of Ireland
CPSMA: Catholic Primary School Managers' Association
DCU: Dublin City University
DIT: Dublin Institute of Technology
FÁS: The Training and Employment Authority
FELLOWS: Senior academic staff in TCD who, along with the Provost, are
    the legal owners of the college
HEA: Higher Education Authority
IBEC: Irish Business and Employment Confederation
ICTU: Irish Congress of Trade Unions
INTO: Irish National Teachers' Organisation
ISA: Irish Schoolmasters' Association
IT: Information Technology
IVEA: Irish Vocational Education Association
JMB: Joint Managerial Body (of Protestant and Catholic secondary schools)
LEC: Local Education Council
MAYNOOTH: St Patrick's College, Maynoth
NCCA: National Council for Curriculum and Assessment
NCEA: National Council for Educational Awards
NCVA: National Council for Vocational Awards
NEC: National Education Convention
NESC: National Economic and Social Council
NUI: National University of Ireland
NUID: National University of Ireland, Dublin
NUIG: National University of Ireland, Galway
NUIM: National University of Ireland, Maynooth
REB: Regional Education Board
RTC: Regional Technical College
TCD or TRINITY: Trinity College Dublin, the sole constituent college of
    the University of Dublin
TEASTAS: The Irish National Certification Authority
TUI: Teachers' Union of Ireland
UCC: University College Cork
UCD: University College Dublin
UCG: University College Galway
UL: University of Limerick
VEC: Vocational Education Committee
WIT: Waterford Institute of Technology

Ministers for Education

Second Dáil:	J.J. O'Kelly	26/8/21 - 9/1/22
	Michael Hayes	11/1/22 - 9/9/22
Provisional Government:	Fintan Lynch	1/4/22 - 30/8/22
Acting Minister:	Michael Hayes	17/7/22 - 30/8/22
	Eoin Mac Neill	30/8/22 - 9/9/22
Third Dáil onwards:	Eoin Mac Neill	9/9/22 - 24/11/25
	John M. O'Sullivan	28/1/26 - 9/3/32
	Thomas Derrig	9/3/32 - 8/9/39
	Sean T. O'Ceallaigh	8/9/39 - 27/9/39
	Eamon de Valera	27/9/39 - 18/6/40
	Thomas Derrig	18/6/40 - 18/2/48
	Richard Mulcahy	18/2/48 - 14/6/51
	Sean Moylan	14/6/51 - 2/6/54
	Richard Mulcahy	2/6/54 - 20/3/57
	Jack Lynch	20/3/57 - 24/6/59
	Patrick J. Hillery	24/6/59 - 21/4/65
	George Colley	21/4/65 - 13/7/66
	Donogh O'Malley	13/7/66 - 10/3/68
	Jack Lynch (Taoiseach and Acting Minister for Education)	11/3/68 - 26/3/68
	Brian J. Lenihan	27/3/68 - 2/7/69
	Padraig Faulkner	2/7/69 - 14/3/73
	Richard Burke	14/3/73 - 1/12/76
	Peter Barry	2/12/76 - 14/7/77
	John P. Wilson	15/7/77 - 30/6/81
	John Boland	1/7/81 - 9/3/82
	Martin O'Donoghue	9/3/82 - 6/10/82
	Charles J. Haughey (Taoiseach and Acting Minister for Education)	6/10/82 - 27/10/82
	Gerard Brady	27/10/82 - 14/12/82
	Gemma Hussey	14/12/82 - 13/2/86
	Patrick Cooney	14/2/86 - 10/3/87
	Mary O'Rourke	11/3/87 - 13/11/91
	Noel Davern	14/11/91 - 11/2/92
	Séamus Brennan	12/2/92 - 12/1/93
	Niamh Bhreathnach	13/1/92 - 17/11/94
	Michael Smyth (Acting)	17/11/94 - 15/12/94
	Niamh Bhreathnach	15/12/94 - 26/6/97
	Micheál Martin	26/6/97....

Michael Woods.

ix

Noel Dempsey
Mary Hanafin.

Introduction

The final quarter of the twentieth century saw extraordinary changes in the Irish psyche and in Irish society. The transformations touched virtually every aspect of life in Ireland – personal, educational, economic and political. Changes that were working their way through the body politic and the body social in the seventies and eighties came to the surface in the nineties, catching many people unawares.

The most obvious changes were economic. Standards of living and GNP rose steadily, and towards the end of the nineties the labour market began to tighten with skill shortages emerging in many growth areas. Job creation agencies proudly boasted that they had attracted most of the international software giants to set up plants in Ireland. These, in turn, heightened awareness of globalisation and the need for further investment in fast moving information technologies.

The boom reversed the migration patterns of decades. It was easy to forget that in the eighties almost 200,000 people left, mostly in the second half of the decade. The demographic and psychological effects of this haemorrhage on the country were noted by Professor Liam Ryan from the National University of Ireland, Maynooth. He pointed out that in Ireland in 1988, probably uniquely among the nations of the earth, the numbers leaving (45,000 approx.) came close to the annual number being born (54,000).[1] The emigrants were not only the poorly educated of earlier decades; a fifth of those who qualified with primary degrees in 1988 obtained employment overseas.[2]

---

[1] Liam Ryan, 'Irish Emigration to Britain since World War II', in Kearney, Richard (Ed.), *Migrations: The Irish at Home and Abroad,* Dublin, Wolfhound Press, 1990.

[2] Higher Education Authority, *First Destination of Award Recipients in Higher Education (1992)*, Dublin, HEA, May 1994.

Governments did much to prepare the ground for the economic success through controls on public spending, while modest pay rises, coupled with infrastructural development and particularly investment in education and training, formed part of successive agreements with the social partners. But the stock of politicians dropped in public opinion following a number of tribunals which found that some were cosying up to big business too much. Governments had more success in Northern Ireland where the outline of a peace agreement began to take hold. Voices that were once banned on the national and UK airwaves were heard around the world proclaiming a new vision of peace for Northern Ireland.

In sexual politics much changed in the latter part of the century. Divorce was introduced after a referendum narrowly agreed a change in the constitution. The provision of information on abortion was legalised even if there was a political reluctance to deal with the issue of abortion itself through legislation. Homosexual practice was legalised, admittedly following pressure from Europe, while few voices were heard in the late nineties objecting to the installation of contraceptive vending machines in public houses and elsewhere.

Europe loomed ever larger in Irish affairs with moves towards greater political and economic union. The country benefited in many respects from membership of the European Union, most obviously in transfers from the EU budget. Agriculture was the major beneficiary but other sectors also received a financial boost. For the period 1994 to 1999, for instance, Ireland agreed with the EU a substantial developmental programme of education measures involving a total expenditure of £1.5b. This funded many schemes at home, providing, for instance, badly needed places for students at third-level courses in institutes of technology and training places in FÁS centres for jobless adults. EU membership also allowed Irish students, teachers and institutions to participate in a variety of transnational projects such as SOCRATES and LEONARDO DA VINCI.

As the nineties drew to a close, Irish people no longer saw themselves as simply being members of a European club – they felt that they had a role on the broader world stage. They developed an increasing confidence in their ability to deal with the world on its own terms. There was great pride in, but no longer surprise over, the success of sportstars, musicians, novelists, poets, and other artists. This confidence was seen most commercially and visibly in the *Riverdance* phenomenon which swept the globe with its modernised version of traditional Irish music.

Throughout this period of sometimes bewildering economic and social change the education system developed exponentially. By the end of the nineties, 82-84 per cent of the relevant age cohort finished senior-cycle programmes in second-level schooling. Proportionately more young people went into further and higher education in Ireland than in the UK although the figure was still some way off world leaders such as the US.

Many initiatives were taken to meet growing concerns over the lot of the disadvantaged in society. The aptly named Breaking the Cycle was perhaps the most significant, targeting primary schools in disadvantaged urban and rural areas. The education and training systems combined forces for other programmes such as Youthreach which was aimed at disadvantaged young people in their mid-teens, yet still a few thousand slipped through the net every year into an uncertain future on the edges of the labour market. A variety of new programmes was introduced in response to other emerging needs, programmes such as Relationships and Sexuality Education; Stay Safe; Civic, Social and Political Education; Social, Personal and Health Education; the Leaving Certificate Applied; and the Leaving Certificate Vocational Programme.

The Irish state had adopted a strongly interventionist role in education in pursuit of economic development since the early 1960s.[3] Successive governments invested heavily in the system, partly to keep young people at school in times of recession and partly because of an innate belief that education would somehow contribute to economic growth. The system, however, needed a coherence and a direction and this began to emerge only towards the end of the eighties and into the nineties. This book seeks to trace the evolution of government policies, particularly during the nineties, and to explain how they were shaped by personalities and politics as well as by a degree of consultation that was probably unique in developed countries. It examines the developments in a chrono-logical and thematic manner.

---

[3] J.J. Sexton and P.J. O'Connell (Eds), *Labour Market Studies: Ireland*, Brussels/Luxembourg, European Commission, 1997, p. 115.

Chapter 1 sets the scene with the draft Green Paper prepared by Mary O'Rourke which, although never officially published, was a seminal document that influenced subsequent deliberations. Minister O'Rourke was succeeded briefly by Noel Davern who in turn was followed by Séamus Brennan, the minister who got to publish a much different document than the one he had inherited. The changes he made and the role of the media in prompting those changes are reviewed. The chapter examines the manner in which some of the proposals, such as removing state aid to fee-paying schools or appointing business people to boards of management, were subsequently dropped. It also looks at the way in which some proposals survived the various drafts and led to what is now accepted policy, such as 30 per cent of Leaving Certificate students pursuing the Leaving Certificate Vocational Programme. Chapter 2 summarises the extraordinary reaction to the Green Paper – over a thousand written responses – and looks at the success of the National Education Convention held in October 1993.

The succeeding chapters examine, in turn, three of the most significant proposals to emerge from the Green Paper and Convention deliberations. Although the book is concerned mainly with developments during the nineties, it is necessary to set some of the major developments in an historical context. For instance, chapter 3 examines the various attempts – all unsuccessful to date – to introduce some form of intermediate structure in education, whether in the form of regionalised bodies or county committees of education. It contains much new material particularly about the attempt to introduce regionalisation in the seventies and about differences that emerged within the Catholic Church in the nineties. Chapter 4 reviews the changes that have taken place in the governance of schools with the moving away from a single manager to representative boards of management in most of the country's schools. Chapter 5 deals with higher education, looking at the expansion of the system, the abolition of tuition fees, proposals for changes in the universities, the controversy over the Universities' Bill, the campaign for upgrading of the Regional Technical Colleges and the Dublin Institute of Technology. It contains information not previously in the public domain about the abolition of tuition fees and about the discussions on the Universities' Bill.

Chapter 6 gives details of the unpublished Education Bill prepared by Niamh Bhreathnach as well as the legal advice which guided sections of the Bill and it examines the reaction to the proposals once they were leaked. Chapter 7 reviews some of the outcomes of the long process of consultation, including the passing of an Education Act by Niamh Bhreathnach's successor, Micheál Martin.

During the period covered by this book, the role of the Churches in education evolved significantly. The Churches have become more open to sharing responsibility for running Church-linked schools with teachers and parents. This occurred at a time when the authority of the Catholic Church progressively weakened, caused partly by a succession of sexual abuse scandals involving clergy and religious and partly by a growing secularisation. Attendance at religious services dropped in many urban areas while seminaries and convents no longer attracted sufficient new entrants to the religious life. The face of Irish education was changing so dramatically that the Conference of Religious in Ireland predicted in 1997 that within a quarter of a century there would be no religious left in Irish schools.[4] This may not necessarily mean an end to Church influence in denominational schools – where the Church will retain trusteeship – or in society generally. As O'Connor has written, it is equally plausible to suggest that the institutional Church will remain important, especially in so far as it continues to retain its control over education and continues to reinforce its structural and ideological power base by forming key alliances with middle class groups.[5] CORI's and O'Connor's views are not necessarily incompatible. Perhaps the OECD best summed up the position when it opined that while the Catholic Church recognised that it could not continue to play its historic role as the *principal* actor, it remained a *major* actor on the educational stage.[6]

In the meantime the teacher unions grew more powerful and formed one of the most effective lobby groups in the country. They exercised much more influence than their counterparts in the UK and USA and were regarded officially as important stakeholders

---

[4] CORI, *Religious Congregations in Irish Education – A role for the future?* Dublin, CORI, 1997, p. 9.

[5] Pat O'Connor, *Emerging Voices – Women in Contemporary Irish Society,* Dublin, Institute of Public Administration, 1998, p. 67.

[6] OECD, *Reviews of National Policies for Education: Ireland,* Paris, OECD, 1991.

in decisions on educational policy issues. They helped keep teachers' salaries relatively high, compared with other developed countries, and this has ensured a steady supply of academically well-qualified young entrants to the profession. Parents also became organised through the National Parents' Council and were represented as equal partners with the unions and managers on various official bodies. A recent OECD report remarked that the various reforms initiated in the nineties meant that Ireland 'will have one of the most parent-participative systems in the world'.[7]

The government that came to power in 1997 changed the name of the Department of Education to the Department of Education and Science and nobody raised a query. The Catholic Church, which might in other times have protested the name change on the grounds that it indicated a utilitarian approach to education, said nothing. In some respects the name change symbolised the direction in which the education system had been heading for the previous two decades, with the increased emphasis on serving the needs of business and high-tech industry while at the same time meeting the needs of a mass education system.

The name change came towards the end of a long consultative process which led to legislation designed to give a sense of direction to Irish education into the twenty-first century. The process gave the wider education community – parents, teachers, students, interest groups – as well as decision-makers a greater sense of ownership of the changes that emerged than would otherwise have been the case. It is a model that other departments, especially those concerned with the social services, might well consider before embarking on major structural reforms.

---

[7] OECD/CERI, *Parents as Partners in Schooling*, Paris, OECD, 1997.

CHAPTER 1

Preparation of Green Paper

The Irish educational system underwent dramatic changes in the latter quarter of the century. Demographic factors exerted a strong influence, with more young people remaining in second-level schooling and increasing numbers going on to higher education. The higher retention rates were in line with similar developments in other countries and were influenced by government policies and by employers' demands for higher levels of education and training from their workforces. Policies of social equity and equality also became increasingly important as did the strongly interventionist role adopted by the Irish state in pursuit of economic development.[1]

The late eighties saw a quickening of pace in debates on educational issues and an unstoppable momentum towards change on many fronts. A succession of reports had touched upon different aspects of educational development, adding to the sense of growth without clear goals. A drawing together of the disparate discussions was becoming increasingly necessary. The catalyst proved to be Mary O'Rourke, one of the most politically astute Ministers for Education of recent decades, who subsequently went on to become deputy leader of the Fianna Fáil party. Although she had left the education ministry by the time a Green Paper on education was published, it was she who prepared the initial draft. Never officially published, the draft was a seminal document that was to have a major influence on the future direction of Irish education.

The first indication that O'Rourke was considering an Education Bill came in August 1990 in an interview with Christina Murphy in *The Irish Times* in which she promised, not a Green Paper, but a White Paper before the end of 1991 which would be used to launch

---

[1] J.J. Sexton and P.J. O'Connell (Eds), *Labour Market Studies: Ireland*, Brussels/Luxembourg, European Commission, 1997, p. 115.

a widespread public debate on education. A Green Paper generally is a discussion document while a White Paper outlines government policy and decisions. It is obvious from the newspaper interview and from discussions the author has had with O'Rourke that she really intended to publish a discussion document that would draw many people and organisations into the debate on education policy. In the original newspaper interview she said:

> It is ten years since the last full-scale debate on education and so many changes have taken place in the meantime. A number of important reports, including a major OECD report on Irish education, will be published over the next few months. I would like a public debate on the issues these raise and on other changes I propose making in the system. I would then, from that debate, like to work out whether an Education Act is desirable, or in what form.[2]

The idea of educational legislation began to take shape in October 1990 when Taoiseach Charles Haughey announced in the Dáil that it was the government's intention to introduce a comprehensive Education Act. The following month, the minister spelt out the rationale for such an Act in some detail. She pointed out that a comprehensive Act, or set of Acts, was a common feature in other developed countries. The need for an Act in Ireland had been raised in a number of quarters she said, citing a call from the Irish Congress of Trade Unions for educational legislation. She said also that there were weaknesses in the existing statutory position. Concern had been expressed about

1 administrative procedures which permit a Minister for Education to issue important policy directives with a tenuous, if any, link to legislation
2 the multiplicity of rules and circulars which have their impact on and set various aspects of policy, and
3 a variety of other issues, including whether some of the current practices in relation to education conform with Article 42 of the Constitution.[3]

[2] *The Irish Times*, 24 August 1990.
[3] Minister for Education Mary O'Rourke, *Press briefing on the question of an Education Act*, 26 November 1990.

As happens frequently in politics, other parties had been thinking along the same lines. The day after the minister's announcement the main opposition party, Fine Gael, published a detailed set of headings under which it said it was drafting its own Education Bill.[4] Launching the headings, Fine Gael leader John Bruton said his party was concerned at the 'relaxed and dilatory time-table proposed by the minister for dealing with the drafting of an Education Act'. Bruton had long been interested in educational issues, having served as a parliamentary secretary (junior minister) in the Department of Education in the early seventies. The seven page document gave an outline of the party's policy on issues such as an administrative structure for education, admissions policies, a Curriculum Review Board, a separate administrative unit for exams, continuous assessment, a special unit for policy development, duties of teachers, the role of parents, and special needs. It envisaged the setting up of Local Education Boards and referred to the Green Paper – *Partners in Education* – issued in 1985[5] by the former Fine Gael Minister for Education, Gemma Hussey, which outlined proposals for such boards. It also referred to the New South Wales Act, Section 30, and to the British Columbia Act, Section 92-104, which dealt with education boards.

The work begins

Having secured the political backing for her proposal, Mary O'Rourke set about the task with enthusiasm. She had the strong support of the Secretary of the Department of Education, Noel Lindsay, an energetic public servant who had worked with the World Bank and who had acted as a consultant on educational developments in a number of European and Middle Eastern countries. Lindsay asked each section head within the department to formulate a paper, outlining what was happening in that section and indicating what policies it was working on. Once the papers

---

[4] Fine Gael, *Press Release*, 27 November 1990.
[5] Department of Education, Green Paper, *Partners in Education*, Dublin, Stationery Office, 1985.

were formulated the minister and the secretary discussed the
situation again and a more sustained process began.[6] Also involved
was the minister's adviser, Margaret Walsh, former president of the
Association of Secondary Teachers, Ireland. O'Rourke wanted certain
issues covered in the Green Paper:

> I wanted some form of devolution down to the local school board,
> I wanted the boards to have their budgets and a lot of autonomy.
> I was strong on separation of Church and State. I wanted on-going
> life-long learning and I was interested in the disadvantaged, in
> women and in parents.

She was very interested also in having a common post-primary
school type, in place of the existing five different types – voluntary
secondary, vocational, comprehensive, community schools and community colleges. She recalled that in the departmental discussions
'good practical ideas' came forward which could be incorporated
into the Green Paper, ideas such as parents' associations in every
school and stronger support for multi-denominational schools. The
first draft was not to her liking, however, and she has an abiding
memory of taking the document on a boat trip with some friends.
'I was tempted to toss every single page into the waves of the
Shannon. It seemed to me that caution had spancelled everything'.[7]

   The minister decided to invite Dr John Coolahan, Professor of
Education at what was then St Patrick's College Maynooth, to join
the team that was engaged in writing the Green Paper. Coolahan
was well known as an educational historian and a contributor to
current debates on educational issues. The minister appreciated
there was a risk that in getting involved in the Green Paper he
might be seen to compromise his academic independence but she
anticipated correctly that an academic of his stature would find it
hard to resist the possibility of shaping the future development of
Irish education. He accepted the invitation and started working
with the department officials during the summer of 1991. Tensions,
however, surfaced between those who wanted a top-down
document that prescribed changes for schools in a very directive

[6] Mary O'Rourke, interview with author, 16 November 1995.
[7] Ibid.

fashion and those who wanted more organic growth in the system with the main stake-holders taking ownership of the changes. These were largely resolved when O'Rourke took a more active part in the discussions and began chairing early morning meetings in the department in September 1991.[8] The team then produced a new and very different second draft the following month.

Draft Green Paper 1991

The revised draft Green Paper contained a host of far-reaching recommendations and was much more than simply a preparatory paper for educational legislation.[9] It was a coherent document, running to over 160 pages and the thrust of the proposals was grounded on six broad principles:

- an educational system based on a philosophy of education which aims at the development of the whole person in a balanced and harmonious way
- the development of education as a partnership between providers and those participating in the process of education
- the devolution of as much decision-making and responsibility as possible to local level and especially to schools
- making quality and equity the guiding principles
- achieving an appropriate balance between the respective roles, rights and responsibilities of the various partners in education
- ensuring that the educational system in this country plays a full part in developments in the European Community, while continuing to preserve and enhance our distinctive national identity.

Later chapters will deal with some of the major proposals, for example the proposed limiting of the department's involvement in the day-to-day operation of the education system, the plans for county committees of education, changes in the boards of management of primary and second-level schools, and university legislation. Apart from these there were many other suggestions put forward in O'Rourke's draft, including

---

[8] Off-the-record sources.
[9] Department of Education, Draft Green Paper, 25 October 1991, unpublished.

- a common form of initial training for all teachers
- a Teaching Council or restructured Teachers' Registration Council
- seven year contracts for principals
- rationalisation of subject options in the junior and senior cycles
- a national vocational certification body
- emphasis on oral competence in Irish at primary level
- modularisation and credit transfer across third-level education
- an academic audit committee within the HEA
- third-level access programmes for the disadvantaged.

One issue addressed in the draft was referred to as 'unsatisfactory teaching'. The draft stated that if in-service training for the teacher did not result in an improvement then the department would assist the board of management: 'In the event that remediation is not successful, it may be necessary to pursue withdrawal of recognition. This may involve recourse to special severance arrangements which would be worked out in Conciliation'.

The standard of teaching in Ireland is generally high by international comparison, but it is inevitable that a profession with 40,000 practitioners attracts people who are unsuited to it. Getting unsatisfactory teachers out of the profession, however, is extremely difficult in Ireland, not least because of the power of the teachers' unions but also because of perceptions of natural justice and fair play among Irish people. It is worth noting that it took six years after the draft before the issue of unsatisfactory teaching was tentatively tackled in a productivity deal for teachers. In early 1998 the matter also figured in discussions among members of a steering committee set up to examine the issue of a Teachers' Council.[10] The committee set out a protracted procedure for dealing with issues of serious professional misconduct or cases where a teacher was the subject of criminal conviction.[11]

Surprisingly perhaps, O'Rourke's Green Paper had relatively little new to say about gender issues in education. It acknowledged problems such as the unequal take-up of subjects in post-primary schools and the relative paucity of women in management in education. But apart from promising that teaching on gender issues

---

[10] Off-the-record discussions with member of the steering committee, February 1998.

[11] Department of Education and Science, *Report of the Steering Committee on the Establishment of a Teachers' Council,* Dublin, Stationery Office, 1998.

would be included in both pre-service and in-service teacher education there were no new proposals in this section.

The school year

Two issues from O'Rourke's Green Paper are worth highlighting at this juncture. One dealt with the length of time in school. It was pointed out that Ireland had a shorter school year than other developed countries, many of which had school years of 200 days or more. In Ireland at primary level the school year at the time of the draft Green Paper was 184 days and at post-primary it was 180 days, including the period of the certificate examinations. Since then the school year has been reduced further by a day. The draft quoted the report published some years earlier by the Primary Education Review Body in which concern was expressed that the school year had been eroded at primary level.[12] It proposed that the relevant *Rules* be clarified on the basis of the following model:

		Days
School in operation for teaching		184
Standard number of closings		
Saturdays and Sundays	104	
permitted vacation days	56	
public religious holidays, etc.	15	
Total		175
Remaining days		6

O'Rourke's draft asserted that the six so called 'remaining days' were intended to be used for school-related activities such as curriculum development, school planning and parent-teacher meetings, as well as special closures. It was proposed that second-level schools would be in operation for 168 days, twelve days allowed for certificate exams, 179 for standard closings with six 'remaining days'. The draft noted that early closures before examinations, mid-term breaks and special closures had eroded

---

[12] *Report of the Primary Education Review Body,* Dublin, Stationery Office, 1990.

the minimum of 168 days. It promised to explore the potential use of the certificate examinations days to complement the use of the 'remaining days' for school-related activities, including in-service education, for those not directly involved in the certificate examinations.

This was the first indication of the department's intention to deal with an issue of growing concern to parents, who had been complaining increasingly about early and frequent closures, especially in post-primary schools. The issue was raised in the final version of the Green Paper and in the subsequent White Paper. Eventually it was the subject of what turned out to be an ill-fated circular entitled *Time in School* which was sent to schools in mid-1995 but which provoked such a strong reaction that it was superseded by a productivity deal for teachers. The productivity deal will be reviewed in the final chapter.

The Senior Certificate

The second issue worth highlighting in O'Rourke's draft concerned the senior cycle in post-primary schools. The major objective of educational policies for the nineties was that 90 per cent of the age group would complete senior cycle, compared with 73 per cent at the time the draft was prepared. A six-year second-level school cycle was being made available for all pupils at that time and this would allow for various options at the senior-cycle level. O'Rourke endorsed proposals put forward by the National Council for Curriculum and Assessment which would permit students to choose subjects from both the Leaving and Senior Certificate programmes, with academic and practical/vocational subject options in each. The Senior Certificate was an experimental alternative to the Leaving Certificate, with more emphasis on practical and vocational subjects. It had been piloted in a small number of schools during the 1980s but had limited currency among employers, and the idea of making it available nationally was certainly a bold one. Few schools, however, would be in a position to offer the Senior Certificate in addition to the Leaving Certificate programme. The Green Paper acknowledged that offering a range of academic and vocational or practical options, and choices between Leaving Certificate and Senior Certificate, would not be feasible except where there was well-structured collaboration between schools in a local area.

The draft also proposed the establishment of county committees of education which would have an important role in facilitating this type of collaboration at local level. Given that there was a poor record of co-operation between post-primary schools in sharing resources over the decades this was always going to be difficult to achieve. It was also not certain that the Senior Certificate would gain the national currency necessary for success. A perception that the Senior Certificate was for weaker students could quickly dampen any hopes of bright students combining both programmes to select a balanced mix of academic and practical subjects.

Other proposals and how they fared

It is interesting to dwell upon some of O'Rourke's other proposals and examine what happened to them subsequently. One of the most significant was provision for mandatory boards of management in all post-primary schools. In the O'Rourke draft it was stated that in order to secure government funding a post-primary school would need to have an admissions policy that did not discriminate on the basis of means, educational level or social background. The school would be expected to establish a representative board of management with the necessary authority to manage. Half a decade later when this same proposal was incorporated into an Education Bill proposed by the Labour Minister for Education, Niamh Bhreathnach, it was interpreted by some as an indication of the Labour Party's desire for statist control of education (see chapter 6). Bhreathnach's successor, Micheál Martin, dropped the compulsion on schools to establish boards, a proposal that had first been put forward by his own party colleague Mary O'Rourke.

There was a further policy issue on which the Labour Party had traditionally held strong views but about which, ironically, it did nothing when it was given the opportunity. This was the provision of state funds to fee-paying secondary schools, payments to which Labour had long been opposed. Figures indicate that in the mid- to late nineties Catholic and Protestant fee-paying schools received around £30m a year in state aid, mainly in teachers' salaries.[13] Yet

---

[13] Information supplied by Department of Education and Science.

O'Rourke's hint of reducing or ending state support to this sector did not survive through to the White Paper, published some four years later when the Labour Party held the education portfolio. O'Rourke's draft pointed out that the payment of salaries meant that fee-paying schools received the equivalent of 85 per cent of the amount of state support paid to non-fee-paying schools. It added that

> The state is, in effect, increasing the total income of such schools substantially above those of schools not charging fees and thereby increasing the disparity in resource allocation. In the interests of equity, therefore, and of avoiding undue disparity in financial provision between schools, consideration will be given to whether continuance of funding on the present basis for fee-paying schools is justified.[14]

It is, of course, a matter of speculation as to whether or not any government would actually reduce or cease paying teachers' salaries to a very powerful and influential sector such as fee-paying schools. Students in these schools do have an advantage over those in the Free Education scheme, which raises issues of equity. But there are also denominational questions involved because Protestant secondary schools are funded in a slightly different way to Catholic schools. It would be politically impossible to move against Catholic schools without also moving against Protestant schools. No government, however, would rush headlong into a disagreement with fee-paying Protestant secondary schools who would, inevitably, argue that a reduction in their state aid would affect adversely the religious minority in the Republic. Successive governments have always been very sensitive to the needs of Protestant schools and have gone to great lengths to avoid any charges of discriminating against them. Indeed, this was one of the reasons why Niamh Bhreathnach did not deal with the issue during her term of office, according to a political source. Another reason, according to the same source, was because of the extra costs to the state if the fee-paying schools were brought into the Free Education scheme. A third was that the issue was seen by Niamh Bhreathnach as peripheral and not worth the effort.[15]

---

[14] Draft Green Paper, p. 23.
[15] Off-the-record political sources.

Attrition rates

The O'Rourke draft promised an annual report from the department which would provide information and comment to the public on the progress of the education system. This has not yet been delivered. The report was to include an analysis of the flow of students to the end of third-level participation and drop-out rates, outcomes of assessment, trends in subject choices and achievements.[16] The department does publish an annual statistical report that contains much useful data; lack of personnel/capacity and data has prevented it from doing more. However, until recently there has been relatively little data officially available to the public about third-level colleges, such as the number of applications to each institution and the attrition rates. This was in spite of the fact that, for example, in 1996-7 the average expenditure by the department on a third-level student was £4,830 per annum.[17]

The year 1998 saw two developments which led to greater openness in a number of areas. One was the enactment of a Freedom of Information Bill, the full benefits of which will not be known for some time. The other was a decision to allow Leaving Certificate students access to their marked scripts. Such transparency is traditionally not found in third-level colleges, where students have no ready access to marking schemes that explain how marks are allocated and where there is uneven provision of appeals procedures. Nineteen ninety-eight was also the first year that the Central Applications Office officially released details of the number of applications to individual institutions; but this was after they had been leaked to a morning newspaper some months earlier.[18]

The tradition of secrecy has been most pronounced when it comes to pass, failure and drop-out rates from colleges. One Regional Technical College, Dundalk, conducted a confidential study of its attrition rate during the mid-nineties and this showed that an embarrassingly high number of students did not transfer into the

---

[16] Draft Green Paper.
[17] Department of Education and Science, *Key Education Statistics,* 1986/87-1996/97.
[18] *Irish Independent,* 7 February 1998.

second year of their courses.[19] The lowest transfer rate was in Experimental Science where three out of five students did not proceed into the second year of a two-year certificate course. The highest transfer rate was in Accountancy where 90 per cent of students went on to the second year of the course. In early 1998 the Minister for Education and Science, Micheál Martin, agreed, in response to repeated Dáil questions from Fine Gael education spokesperson Richard Bruton, that he favoured a national survey into drop-out rates. Deputy Bruton's brother, and Fine Gael party leader, John Bruton, subsequently called for such information to be made public.[20]

The matter came to the fore in mid-1998 in a report prepared by an expert group on Future Skills Needs. Figures were made available to the group and on the basis of these it concluded that the completion rate for technology degree courses was 80 per cent but that it was only 65 per cent for technician-level diploma courses. The report stated that the Department of Education and Science was carrying out a qualitative study of completion rates among technicians, while the Higher Education Authority was carrying out a similar study amongst university degree students.[21] It is ironic that it was economic rather than educational concerns that propelled the issue into the policy domain, because the group was anxious that the colleges might not be able to meet the growing skill needs unless they could improve their retention rates.

Further information came a few months later in the form of research conducted for the Points Commission which had been set up by Minister Micheál Martin on 15 October 1997. The Commission, chaired by Professor Áine Hyland of UCC, was established to review the existing method of choosing students for third-level colleges and to make recommendations as appropriate. A study carried out on its behalf sought to establish the predictive validity of the points system in relation to the intake of students into third-level education

[19] Dundalk Regional Technical College, *Study on transfer and output rates*, 1997, unpublished.
[20] *Irish Independent*, 6 February 1998.
[21] *Responding to Ireland's Growing Skills Needs: The First Report of the Expert Group on Future Skills Needs to the Tánaiste and the Minister for Education and Science*, 1998.

in 1992. The study of a representative sample of 1,040 students found that 26 per cent of students who had entered college in 1992 had not been awarded any qualification from their college of entry by 1998; most had left or failed.[22] At the press conference to launch the Commission's report, the minister reiterated his support for a national study.[23] Some months later the OECD in its annual *Education at a Glance* report gave a non-completion rate of 23 per cent for Irish university students, an outcome which compared favourably with the non-completion rates in many other countries.[24] The rate was worked out by statisticians at the OECD in Paris from raw data supplied by the Irish education authorities.[25] In February 1999 the Institute of Technology in Tallaght took the bold decision to put its *Institutional Review* on the internet. This self-study review included details of pass, failure and non-completion rates.

Revised draft Green Paper 1992

According to Professor Coolahan, it was Mary O'Rourke's intention to publish her draft Green Paper on 13 December 1991.[26] Before she had time to do so she was moved to another department in a cabinet reshuffle in November 1991 and was succeeded in Education by a Tipperary deputy, Noel Davern. Davern was an unexpected choice; his background was that of a cautious local politician but he was astute enough to realise that he needed guidance from somebody who knew the education scene well and upon whom he could rely. He appointed as his full time adviser the local Chief Executive Officer of the Co. Tipperary South Riding Vocational Education Committee, John Slattery. Slattery, who was subsequently to become the acting head of development of the Tipperary Rural Business and Development Institute, was familiar with the North American education system and held strong views on the issue of

---

[22] K. Lynch, T. Brannick, P. Clancy, and S. Drudy, 'A study on the predictive validity of the points system', in Commission on the Points System, *Consultative Process – Background Document*, Dublin, Stationery Office, September 1998.
[23] *Irish Independent*, 2 September 1998.
[24] OECD, *Education at a Glance: Indicators 1998*, Paris, OECD, 1998.
[25] Interview with OECD officials, Paris, 23 November 1998.
[26] John Coolahan, address to Society for Management in Education in Ireland, TCD, 17 October 1998.

technical versus academic education. His ideas were to make a lasting impact on the redrafted Green Paper and on the subsequent White Paper.

At that time much of the debate on education was influenced by a report on industrial policy – the Culliton Report – which had claimed that there was not enough emphasis in Irish second-level education on technical and vocational training. 'Over the years the prestige of the academic Leaving Certificate programme has diverted students who would be much better adapted to technical training', it claimed.[27] The report recommended a parallel stream of non-academic, vocationally oriented education at second level which would command widespread recognition, respect and support.[28]

Slattery, however, had other views and the main change made to O'Rourke's draft during Davern's term of office was an entirely rewritten section on vocational education and training.[29] This section acknowledged the need for an improved vocational and technical orientation to education at the second level. It warned that

> There is a strong possibility, however, that to seek to do so through a separate non-academic vocational stream would be regarded as providing only for less able children, and would not meet the objective of ensuring a broadly-based education for all, with vocational options and orientation, to completion of the secondary stage.[30]

It proposed instead to build on and expand the range of vocational options within the existing Leaving Certificate Vocational Programme (LCVP), with the intention of increasing the numbers of Leaving Certificate participants in that programme from 5 per cent of the total in 1991 to at least 30 per cent from 1994. It is interesting to note that this target was retained in the final version of the Green Paper that was officially published in June 1992.[31] Considerable progress has been made towards reaching this target. In 1998-9

---

[27] The Industrial Policy Review Group, *A Time for Change, Industrial Policy for the 1990s*, Dublin, Stationery Office, 1992.

[28] Ibid.

[29] Department of Education, Draft Green Paper, 29 January 1992, unpublished.

[30] Ibid.

[31] Department of Education, Green Paper, *Education for a Changing World*, Dublin, Stationery Office, 1992, p. 78.

there were just under 90,000 students taking the two-year traditional Leaving Certificate programme and 5,481 others were repeating the Leaving. At the same time there were just over 26,000 taking the LCVP route.[32] The projected target for 1999-2000 was for 40,000 places in 700 schools.[33] The LCVP may have made some difference as far as practical subjects were concerned, although it could be argued that the assessment of students was not that radically different from the traditional mainstream Leaving Certificate, relying in the main on a written terminal examination.

The main innovation in the LCVP was the introduction of three link modules in enterprise education, preparation for work and work experience. The activities involved include the organisation and running of mini-enterprises, visits to business and industry and investigations of the local community. The link modules are assessed by the National Council for Vocational Awards. The assessment comprises two elements: written examinations (40 per cent of marks) and portfolio of coursework (60 per cent of marks). LCVP students receive the same certificate as established mainstream Leaving Certificate students. In addition, their certificates include a statement of results of the link modules (pass, merit or distinction). In February 1999, the Conference of Heads of Irish Universities announced its intention to recognise the link modules for points purposes, a decision which was seen as giving a boost to the LCVP, although the Institutes of Technology gave more points for the modules than the universities.

It is also worth noting that in 1997-8 some 165 schools/centres were providing about 5,500 Leaving Certificate Applied (LCA) places and that it was estimated that up to 9,000 places could be provided in 1998-9. The LCA is another alternative to the mainstream Leaving Certificate which is still taken by the vast majority of students. The LCA, which is modular-based, is designed to prepare young adults for adult and working life and to enable them to make decisions about further education and training. They undertake a number of tasks over the two years of their programme. These tasks, which

---

[32] Department of Education statistics.

[33] Commission on the Points System, *Consultative Process – Background Document,* Dublin, Stationery Office, 1998, p. 41.

are examined by the Department of Education, are practical activities which allow students individually and in teams to apply classroom experience to real-life situations. A maximum of 100 credits is available to students on successful completion of the programme; two-thirds can be gained during the two years of the programme and the remaining third at the final examinations. The development of the LCA is due in large measure to Niamh Bhreathnach, who expanded it nationwide in the face of some internal department opposition, although the inspectorate was supportive of it: she also took a policy decision to 'ring-fence' the LCA so that it would not be 'corrupted' by the mainstream Leaving Certificate programme.[34]

However, to return to Davern's draft, it stated that the proposed County Committees of Education would be responsible for the provision of all off-the-job vocational education and training, within a regulatory framework established by FÁS and CERT. It stated that the existing National Council for Vocational Awards would be placed on a statutory basis and its remit extended to include the certification of programmes provided by FÁS and CERT.

There would be a co-ordinated set of national arrangements for the provision of vocational education and training programmes and for the assessment, certification and accreditation of levels of knowledge, skills and competencies attained. Such arrangements would enhance the transfer of students between programmes, the credibility and acceptability of qualifications and the mobility of personnel in the wider European labour market, it added. This was always going to be difficult to achieve, given the traditional 'turf-wars' between the Department of Education and the Department of Enterprise and Employment which was responsible for FÁS, the training and employment authority. It took six years before a subsequent minister, Micheál Martin, got to the stage that draft heads of a Bill to set up a national qualifications authority were prepared.[35]

To help achieve this objective, Davern's draft suggested that all vocational training programmes should be reconstituted progressively under an extended apprenticeship system. In Ireland the apprenticeship system is confined to training mainly in designated

---

[34] Off-the-record sources.
[35] Micheál Martin, Opportunities '98 Conference, RDS, Dublin, 4 February 1998.

trades whereas it covers a much wider range of economic activity in many other European countries, notably Germany and the Scandinavian countries. The redrafted Green Paper indicated that the basis for an extended system was already in place through the development work of vocational preparation and training courses in vocational schools since the mid-eighties, particularly for post-Leaving Certificate participants. Courses at levels below those acceptable for apprenticeship would be reorganised as potential stepping stones to apprenticeship for successful trainees, within a graduated certification process.

It could, however, be difficult to get widespread acceptance for the concept of apprenticeship as articulated in Davern's paper. The Dual System as it is called works well in Germany where employers across all sectors are much more willing to invest in training for their apprenticed employees than are Irish employers. The divisions between education and training and the lack of close co-ordination between the Departments of Education and Science and the Department of Enterprise and Employment are also factors inhibiting development in this regard.

Media intervention

It is not often that newspaper reports prompt a rewriting of government policy but this appears to have transpired when *The Irish Times* decided to publish a series of articles about the draft Green Paper in February 1992.[36] Séamus Brennan had just taken over the education portfolio from Noel Davern following a further cabinet reshuffle.

The author was education correspondent with *The Irish Times* at the time and had spent almost a fortnight in mid-February working on a three-part series on the Green Paper. During this time the author was able to secure leaked drafts of both O'Rourke's and Davern's Green Papers. These had not been published and the newspaper recognised that they would be of considerable public interest. Radio advertisements were due to be broadcast from Tuesday 25 February, announcing the commencement of the series

---

[36] *The Irish Times*, 25-27 February 1992.

that morning. The night before there was an unexpected telephone call to the author from the minister's press officer, Joe Jennings, to say that the minister would have something important to announce the following afternoon regarding the Green Paper. The author advised the editor Conor Brady that the minister was bringing the issue of the Green Paper to cabinet the next morning and that the newspaper's plans would certainly come into the reckoning if the series was published. The decision was taken to go ahead with the series.

The timing was purely coincidental but the newspaper series caused a major political difficulty for the new minister. Two sources have told the author that Brennan was prepared to 'run' with what he had inherited – in other words he was willing to publish, as an official government discussion document, the draft he had inherited, even though he had not put his own 'stamp' on it. One spoke of the 'panic reaction' in the Department of Education on the morning the first part of the series appeared and said that invitations for a press conference at which the Green Paper was to be launched were already printed at that stage. The launch was to be held on 5 March according to one source who said that the minister was furious because he did not want to be seen as a mere 'messenger boy' for somebody else's Green Paper.

In an interview with the author in 1997 Séamus Brennan agreed that there was 'some truth' in the reports that he had been prepared to 'run' with what he had inherited.[37] He disputed accounts that he was due to bring the full Green Paper to cabinet on the morning the first instalment of the series appeared but agreed that he was due to bring some issue arising from the Green Paper up for discussion. No announcement was made that afternoon but instead the minister assembled a team and spent several weeks rewriting the Green Paper at a series of meetings in Barrettstown Castle. 'The leaks did goad me into looking at the Paper more closely, but it was not done in a fit of pique' he told the author.[38]

Coolahan has argued that the leaks of the drafts did not foster the public good, particularly because some of the new proposals

---

[37] Interview with author, 10 April 1997.
[38] Ibid.

that were incorporated into the Green Paper led to suspicions among teachers that took some considerable time to allay.[39] Certainly, the draft that he inherited was changed radically by Brennan and it was changed in a way that alienated the teaching profession instead of encouraging the profession along to meet the challenge of change.

Green Paper 1992

Brennan had engaged the services of a 'word-smith' named Noel Jones to help write the Green Paper in a direct style that would make it accessible to the general public. A short introduction to the Green Paper was published in April, just in time for the annual round of teachers' conferences.[40] It outlined six key aims:

1 to establish greater equity in education – particularly for those who are disadvantaged socially, economically, physically or mentally
2 to broaden Irish education – so as to equip students more effectively for life, for work in an enterprise culture, and for citizenship of Europe
3 to make the best use of educational resources – by radically devolving administration, by including the best management practice and by strengthening policy-making
4 to train and develop teachers so as to equip them for a constantly changing environment
5 to create a system of effective quality assurance
6 to ensure greater openness and accountability throughout the system, and maximise parent involvement and choice.

The full text of the Green Paper was published in June 1992.[41] It introduced many new features but it also retained many of the original provisions from O'Rourke's draft which have been highlighted in this chapter. One that was dropped, however, was O'Rourke's proposal for a general extension of the Senior Certificate. Brennan opted instead for Davern's suggested target of 30 per cent of Leaving Certificate students taking the Vocational programme.

---

[39] John Coolahan, address to Society for Management in Education in Ireland, TCD, 17 October 1998.
[40] Department of Education, *Introduction to Green Paper*, 21 April 1992.
[41] *Education for a Changing World.*

O'Rourke's proposal for county committees of education was also dropped, in favour of executive agencies, for example a payroll agency, an educational property management agency, a curriculum and assessment agency etc.

Brennan had come from a business background and had served in a number of economic ministries. He was not an obvious choice for the education portfolio and was impatient with the manner in which the department operated and the slowness of decision-making as he perceived it.

> I came from departments where decisions were taken every day of the week, often involving spending millions of pounds. In Education I found a department that was the biggest property holder in the country. Too much time was spent on decisions about fixing slate roofs. I felt all that should be contracted out and that the department should concentrate on deciding policy.[42]

He told the author that he had gone as far as preparing detailed proposals for an interim board for a property management agency which would have its own chief executive and staff and that he even had a person in mind for the post of chief executive. This was to be followed by proposals for an agency to handle school transport, an area he has long felt should be devolved from the Department of Education.[43] However, he did not remain in office long enough to bring his ideas to fruition and the 'agency' idea did not feature in the White Paper which was published by his successor, Niamh Bhreathnach, and which will be reviewed in the next chapter.[44] Indeed, few of the major additions made by Brennan to the draft Green Papers survived to the White Paper. He proposed, for example, that not less than 60 per cent of the marks in certificate examinations in Irish and in modern European languages should be allocated to the oral/aural component. Brennan was correct in identifying a need for improvement in oral and aural comprehension skills but allocating only 40 per cent of marks to the written examination was an extreme reaction to this concern.

---

[42] Interview with author.
[43] Ibid.
[44] Department of Education, *Charting our Education Future – White Paper on Education,* Dublin, Stationery Office, 1995.

The enterprise culture

Another ill-fated proposal was that a subject to be called Enterprise
and Technology Studies would become obligatory for all students,
initially in the junior cycle and then in the Leaving Certificate. This
particular proposal ran into a storm of criticism later and was
dropped by Brennan's successor, Niamh Bhreathnach. Also dropped
was his proposal for the appointment of a business person to each
board of management of primary and second-level schools. (As we
shall see in chapter 4, O'Rourke had first proposed this notion.) A
similar fate greeted his designation of school principals as chief
executive officers, another move which was redolent of a business-
type approach to education. However, the Green Paper promised
that an enterprise dimension would be introduced progressively
into business studies programmes through the junior and senior
cycles and this has since been implemented.

With hindsight Brennan acknowledges that he gave critics an
issue to 'jump' on when he talked of the need for an enterprise
culture in schools. He believed that the education system traditionally
prepared people for employment but not to create employment.
What he had in mind was that the education system should help to
create enterprising individuals. He stated the following:

> But this was not just a Séamus Brennan philosophy. At that time
> we were accused of not having enough small businesses in Ireland,
> of not having enough risk takers. This was the view of the
> Confederation of Irish Industry and was mentioned in the Culliton
> report.[45]

As well as a school plan, Brennan's Green Paper envisaged that
each school would issue an annual written report on all aspects of
its work. This should include curricular policy and initiatives, and
the outcomes of assessment and staff development policies. 'It should
contain, as an appendix, a summary analysis of relevant statistical
data'.[46] This was interpreted by some observers as a code, enabling
each school to make its exam results available to parents. Although
Brennan insisted at the time that he was not looking for league

---

[45] Interview with author.
[46] *Education for a Changing World*, p. 114.

tables, the availability of individual school reports would inevitably lead to the compilation of such tables. Comparisons between half a dozen schools in an area would be relatively easy to compile by the local press and with a bit of initiative a national newspaper could draw together enough information to give a reasonable national picture.

Little has been heard either about Brennan's proposal for testing pupils at ages seven and eleven. The Green Paper made the point that the first formal examination which students encounter is the Junior Certificate, taken after they have completed nine to eleven years of formal schooling. It stated that the use of standardised tests at seven and eleven would be for diagnostic purposes to identify those in need of special assistance, including those who might be experiencing basic literacy or numeracy problems. However, the idea was opposed by those who feared a return to the old written primary certificate and by those who saw the negative effects of too much testing in UK schools.

A section in the final version of the Green Paper dealt with the large number of primary schools. At the time of publication in 1992 there were 3,224 primary schools of which 1,380 had three teachers or less. It was estimated that the number of primary schools with three teachers or less would increase by 450 if existing trends continued and the need for the reorganisation of school facilities would become increasingly relevant. The Green Paper announced a new policy aimed at maximising the number of schools of four teachers and more in rural areas and schools of eight teachers or more in urban areas.[47] This was a totally unexpected proposal that represented a sharp break in traditional policy and it was quietly buried by Niamh Bhreathnach. However, Bhreathnach did establish a Commission on School Accommodation to look at this and other issues – the question of rationalisation of primary schools will have to be addressed sooner rather than later given the rapid decline in the primary school-going population.

---

[47] Ibid, p. 71.

Fee-paying secondary schools

Brennan's Green Paper watered down O'Rourke's threat to the funding of fee-paying schools. It stated that discussions would be held with these schools on the possibility of their joining the Free scheme or setting up boards of management, allowing community use of buildings, and introducing non-selective admissions policies. Brennan informed the author that the decision to alter O'Rourke's proposals was taken on cost and philosophical grounds.[48] He believed in the state providing a certain level of services and in the right of people to pay more if they wished for additional services. 'We don't all have to travel second class on a train' was his analogy. He added that there would have been few if any savings made by ending the subsidy to fee-paying schools because there would be costs associated with their joining the Free Education scheme. He argued that consideration of his views in this regard should be balanced against the views expressed in the Green Paper on the need for targeting resources at the disadvantaged.

> I am seen as pro-enterprise but I have always said that we have to face up to our responsibilities to the disadvantaged. Throwing money at the problem will not solve it if the money is spread too thinly. That's why it has to be targeted.[49]

It must be said that more attention is given in Brennan's Paper than in the earlier drafts to the issues of equity and equality. The Paper emphasised the need for links between the home and the school, provision for the needs of travellers and others with special needs. It also contained a section on gender issues and promised a campaign for gender equity in education. Brennan acknowledged the role played by Dr Sheelagh Drudy in helping to formulate policies in these areas.

One further issue highlighted in the Green Paper was the need for regulation of the private colleges' sector in the interest of consumer protection. The Paper proposed the setting up of a new body, the Council for Educational and Vocational Awards, which would have a wide remit covering all aspects of vocational training

---

[48] Interview with author.
[49] Ibid.

outside the university sector. The body would have an overall registration function for private colleges and for specific courses offered by them. The intention was that the department would agree a comprehensive code of quality control for the colleges. Given the collapse of three private colleges over the past few years such controls would seem essential but there has been a long delay in introducing them.

The author can take some small credit for the inclusion of the proposed controls of private colleges. It was suggested by the author to Brennan the day after he was appointed minister that this was something that needed to be addressed in the interests of consumers. A second suggestion offered by the author to the minister's adviser, Dick Doyle, three weeks before publication of the Green Paper was not, however, acted on. The author had been lucky enough to have read the penultimate draft of the Green Paper. While not in a position to alter the philosophical approach of the Green Paper, he adverted to the strikingly obvious absence of any worthwhile reference to the role of the arts in education. This issue was not of key importance in O'Rourke's draft but it could be argued that a focus on the arts was more necessary in Brennan's document to balance the perceived bias towards a utilitarian view of education. An undertaking to look again at this issue for the final version was forgotten in the subsequent busy weeks with predictable consequences for the minister who was roundly condemned for the lack of reference to the arts. A section on the arts in education might have been perceived as an attempt to put a gloss on a very utilitarian document but, had it been included, it might have tempered some of the subsequent criticism of the Paper. Such is the manner in which policy is formulated!

CHAPTER 2

The Consultation Process

Séamus Brennan was a man in a hurry to take decisions. Initially he wanted all responses to the Green Paper submitted within three months but was persuaded by department officials to allow at least six months for submissions.[1] The Green Paper had been published in June 1992 and a three-month deadline would, therefore, have been impossible to adhere to because of the intervening summer holidays. A general election delayed the deadline even further and a new centre-left administration was installed, comprising Fianna Fáil and the Labour Party. The government took office on 12 January 1993 and the Labour Party secured the education portfolio for the first time in its history. Niamh Bhreathnach became the new minister and one of her first acts was to extend the deadline for the final receipt of submissions to Easter 1993.

It is not an exaggeration to describe the response to the Green Paper as extraordinary. There were innumerable seminars and conferences, some private, the others public, up and down the country, including a number organised by the department. The seminars organised by the department, initially at any rate, worked very well in opening up the discussions to a much wider audience than might otherwise have been secured. However, as the department-organised sessions continued around the country, they were increasingly dominated by interest groups who tended to reiterate their official positions and invariably seek additional resources for their sectors.

The most remarkable feature of the consultation process was the volume of written submissions to the department, almost 1,000 in all by the revised deadline. This was probably more than any government document had prompted in many years and was a measure of the growing public interest in education as a vehicle

---

[1] Séamus Brennan, interview with author, 10 April 1997.

for personal and societal advancement. The list of organisations that made submissions gives an insight into the extent to which Irish society felt that education had a role to play in a diverse range of areas. It included, naturally, all the main education players but submissions came also from dozens of individuals involved in education while about a fifth of submissions came from school boards of management.[2]

The list included organisations as diverse as the following: Community Addiction Counsellors; Irish Society of Medical Officers of Health; Irish Children's Book Trust; Missionary Society of St Columban; Area Partnerships Co-ordination Office; Disability Federation of Ireland; Conradh na Gaeilge; Geographical Society of Ireland; The Giraffe Play Centres; Business and Professional Women's Group, Galway; SIPTU; Dance Council of Ireland; Irish Heart Foundation; Industrial Development Authority; Lesbian and Gay Youth Federation of Ireland; Parents against Stay Safe; Mothers Working at Home; Dublin All Stars Marching Band; National Safety Council; Federation of Services for Unmarried Parents and their Children; Motor Cycle Union of Ireland; Council for the Croquet Association of Ireland; and the Bowling League of Ireland.

Some of the organisations might seem esoteric in the context of a debate on the formulation of government policy on education but their inclusion reflects a sense of public 'ownership' of the debate on the future of Irish education. One wonders, however, what would have happened had Séamus Brennan published the draft Green Paper that he inherited and had he not amended it in such an obviously controversial fashion. Would an unamended Paper have produced the same healthy response and discussion? Alternatively, did the controversy over the business and enterprise thrust of the Paper take from discussion on more important quality and curriculum issues at all levels?

A summary of all the responses is beyond the scope of this chapter. Some of the issues raised, such as intermediate structures and school governance, will be taken up in subsequent chapters and this chapter will concentrate on several other topics raised in

[2] Department of Education, *Education Green Paper 1992: List of Submissions*, 1993, unpublished.

the responses from the education players. It relies in the main on a report prepared by the department entitled *Summary of Main Issues – What the Partners are Saying.*[3] In the summary the department listed the issues it felt were sufficiently important to pick out from the submissions. They are: local structures; ethos and religion; boards of management; owners/trustees/patrons; assessment of primary pupils; teacher pre-service training; curriculum – primary and post-primary; philosophy; resources; disadvantaged/equality; sport; youth services; adult and community education; school-based assessment at post primary level; principal's role; Teachers' Council; emphasis on oral language skills; in-service teacher training; school plan and report; integration of special needs pupils; role of inspectors; and role of the department.

Responses to the Green Paper 1992-3

The Green Paper had a number of broad educational aims but no stated philosophy and this lacuna was adverted to in a number of the responses. The ASTI suggested that the pervasive philosophy in the Paper was that education for enterprise and education for work should be the driving force of the system. The CMRS felt that the absence of an explicit philosophy of education was a serious weakness while the AMCSS felt that the essential thrust of the Paper was inspired and driven by 'economic pragmatism, acquisitive individualism and functional efficiency'. The CPSMA said that there was a disproportionate emphasis on the obligation of schools to prepare young people for work and for the promotion of an enterprise culture. The INTO said that 'Pragmatic and utilitarian approaches, while superficially attractive, in that they facilitate a proximate response to a pressing demand, can lead to a lack of direction and ultimately to bad practice'.[4]

The overemphasis on enterprise and individualistic values was contrasted with the underemphasis on artistic and cultural aspects of educational development. Subsequently Minister Brennan, in a speech in the Seanad, enunciated a deeper and more liberal concep-

---

[3] Department of Education, *Summary of Main Issues – What the Partners are Saying,* 1993, unpublished.
[4] Ibid, pp. 20-21.

tion of 'enterprise' and also set out what Professor Coolahan has called a much more enriched view of the arts as part of a balanced education. A commitment to a balanced education was again in evidence in a policy speech delivered in Tralee in October 1993.[5] According to Coolahan:

> It would seem that perceived imbalances of outlook in the Green Paper have been addressed in favour of a reinstatement of a view of education emphasising the moral, spiritual, intellectual, aesthetic, social and physical education of people in a harmonious way. It is also felt that the value of enterprise, innovation, self-reliance, among other personal qualities, can be fostered through the range of educational experiences made available to people, without detriment to an initiation into Ireland's rich cultural heritage.[6]

A related area which many submissions dealt with was that of ethos and religion. The Green Paper had stated that the school would seek to establish values and behaviour consistent with its own ethos. It stated that in all circumstances the school must have due regard for the rights and wishes of parents. Religious education should form part of the available programme for all students, with due regard to the constitutional rights of parents in regard to the participation of their children, it added.

The AMCSS felt that the understanding of religious education revealed in the Paper was 'seriously deficient'. The Church of Ireland Board of Education was disappointed that the emphasis in the discussion of religious education was almost completely concerned with whether religion should or should not be integrated into the curriculum. The Board stated that ethos related to the unwritten curriculum in schools – religion was just one of the elements which contributed to school ethos. The CPSMA said it expected that the proposed Education Act would enshrine the right of denominational schools to exist. The Association said it also recognised that multi-denominational schools could be established. Educate Together – in answer to Minister Brennan's suggestion that the ethos of a school might be set out in a charter – forwarded a copy of the charter to which all its schools subscribed.

---

[5] John Coolahan (Ed.), Background Paper for the National Education Convention, 11-21 October, 1993, p. 7.
[6] Ibid.

The Catholic bishops and CMRS felt that in the case of each type of school there must be a distinction between the management of the foundation or institution (the executive role) and the management of the school (the administrative role). They felt that the Paper did not take sufficient cognisance of this distinction. They pointed out that the state was responsible for the setting and planning of the curriculum but since it did not provide the education itself in schools it could not dictate in what fashion and with what values a child should be educated. They felt that it would be contrary to any understanding of the constitution if a denominational school could only be denominational in the sense that it could only teach religion in a formal setting but could not promote religion in the everyday life of the school.

The issue of resources

The Green Paper did not make any commitments to provide extra resources but both Séamus Brennan and Secretary Noel Lindsay agreed at the department-organised seminars that the primary sector was underfunded. Predictably, most of the education partners referred to the lack of commitment to additional resources. A Green Paper, however, is by definition a discussion document on future policy directions and it is hardly appropriate for a government to give specific commitments in advance of decisions on such directions. To give commitments would be to undermine the discussions and negate the very basis for issuing a discussion document in the first place. One organisation that did not espouse the general criticism was the CMRS which argued that the Paper was not defective by virtue of its failure to spell out the resource implications of the various proposals. The department's summary of the response from the CMRS was that:

> They believe that it is perfectly reasonable to first achieve consensus on general principles which could then be the basis to setting priorities about the allocation of resources. They do note, however, that there is a serious danger which results from the fact that there are some very specific proposals in the Green Paper which will require extra resources if they are to be effective.[7]

---

[7] *What the Partners are Saying*, p. 23.

One area that would obviously require additional resources was the targeting of education disadvantage and there was a general welcome for the priority afforded in the Green Paper to tackling this problem. The Catholic bishops and CMRS felt that while the education system could not be blamed for inequity in society it did contribute to and reinforce inequalities. The Church of Ireland Board of Education felt that initiatives to improve access and equity would, in most cases, require specific and closely targeted proposals rather than 'broad brush' policies.[8]

There was strong negative reaction to the notion of the principal as a chief executive of the school. Many organisations pointed out that the principals were already overworked without the addition of the extra duties proposed in the Green Paper. The AMCSS said the principals would require an adequate and effective middle management structure; in-service training in the areas of administration; pastoral care; plant maintenance; ancillary staff and services; an enhanced salary and allowances.

Overall there was a very mixed response to the Green Paper. There was a general welcome for its official publication but criticism of many of those elements that Séamus Brennan had introduced – these have been identified in the preceding chapter. The publication and submissions were useful in stimulating debate about the type of education system best suited to the needs of the country. They also made many people in the education system appreciate that change was coming, whether they liked it or not, and that it was far better to anticipate change than have it imposed.

The National Education Convention, October 1993

In the normal course of events the government would have prepared a White Paper setting out its decisions after a study of the responses to the Green Paper. However, Brennan's successor, Niamh Bhreathnach, decided to prolong the consultation process in a unique manner by holding the National Education Convention which took place in Dublin Castle on 11-21 October 1993. The Convention brought together representatives from forty-two organisations –

---

[8] Ibid, p. 25.

educational bodies, the social partners and the department – to discuss key issues of educational policy in Ireland. It consisted of plenary sessions, all of which were attended by the minister, and analysis of issues sessions. The Convention attracted significant interest abroad.

The logic of the Convention was to remove the department as the buffer between the various educational interests. Until the Convention each group came to the minister or the department with its position, and largely ignored the position of others. The idea of the Convention was to encourage 'win-win' solutions through multilateral dialogue. According to Pat Keating, the minister's programme manager, the Convention was basically Niamh Bhreathnach's idea, supported and developed by Department Secretary Dr Don Thornhill. Keating has argued that it was not fully understood or appreciated, initially at any rate, by other participants who wanted to get on with the White Paper in the traditional manner.[9]

The contributing organisations largely reiterated or elaborated upon their known positions. It would be unfair, however, to categorise the NEC as simply a forum for set speeches. The members of the secretariat – all distinguished academics – probed behind the stated positions. This process ensured that over the nine days the representatives of organisations had to think deeply about and defend their positions. It was partnership in education at its finest.

As a journalist covering the NEC, the author found the process fascinating. Among the lasting impressions are the following: a speech by Anne Colgan of the National Parents' Council (Primary) in which she made a powerful plea for partnership at all levels in education; the close questioning of the Catholic bishops about their views on education; the acceptance of the difficulties faced by multi-denominational schools; the recognition of the rights of those represented by the Campaign to Separate Church and State which pointed to the dilemma faced in a largely denominational system by parents of no religious views; an impressive contribution by the Union of Students in Ireland; the strong defence of the National Council for Educational Awards by its then director, Dr Padraig MacDiarmada; detailed costings of all the desirable improvements

---

[9] Pat Keating, interview with author, October 1998.

in education given by the Department Secretary, Dr Thornhill; the apparent 'writing on the wall' for the vocational education committee sector; and the convergence of views on the need to seriously tackle educational disadvantage.

There was extensive coverage of the event by the newspapers, television and radio, which helped highlight the importance of the NEC for the general public and for the participants. The participating journalists agreed not to report any information given to them about the private sessions. This may seem unusual for professionals who are constantly seeking to extract information from private meetings. It would have been relatively easy to find out what disagreements had developed behind closed doors but the author persuaded colleagues that reporting these tensions would make it more difficult to secure consensus on the issues and make progress.

A report on the convention was compiled by the NEC secretariat, whose secretary-general was Professor Coolahan.[10] The report summarised and analysed the discussions under various headings: philosophy of education and policy formulation; administrative change and the role of the department; intermediate educational tiers; the governance of schools; provision of multi-denominational and secular education; school rationalisation; the internal management of schools; the quality of education within schools; curricular issues; the Irish language; the teaching profession; higher education; adult and community education; equality issues; Irish education within its international context; legal aspects; the resourcing and implementation of educational change. Recommendations or pointers to the future were offered under each of the headings.

Some of these issues will be examined in later chapters. So also will the position papers on school governance and regional education councils as well as the round-table conferences on both those matters which were also held at Dublin Castle.

The report noted that the proposals for change set out in the Green Paper and the educational commitments in the *Programme for a Partnership Government 1993-1997*, if they were to be realised, would involve very significant additional expenditure on education:

---

[10] John Coolahan (Ed.), *Report on the National Education Convention,* Dublin, Stationery Office, 1994.

'As issues were explored at the Convention, it became clear that many reforms were being recommended by participants which would have significant cost implications. High expectations of improvements were also in evidence'. The secretariat, chaired by Professor Dervilla Donnelly from UCD, accepted that it would be extremely difficult to undertake all proposed improvements contemporaneously and that a planned prioritisation policy would be necessary. Nevertheless, it emphasised that the process then underway could not hope to be successful without significant extra resources being available for educational expenditure.[11]

Preparation of the White Paper

The lengthy process of consultation culminated in the publication of the White Paper.[12] Before examining the Paper in any detail a few remarks are worth making about the secrecy surrounding its preparation – secrecy that seemed at times touched with paranoia about the dangers of leaks. For several months officials of the department worked on the draft on weekdays in an office at the Marino Institute of Education. One reason was that the people involved would be able to get on with the work without too much interruption. But even the venue was not generally known about within the department's headquarters in Marlborough Street lest any hint of the contents become known. At weekends the minister worked on the paper in her home with her programme manager, Pat Keating, who was on secondment from his post as principal of the Christian Brothers' secondary school in Monkstown, Co. Dublin. According to Keating the minister 'took a hands-on approach to it and wrote and structured a good deal of the White Paper herself'.[13]

Extraordinary as it seems, the draft was typed on a paper that could not be photocopied. The gardaí had been consulted and they had recommended the use of a purple paper called *No Copi* paper. However, because of its colour it was difficult to read what was typed on it in certain light. This had one humorous result when

[11] Ibid, p. 5
[12] Department of Education, *Charting our Education Future – White Paper on Education*, Dublin, Stationery Office, 1995.
[13] Pat Keating, interview with author, October 1998.

the drafts were circulated for observations and the secretary of another department complained that Minister Breathnach's department was trying to blind him![14] Each chapter in the draft was preceded by a printed page warning that it might be an offence under the Official Secrets Act to read the chapter unless one had obtained the necessary permission. A shorter warning to the same effect was contained on every page of the draft. Keating has confirmed that the measures were prompted by concerns about the reaction of the Department of Finance if the White Paper was leaked – the apprehension was that Finance would blame Education for the leak and this might adversely affect its reaction to proposals that had cost implications.[15]

Despite the, at times ludicrous, lengths the department went to, the *Irish Independent* reported considerable detail from the White Paper around the time it was due to go before cabinet for final noting.[16] This prompted an early morning telephone call from Taoiseach John Bruton who asked the minister if her department had leaked the White Paper in order to ensure that it went through cabinet. This she vehemently denied. Her programme manager analysed the newspaper articles line by line and concluded that they were based on 'intelligent reading' of the minister's speeches, the NEC report, the Green Paper responses and criticisms, department position papers on regionalisation and governance, and a correct anticipation of what might be in the White Paper. The Taoiseach was so informed![17]

The White Paper

The White Paper built very directly on the work of the NEC which had achieved a fair degree of consensus and which had given the various stakeholders a sense of ownership of the proposals. The three-year period from the Green Paper to the White Paper also allowed people time to get used to the new policy proposals and ideas that had emerged.

---

[14] Off-the-record sources.
[15] Pat Keating, address to Society for Management in Education in Ireland, TCD, 17 October 1998.
[16] *Irish Independent*, 11 April 1995.
[17] Off-the-record sources.

The White Paper was divided into seven parts. The first part set out the philosophical framework. It identified the core concerns of the state in relation to education as being the promotion of pluralism, equality, partnership, quality and accountability, together with the protection of fundamental civil and human rights, and the promotion of social and economic well-being. The first few were insisted upon by the minister while the latter two were part of the inherited official ideas with which she agreed.[18] The Paper recognised the rights of individual schools, colleges and other institutions to develop and give effect to their own ethos and philosophical approach to education.

Part two was the most extensive, covering all levels of education as well as sport activities and youth. The primary education section dealt with pre-schooling; the revision of the curriculum; the need for 'sensitive and systematic' assessment of students' potential; the needs of children with disabilities; and provision for traveller children. The second-level section specified a target of 90 per cent completion rate of the senior cycle by the year 2,000 (the current level was 82-84 per cent); responsibility for tracking and monitoring school attendance to be given to new regional Education Boards; reforms of the curricula; a shift towards school-based assessment in the Junior Certificate; and increased emphasis on oral/aural assessment in languages.

Part two also contained a commitment to raising the legal school-leaving age from 15 to 16 and stated that Education Boards would have statutory responsibility for ensuring that regulations in regard to the length of the school year and day were adhered to by all schools. Boards would own new school buildings and a Commission on School Accommodation Needs would be established to advise on criteria and procedures for school rationalisation and amalgamation. In future, full recognition and entitlement to capital grants would be given to all schools, including all-Irish and multi-denominational schools, from the date of their establishment.

A Further Education Authority was promised as was new university legislation and more rigorous control procedures for private commercial colleges. A Youth Service Act was also promised

---

[18] Pat Keating, interview with author, October 1998.

and Education Boards were to be given a statutory role in the co-ordination and development of youth work.

Part three dealt with the teaching profession and promised a review of pre-service education for second-level teachers; a school-based scheme for the appraisal of teachers; a statutory Teaching Council; a welfare service for teachers; and priority to ensure teacher mobility between both parts of the island.

Part four dealt with the role of parents. It promised statutory entitlement to representation on all school boards of management and Education Boards; statutory right of access to their children's records in schools; a statutory duty on boards of management to promote the setting up of parents' associations; the involvement of parents in the preparation of school plans; right of appeal to the Education Boards; the rights of parents, through the National Parents' Council, to be consulted on important educational matters; and training programmes for parents.

Part five dealt with new organisational arrangements, in particular setting out the devolution of power and responsibilities to ten Education Boards and to individual school boards of management. The intention was to establish the Education Boards on a phased basis. They would be given responsibility for the systematic planning and co-ordination of educational provision in their regions at first and second level and in relation to vocational education and training, and adult education. In addition they would provide a wide range of services to schools. The Boards would be representative of the education partners and of the wider community, they would include public representatives and ministerial nominees. Side by side with the phasing in of the Boards the rationalisation of the state's thirty-eight Vocational Education Committees would be undertaken – this issue would be addressed by the Commission on School Accommodation Needs.

The individual schools would develop and publish a school plan and would be required to develop explicit policies for the promotion of health and well-being among their students.

The White Paper promised that the department would be restructured to focus on core responsibilities – policy formulation, national budgetary formulation and evaluation, national budgetary management and the evaluation and maintenance of the highest standards of quality. The role of the department's inspectorate would be changed. Some inspectors would be assigned to the Education Boards, with the primary task of evaluating the effectiveness of schools and providing advice on best practice, while a small core inspectorate would remain in the department with responsibility for the evaluation and maintenance of standards at national level.

Part six dealt with international issues, including the continued participation of the Irish education system in initiatives and programmes within the European Union. It promised the systematic promotion of active co-operation between the education systems on the island of Ireland. It also promised the promotion of an awareness of world issues, including development and environmental issues.

The final part of the White Paper dealt with the legal framework and the agenda for the implementation of change. The section did not attempt to interpret the constitution but instead identified the variety of constitutional rights which exist, for instance in relation to parents, children, religious denominations and property, as well as the overall framework of human and civil rights. In attempting to establish coherence and consistency between conflicting rights, one approach is to place those rights in a hierarchy where each right is given a priority relative to the other. The Paper argued, however, that alternatively the doctrine of constitutional interpretation known as 'harmonious interpretation' should be employed and that it had a special role to play in drafting legislation relating to education.[19] This 'harmonious interpretation' approach was indeed to play an important part in the drafting of the subsequent legislation.

The final section also promised that the implementation of change would be characterised by a firm commitment to the key directions set out in the White Paper. Change would be implemented as far as possible on a partnership basis in consultation with the concerned interests as appropriate and necessary.

Commentary

Professor Áine Hyland has noted that the 'unprecedented' success of the National Education Convention and of the subsequent round-

---

[19] White Paper, p. 214.

table discussions in Dublin Castle was evidenced in the acceptance by the different groups of the NEC report issued in January 1994 and, subsequently, of the White Paper.[20] The publication of the White Paper was the culmination of a long process of consultation and discussions. The process was characterised by much more openness and transparency than that leading up to the publication of the previous White Paper in 1980 by a Fianna Fáil minister, John Wilson.

There were no real surprises in the 1995 White Paper, arguably the most comprehensive and coherent document issued by the department to date. It set out a framework for development into the next century. It defined the roles and responsibilities of each of the education partners and proposed statutory enshrinement of the rights of parents.

It dropped many of the more controversial changes introduced by Séamus Brennan and reintroduced the notion of an intermediate tier. It avoided certain controversial issues such as how many VECs would be amalgamated and how many post-primary schools would have to close, given the need for rationalisation. The Paper could be faulted for not containing any costings, particularly for the proposed Education Boards. It could be faulted also for not having a separate section on Information Technology, given the growing importance of information and communications technologies in schools and society generally. These reservations aside, it was a document that any minister would have been proud to publish and one that was justifiably well received by all sides in the debate.

---

[20] Áine Hyland, 'A legacy to education that is real and tangible', in *The Examiner*, 22 May 1997.

CHAPTER 3

Intermediate Bodies/Regionalisation

The different types of schools in Ireland – primary, voluntary secondary, vocational, community and comprehensive – came into being independently of each other at different periods in history. They are managed, funded and administered differently. Each type has a different relationship with the Department of Education and Science in Dublin which has exercised considerable control over the day-to-day running of the majority of the schools.

The entire primary education system and most of the second-level education system in Ireland has been centrally administered for over 150 years. This centralised system in Ireland is in contrast to the situation in Great Britain and Northern Ireland where local education structures (e.g. Local Education Authorities in England and the Education and Library Boards in Northern Ireland) have been in existence since 1902 and 1922 respectively.[1] Before 1922 the central administrative bodies were the National and Intermediate Boards and these boards were replaced in 1922 by the Department of Education in Dublin.

The only regional administrative structures for education are the Vocational Education Committees (VECs) which were set up under the 1930 Vocational Education Act. They replaced the Technical Education Committees set up under the 1899 Agricultural and Technical Instruction (Ireland) Act.[2] Vocational schools, however, represent only a small proportion of the total number of schools in the country; in 1996-7 there were 243 VEC schools and colleges compared with 80 community and comprehensive schools, 440 voluntary secondary schools and 3,192 national schools.[3]

---

[1] Áine Hyland and Kenneth Milne, *Irish Educational Documents Volume II*, Dublin, Church of Ireland College of Education, 1992, p. 287.
[2] Ibid, pp. 287-288.
[3] Department of Education and Science, *Education statistics 1986/87-1996/97*.

Various proposals have been put forward over the decades to regionalise educational administration and these came closest to enactment in draft legislation in 1997. On each occasion, the proposals provoked strong reaction from interests opposed to the concept of regionalisation. This chapter will examine the proposals and review how they fared. Such a review may help to put the most recent discussions on regionalisation into their historical context.

Earliest proposals

At the turn of the century the quickening political tempo was reflected in the tensions between the Catholic Church and the British administration over educational issues. Matters came to a head in 1904 when Chief Secretary George Wyndham proposed that technical and intermediate education be co-ordinated and local control and rate-aid introduced – with an extension of this system to the primary level at a later date.[4] When the bishops met at Maynooth on 22 June 1904 they issued a statement in which they suggested that the proposals were but a guise for an attack on clerical power in the schools. As for democratic structures and parental involvement, they pointed out that parents showed little desire to interfere in schools 'from the conviction, which we regard as, on the whole, sensible on their part, that these things are somewhat outside of their competence'.[5]

Further attempts at changing the financing and administration of Irish education which were included in the Irish Councils Bill of 1907 were lost in the rejection of that measure.[6] In 1919 Ireland was given a new Chief Secretary, James MacPherson, a Scottish Presbyterian who attempted the most radical transformation of the Irish education system. His Bill, which was introduced into the House of Commons in November 1919, proposed the amalgamation

---

[4] E. Brian Titley, *Church, State and the Control of Schooling in Ireland 1900-1944,* Montreal and London, McGill-Queen's University Press, Dublin, Gill and Macmillan, 1983, p. 19.

[5] Ibid, p. 20.

[6] John Coolahan, *Irish Education: history and structure,* Dublin, Institute of Public Administration, 1981, p. 37.

of the National and Intermediate Boards and the Department of Agriculture and Technical Instruction into a single Department of Education for the whole country.[7] Authorities for local administrative purposes would be created for every county and county borough. They would take over the complete operation of the technical schools but would not interfere with the managerial system in primary or secondary schools nor have any role in teacher appoinments. The Bill also included clauses on compulsory attendance, evening and continuation classes, provision of an education rate to be added to departmental funds, abolition of the payment by results system and the introduction of superannuation schemes for all teachers.[8]

The Bill was, as Akenson has noted, 'as educationally desirable as it was politically unpalatable: it provided logical, inclusive and efficient solutions for most of the educational problems bedevilling Ireland; but it stood no chance of success because it aroused the ire of the Catholic bishops'.[9] The public reaction to the Bill divided along denominational lines; the Catholic clergy, the Catholic educational bodies and the Catholic-oriented press thundered against it while the Protestant churches, the Protestant managerial bodies and the Northern press generally stoutly supported it.[10] Because of the pressure on parliamentary business the Bill was withdrawn without a second reading in December 1919 but an identical Bill was reintroduced in February 1920, once again arousing great public controversy. Cardinal Logue issued a pastoral letter describing the 'pernicious Education Bill' as threatening the eternal and temporal interests of generations of Irish children.[11] The UK Government, already engaged in passing what was referred to as the 'Partition Act', was unwilling to become involved in another contentious

---

[7] Titley, p. 60.

[8] Coolahan, p. 72.

[9] Donald Harman Akenson, *A Mirror to Kathleen's Face – Education in Independent Ireland 1922-1960*, Montreal and London, McGill-Queen's University Press, pp. 18-19.

[10] Séamus Ó Buachalla, 'Education as an Issue in the First and Second Dáil', in *Administration*, Spring 1977, Vol. 25, No 1, Dublin, Institute of Public Administration, p. 59.

[11] *Irish News*, 16 February 1920.

Irish measure.[12] At the same time the Irish Nationalist Party was using delaying tactics against the Bill which was eventually withdrawn in December 1920 – the last effort at educational legislation for the whole island.[13]

The Duggan Report 1962

The Irish Free State inherited a rather run-down education machine in February 1922. Regionalisation was not a priority although the idea did surface in both Fine Gael and Labour Party documents in the period from the 1920s onwards.[14] The attitude that generally prevailed towards regionalisation of education in this period was captured by Atkinson when he wrote:

> The degree of centralisation in any education system should not be measured only against a background of population and geographical extent. It happens that the Irish Department of Education serves a population which is roughly comparable with that of one of the larger London boroughs, and an area which is smaller than that of some American School Districts.[15]

Yet the idea of regionalisation was examined officially by the Department of Education as early as 1962. The then minister, later President of Ireland, Dr Patrick Hillery, set up a committee of civil servants to study the education system and to advise on the changes needed.[16] The report was never published and its existence at the time was unknown to the teacher unions, managers and the public generally; even members of the OECD Investment in Education team were unaware of its existence.[17] In this context it is worth noting that the OECD study arose from a conference in Washington at the behest of the Department of Finance, rather than the Depart-

---

[12] Akenson, pp. 20-21.
[13] Coolahan, p. 73.
[14] Hyland and Milne, p. 288.
[15] Norman Atkinson, *Irish Education: A History of Educational Institutions,* Dublin, Allen Figgis, 1969, p. 195.
[16] Imelda Bonel-Elliott, 'The Role of the Duggan Report (1962) in the Reform of the Irish Education System', in *Administration,* Vol. 44, No 3. Autumn 1996, pp. 42-60.
[17] Ibid.

ment of Education. Five senior school inspectors sat on the committee, which was chaired by Dr Maurice Duggan.

It has been argued that the unpublished Duggan report played a key role in formulating the major structural reforms of the post-primary education system since the early 1960s.[18] The report recommended free post-primary education, which was highly significant in itself, but it also proposed the introduction of local statutory committees for post-primary education.[19] These committees would have power to raise funds from the rates and the right to supplement these funds from the central authority. The committee members would be nominated principally by the local authorities and would have, in addition, nominees of the local Catholic bishop and of religious minorities. The committees would take over all the existing functions of VECs and arrange for the disposal of funds to the post-primary education system in operation in their areas. The committees would take decisions about new school buildings but the managers of privately owned secondary schools would have the right of appeal to the minister against any adverse decision taken by the committees.[20] It is not known if the proposals were ever mentioned to the Catholic Church but it has been speculated that senior civil servants may have presumed that the Church would be against the proposals.[21]

Regionalisation proposals in the nineteen sixties and seventies

The middle to late sixties in Ireland saw much public discussion about regionalisation, not especially in the context of education but in terms of devolving power generally to the regions. The health and tourism services were being reorganised on a regional basis for instance, while in the education area Regional Technical Colleges were being introduced. A Labour Party policy document on edu-

---

[18] Ibid.
[19] Department of Education, *Tuarascáil Shealadach Ón Choiste A Cuireadh I mBun Scrúdú A Dhéanamh Ar Oideachas Iarbhunscoile*, December 1962, unpublished.
[20] Ibid.
[21] Imelda Bonel-Elliott, *Administration,* Autumn 1996.

cation in the late sixties called for Regional Education Authorities and Local Education Committees.[22]

Within the Department of Education some civil servants still regarded regionalisation as a solution to many of the problems of the education system. Although he was not on the Duggan Committee, Sean O'Connor, an energetic civil servant who was open to new ideas and willing to express them publicly, had prepared a paper on regionalisation in the latter half of 1967. In it he proposed that many of the minister's functions with respect to national schools and secondary schools be devolved to regional councils.[23] The then Minister for Education, Donogh O'Malley, who got on very well with O'Connor, decided to seek Cardinal Conway's reaction to the scheme. According to O'Connor:

> He told me he had gone to Cardinal Conway and left him a copy of the scheme. However, Mr O'Malley died soon afterwards and I never heard anything about the scheme. It may well be that Mr O'Malley did not like the scheme and had quietly buried it. Not until Richard Burke's appointment as Minister for Education was I able to interest any other minister in regionalisation.[24]

Indeed, little was done about regionalisation of education structures until Dick Burke became Minister for Education in March 1973, the same year O'Connor was appointed secretary of the department. Burke, later an EEC Commissioner, was a complex man, a very strong Catholic and at that time a public proponent of the principle of subsidiarity, which states that it is wrong for a larger and higher organisation to arrogate to itself functions which can be performed efficiently at a lower level.

Unusually, it was a civil servant – O'Connor – who made the initial running in public on two of the reform proposals most associated with Burke. It was he who first put forward the proposals for boards of management in primary schools (see chapter 4), in a speech to the Catholic Primary School Managers' Association in 1973. In the same speech he also proposed the introduction of

---

[22] Labour Party, *Outline Policy on Education*, 1969.
[23] Sean O'Connor, *A Troubled Sky – Reflections on the Irish Educational Scene 1957-1968*, Dublin, Educational Research Centre, 1986, p. 157.
[24] Ibid.

county and regional educational authorities.[25] These new bodies would look after every facet of education locally – primary, secondary, vocational and community schools and third-level colleges. The universities would be excluded, he said, 'only because we can't get them in'. He said that the department would simply give budgets to the new committees. All it would be concerned with was the amount to be given, a general indication of what it would be used for, and after that the committees were on their own.[26]

This was radical stuff indeed and bound to run into opposition, given the cautious nature of the education system at that time. O'Connor's proposals were fleshed out the following month.[27] An official document suggested the creation of county committees which would be composed half of teachers and school management and half of elected representatives. The functions of the committees might include the employment and payment of teachers; supervision of school transport services; development of adult education; maintenance and equipping of schools; provision of specialist services; allocation of school budgets; and preparation of county budgets for submission to the regional authority. The regional authority would have supervisory functions over county committees; it would approve applications for new schools; encourage innovation etc.

At first glance the document seemed to row back somewhat from O'Connor's original idea because it stated that the management of national and private secondary schools 'would not be interfered with by this scheme'. But the services to be provided by the proposed intermediate bodies, such as school transport and specialist services, would impact directly on the private Church-linked schools. Besides, both primary and secondary school teachers and managers were being invited to nominate people onto the new bodies. In addition the Churches were invited by the minister to join discussions on regionalisation.

It was made quite clear at the first meeting called by the minister on 3 October 1973 that the voluntary schools would come under

---

[25] *Irish Independent,* 13 June 1973.
[26] Ibid.
[27] Department of Education, *Regionalisation Draft for Discussion,* 25 July 1973.

the proposed education authorities. O'Connor told the meeting, which was attended by representatives for seventeen organisations, that 'unless the primary and secondary schools are in this scheme there just isn't any scheme, as far as I am concerned'.[28] The minister agreed that the document on regionalisation was vague but said he had two choices. 'One is to give you a worked out thing which would negate the idea of consultation, or to throw out broad principles on which we could work'.[29] Judging by the official minutes the morning session went reasonably well, with a fair measure of support from many of the organisations for the concept of regionalisation. But the atmosphere seems to have changed in the afternoon as a memorandum subsequently prepared for the Catholic Church school authorities showed. O'Connor apparently indicated that if schools remained out of the scheme their grants would be frozen. According to the memorandum prepared by Fr John Hughes SJ from the Secretariat of Catholic Secondary Schools the minister was asked to restore the good atmosphere which prevailed before lunch and which was dissipated by O'Connor's remark on 'freezing grants'. The memorandum reported that O'Connor rephrased his statement thus: 'there will be financial incentives for those who wish to enter the scheme as fully as their interests allow. These incentives will not be available for those schools (individual schools) which opt out'.[30] Fr Hughes also made a number of observations that are worth recording.

> The minister seemed to me to be over forceful in many of his statements and comments: this I would attribute to his desire to calm the IVEA and, possibly, the CEOs. ... No delegation rejected devolution: all asked for more information. The IVEA seemed very concerned. The minister blocked them developing their rather obvious demand for complete uniformity of management. He said: Private Schools will not be abolished.[31]

---

[28] Department of Education, *Minutes of Meeting with the Minister on 3 October 1973,* unpublished.

[29] Ibid.

[30] Secretariat of Catholic Secondary Schools, *Report on Minister's Meeting on Regionalisation, 3 October 1973,* unpublished.

[31] Ibid.

A committee was appointed and held its first meeting on 19 October. The minutes of the meeting reported that the majority of members considered that the committee's task was to consider, weigh and evaluate the proposals, including the basic one of the desirability of or necessity for decentralisation.[32] A second meeting was held on 9 November 1973. The co-chairman, Tomas O'Floinn from the department, said that 1 December was the deadline for the provision of a report, but several delegates said it was virtually impossible to deal with the various items on the agenda without first reaching some form of agreement on structures.[33] By the third meeting it was obvious that major differences were emerging between the various parties. The constitution of the proposed county committees was one source of disagreement as was the issue of representation of the regional authority on school management boards.[34]

In the meantime the Catholic and later the Protestant education interests involved began to hold their own meetings. The minutes of the first of these lists four key points that had emerged from the initial discussions with the minister and his officials; they also give a fascinating insight into the concerns of the Churches.

1 Statement that unless the Voluntary Schools are prepared to join the scheme, the scheme is not on.
2 Those who opt out will have grants frozen at their present level.
3 Departmental device: if a Working Party is established from a reduced meeting, interests could be conveniently split and divided.
4 Could be the means of requiring expression of orientation NOW, illustrating a divergence of opinion which would give department excuse to make own mixture without paying heed to higher or lower opinion.[35]

---

[32] Department of Education, *Minutes of first Meeting of Committee on Regionalisation, 19 October 1973*, unpublished.
[33] Department of Education, *Minutes of Meeting of Committee on Regionalisation, 9 November 1973*, unpublished.
[34] Department of Education, *Minutes of Meeting of Committee on Regionalisation, 27 November 1973*, unpublished.
[35] Secretariat of Secondary Schools, *Minutes of Meeting of Church Management Bodies, 12 October, 1974*, unpublished.

A subsequent meeting of the Church interests was informed of the
existence of an Educational Policy Group comprising representatives
of the Catholic hierarchy, the Conference of Major Religious
Superiors and the Working Party on the Future Involvement of
Religious in Education. This group was formed 'to meet the need
for a co-ordinated approach in negotiation at government levels
on policy matters of specific importance to the interests of Catholic
education'.[36] As well as some members of the hierarchy its membership included Rev. Paul Andrews SJ and Bro. Declan Duffy of
the Teaching Brothers Association. Its two chief concerns were to
safeguard pluralism in education and the maintenance of Catholic
schools, both religious and lay. The meeting was told that the
co-ordination of objectives was of immediate importance in the
regionalisation debate, 'lest a splintering should result in any
weakening of negotiating strength'. A Bro. Maurice stressed the
need for strictly confidential treatment of this information because
of 'the negotiation procedure'.[37]

    In further discussions the managerial associations agreed that
there should not be more than one administrative structure between
the schools and the department, that teacher employment should
remain in the hands of school managers, and that the new bodies
should comprise one-third teachers, one-third managers and one-
third public representatives.[38] By January the Church bodies, with
the support of the Protestant managerial organisations, had set down
minimum conditions for consideration of regionalisation. They called
for effective statutory guarantees:

    1 as to the continued existence of Church schools
    2 as to equality of opportunity as between Church schools and
       other schools:
       a) in the establishment of new schools
       b) in the renovation and extension of existing schools
       c) in the allocation of facilities for administration, libraries,
          laboratories, etc.

---

[36] Secretariat of Secondary Schools, *Minutes of Meeting of Church Management
    Bodies, 8 November 1973*, unpublished.
[37] Ibid.
[38] Secretariat of Secondary Schools, *Letter to Managerial Associations and other
    Church-linked School Organisations, 23 November 1973*, unpublished.

    d) in the availability of teachers

    e) in the provision of free transport

3 as to the provision of adequate state grants for capital and maintenance costs

4 as to comprehensive religious instruction, formation and worship in accordance with the wishes of parents in all schools.[39]

The document was tabled by Bro. Declan Duffy at what turned out to be the last meeting of the committee on regionalisation. Coolahan has argued that meeting these demands would have meant a full copperfastening of the private schools separate from the schools under the proposed regional authorities.[40] The meeting was again chaired by Tomas O'Floinn who said he would report to the minister that progress was imperceptible – it seemed to him that schools and teachers wanted to remain as they were in relation to the department. In the light of that he was not sure of the purpose of going on with the exercise.[41] The minutes report that

> The chairman did not know whether the committee would continue or not. He felt in all fairness that he had to put it in these terms as he didn't see much point in carrying on with the discussions aimed at agreeing on a set of proposals for the minister's consideration in the context of the reconstruction of the educational system on a regional basis. This was not emerging; he had sought not to lead them in any way but there was disagreement on fundamental issues and to go on would not provide anything worthwhile to the minister.[42]

One of those who attended the talks told the author at that time that it seemed impossible to reconcile the conflicting demands of the private and public sectors at post-primary level.[43] This proved to be indeed correct and the talks were not resumed.

    There is evidence, however, that progress was possible and that the minister was willing to meet at least some of the Church

---

[39] Statement by Clerical/Religious Representatives, *Statutory Guarantees to Voluntary Secondary Schools,* 11 January 1974.

[40] John Coolahan, *Regionalisation of Education: A Recurrent Concern,* address to seminar on the Green Paper, Tralee, 25 January 1986.

[41] Department of Education, *Minutes of Meeting of Committee on Regionalisation, 11 January 1994,* unpublished.

[42] Ibid.

[43] *Irish Independent,* 15 January 1974.

demands. It is known that the minister indicated his readiness to give certain assurances sought by the Educational Policy Group, including recognition of the Church's right to provide new schools and to afford equality of opportunity as between Church and non-Church schools. But he demurred at two of the demands on the grounds that they were financial and would need to be discussed by the full cabinet. These related to entitlment to state capital and maintenance grants equivalent to what was available in Northern Ireland and the application of the same standards, as between Church and non-Church schools, in determining schedules of accommodation and grants.[44] A document prepared some months later by the department also made it clear that the minister was prepared to concede some of the legislative guarantees sought by the Churches.[45] The document provided a very good analysis of the arguments for regionalisation. It indicated that the minister was satisfied that a system of regionalisation which would combine counties into units and divide the country into nine geographical areas would be the most suitable system. The document ended the polite fiction that primary and voluntary secondary schools would remain outside the ambit of the proposed structures, because it proposed that the department would delegate to county education committees functions affecting these schools, such as payments of salaries and grants.[46]

It would be unfair to blame the Churches for the collapse of the talks, because the vocational sector, which would be absorbed into the new structure, was not enamoured of the proposals either. At the final meeting of the committee on regionalisation B.B. Little submitted a statement on behalf of the IVEA. This document stated that the Association was vigorously opposed to regionalisation which would involve a plurality of counties. 'We believe that the big regional organisation would not be any closer to the department than the organisation based on the county and would be far removed from the school'.[47] The IVEA along with the Teachers' Union of

---

[44] Off-the-record sources.
[45] Department of Education, *Regionalisation of the Education Sector, Analysis and Recommendations,* 1974, unpublished.
[46] Ibid.
[47] Irish Vocational Education Association, *Statement submitted to Committee on Regionalisation, 11 January 1974.*

Ireland and the Chief Executive Officers' Association later drew up a response which suggested county committees to service post-primary schools and Regional Technical Colleges.[48] The local education authorities would be composed half from the local authorities, quarter from the teaching unions and quarter from managerial bodies. Their response asserted that 'it is our firm view that the principles of the 1930 (Vocational Education) Act must be incorporated in any proposed legislation or changes to which we can give our assent'. The document was adopted by the IVEA Congress in Bantry in June 1975 but not before it provoked some strong comments from the floor. A Co. Dublin delegate, John Boland, later Fine Gael Minister for Education, was quoted as saying that delegates were being asked to vote to phase themselves out of existence and that future congresses would have very few public representatives present.[49] In his presidential address to the Congress Jack McCann said that any revised scheme of reorganisation must be based unequivocally on the local elective process and he added that 'Until we feel reassured on this aspect of the proposed reorganisation, we are not prepared to agree to any proposals which would have the effect of limiting or changing the present functions of vocational education committees'.[50]

Dick Burke remained in office until the end of 1976 but little more was done to progress his regionalisation plans.

Further proposals on regionalisation

The issue of regionalisation did not, however, entirely disappear from the agenda during the late seventies and early eighties. *Patterns of Education in the British Isles*, which was published in 1977, rather archly noted that

> From time to time there is talk of a move towards the establishment of English-style local education authorities or possibly, as a compromise, regional education authorities. Indeed one of the

---

[48] Irish Vocational Education Association, '*Reorganisation of Educational Structures*'. Annual Report to Congress (Bantry), Appendix V, 1975.
[49] *Education Times*, June 1975.
[50] Ibid.

partners in Cosgrove's Coalition Government (the Irish Labour Party) openly advocates the latter. But it is realistic to remember that, whatever the infrastructure that might be established, real powers would first have to be wrested from the hands of the bishops and the religious orders on the one hand and of the minister on the other given that they, between them, supply the funds for what are essentially the schools of a developing country. There has even been a suspicion in recent years that decision-making could pass outside altogether – to the World Bank, for example, one of the main suppliers of funds for the development of the Republic's second-level system'.[51]

Regionalisation was not mentioned at all in the 1980 White Paper on Education published by a Fianna Fáil government when John Wilson was Minister for Education.[52] However, the coalition of Fine Gael and Labour that came to power the following year agreed a programme which included provision for a 'more decentralised and more democratic' system of administrative structures within the education system.[53] The *Programme for Action in Education* contained a brief reference to the idea when it stated: 'Consultation will take place with a view to the establishment of local co-ordination committees representative of all educational interests in a given area to facilitate initiative in promoting co-operation in educational provision in that area'.[54]

The National Planning Board in its proposals published in April 1984 was more specific when it recommended that 'the establishment of a unified system of local education and training boards should be considered in the context of local government reform'.[55] The recommendation was supported in the report of the committee on youth policy headed by Mr Justice Declan Costello.[56] The report of

[51] Robert Bell and Nigel Grant, *Patterns of Education in the British Isles*, London, Unwin Education Books, 1977, p. 95.
[52] Department of Education, *White Paper on Educational Development*, Dublin, Stationery Office, 1980.
[53] Fine Gael/Labour coalition, *Programme for Government*, December 1982, p. 24.
[54] Fine Gael/Labour coalition, *Programme for Action in Education 1984-87*, p. 24.
[55] National Planning Board, *Proposals for Plan, 1984-87*, Dublin, 1984, p. 296.
[56] National Youth Policy Committee, *Final Report*, Dublin, Stationery Office, 1984, pp. 28, 129.

the Commission on Adult Education supported county adult
education boards[57] and the report of the Committee on In-service
Education recommended local councils for in-service education
for teachers.[58]

This time the Catholic Church was not going to be caught
unawares and its Episcopal Commission on Education established
a working party on regionalisation whose report was presented to
the Episcopal Conference in June 1982.[59] It was a curious document,
combining some cogent arguments against regionalisation with a
nervous defensiveness as shown in this quotation from the two-
page introduction:

> It is timely to highlight the necessity for the Church to have done
> its homework in areas where it might be accused of having a
> 'privileged position' given the atmosphere and attitudes which are
> being shaped by those who propagate 'crusades', 'pluralism',
> 'democracy', 'egalitarianism' etc.

The document questioned the relevance of regionalisation – more
'red tape' etc. – and put forward arguments for use in any debate
about how the Church-linked schools met the advantages claimed
for regionalisation. For instance on the accountability argument it
pointed out that schools receiving state monies were held
accountable by the department for the ways in which the money
was spent. It added that:

> It is interesting to speculate that those who advocate more
> accountability for Church-linked schools would be satisfied only if
> such schools were brought into a total system of education. This is
> the drift which seems to be favoured by the proponents of region-
> alisation. If these points are conceded, then what they desire is the
> antithesis of what they claim to desire, i.e. 'a more democratic
> system of education'.

---

[57] Commission on Adult Education, *Lifelong Learning*, Dublin, Stationery Office,
1983, pp. 129-133.
[58] *Report of the Committee on In-service Education*, Dublin, Stationery Office,
1984, p. 54.
[59] Working Party from the Episcopal Commission on Education, *Report on
Regionalisation of our Education Structure*, presented to the Episcopal
Conference, June 1982, unpublished.

The final appendix listed the same statutory guarantees that had been sought eight years earlier from Dick Burke. It emphasised that these still represented the basic position of the Church side in the 'undesirable event' that regionalisation proposals might be resurrected by another Minister for Education.

Green Paper 1985, *Partners in Education*

Regionalisation was indeed resurrected three years later – in November 1985 – by Gemma Hussey, the Minister for Education in the coalition government. She issued a Green Paper which proposed the establishment of thirteen Local Education Councils.[60] The LECs would consist of 30-32 members each. About a third of the members would be drawn from local authorities. Primary and post-primary school managers, teachers and parents would be represented as would the youth services, training/manpower agencies, adult education agencies and economic interests including the social partners. The Green Paper envisaged each post-primary school having a board of management which would retain rights over the appointment and dismissal of teachers.

The LECs could undertake a number of functions including, perhaps, the provision, planning and development of second-level education, payment of teachers, maintenance of second-level schools, promotion of liaison between the primary and post-primary sectors. Consideration might also be given to the transfer of responsibility for the public library service to the LECs.

The publication of the Green Paper provoked a strong reaction from the Council of Managers of Catholic Secondary Schools which expressed amazement at the priorities of the minister.[61] It claimed that the timing of the proposals was inopportune for three reasons. One was the tension arising from a teachers' pay dispute taking place at that time. Another was the introduction of boards of management in secondary schools then taking place. Thirdly a climate of financial cuts had just been introduced 'with such

[60] Department of Education, Green Paper, *Partners in Education,* Dublin, Stationery Office, 1985.
[61] Council of Managers of Catholic Secondary Schools, *Press Release,* 13 November 1985.

disastrous results for our young people'. The Council subsequently turned down an invitation to talks stating that it would not be prepared to discuss the Green Paper with the minister and the department until there was movement towards redressing the cuts in secondary education.[62] However, the Catholic school managers did prepare their own response in which Bro. Declan Duffy argued that if there were to be an Education Act it should be preceded by a White Paper. He said it should also incorporate the statutory guarantees listed earlier for the continued existence of Church-linked schools.[63] The Conference of Major Religious Superiors claimed that the Green Paper gave no promise of real democratisation, because all the major decisions were made elsewhere. 'We favour real democracy, which would involve all the interested parties participating in decision-making with regard to education at local level'.[64]

A response which was very critical of the Green Paper was prepared by three organisations, the CMRS, CMCSS and the Episcopal Commission for Education. The response stated it was quite remarkable that a document proposing a regional structure for education should issue at a time when the Department of Health was frantically attempting to restore some order to a (regionalised) health service which had gone out of control.[65]

> The discussion document fails to make an adequate case for such far-reaching changes. One of the most compelling reasons given for the proposed new structures is 'in the context of the rationalisation of school facilities' and the hope is expressed that the establishment of a regional body would 'eliminate friction' and provide a 'better framework for the rationalisation of post-primary facilities and for the delivery of other services'. Nothing in the proposed structures or role for the LECs leads one to believe that this will be achieved.

---

[62] Bro. Declan Duffy, *Letter from Council of Managers of Catholic Secondary Schools to Department of Education,* 2 December 1985.

[63] Bro. Declan Duffy, *Response to the Green Paper on Regionalisation,* 17 February 1986.

[64] Fr Paul Byrne OMI, Conference of Major Religious Superiors, *General Comments on Green Paper,* 1986.

[65] Episcopal Commission for Education/Education Commission of the CMRS/ Council of Managers of Catholic Secondary Schools, *Response on Local Education Structures,* 10 March 1986.

The Green Paper had suggested that LEC representatives would sit on the boards of management of all schools and this proposal particularly alarmed the Protestant sector. The Secondary School Council of Governors gave this response:

> Within the terms of the Green Paper any LEC members appointed cannot be guaranteed to be those who would share the aims and objectives of the particular school. Inevitably some appointees would be Roman Catholics. The Council presumes that the implications for Protestant schools had not been appreciated. It can not imagine that the government would contemplate, against the expressed will of the Church of Ireland, the Methodist Church, and the Presbyterian Church, imposing Roman Catholics on Protestant schools. The Council would wish to have definite assurances that any such imposition of members to our boards is not intended and will be explicitly guarded against.[66]

Reaction from the vocational education sector was even stronger, understandable given that the proposals meant the elimination of the VEC system. The Irish Vocational Education Association concluded that the LEC proposal was the antithesis of the Green Paper's stated objective. The proposed regions were 'hopelessly large', they would lack a sense of identity and would not accommodate communities within the region relating to the authority in any meaningful way. It added that the paper 'represents a set of proposals whose main purpose is to cut back existing resources while reorganising and strengthening centralised control of all post-primary education'.[67]

The INTO warned that the minister's objectives could not be achieved without the inclusion of the primary sector.[68] But the Catholic Primary School Managers' Association argued that a regionalised system of education, such as that proposed in the Green Paper, 'would not be of any educational value or advantage to primary schools.[69]

---

[66] Secondary School Council of Governors, *Partners in Education*, Submission to the Minister for Education, February 1986.
[67] Irish Vocational Education Association, *The VEC Response*, 26 February 1986.
[68] *INTO Response to the Green Paper*, November 1985.
[69] Catholic Primary School Managers' Association, *Solus*, Uimhir 9, Fomhar 1986.

The minister spoke at some length about the Green Paper when she delivered the John Marcus O'Sullivan Memorial Lecture in Tralee in January 1986. She said that Ireland had a system of post-primary schools whose different structures did not always harmonise melodiously and added that

> I have been greatly distressed by the bitter divisions which have shattered communities locked into battles of argument about the relative merits of community schools and community colleges. The distinctions centre on issues of control and management where painful power struggles are sometimes acted out which are in no one's interests – least of all the children's. Inevitably someone has to make a decision – usually the unfortunate minister – a decision which inevitably leaves one faction aggrieved and disappointed. This is no climate to establish a school, which should be a beacon of hope and unity in the community. The proposals in the Green Paper seek to overcome this problem, essentially by eliminating the distinction between these two types of schools.

She said it was her target to go back to government in the early summer with recommendations arising from the discussions and submissions. If it was decided to proceed along the lines outlined in the Green Paper it would be her hope that the necessary legislation would be enacted towards the end of the year, she said.[70] However, no further action was taken to implement the proposals while she was in office.

She was succeeded by Paddy Cooney, a conservative politician whose main contribution to education was to settle a long-running and increasingly bitter teachers' pay dispute. Officially he intended to press on with the implementation of the Green Paper proposals but he never got around to it.[71] One suspects that he was not exactly sold on the idea and that he saw his main function as taking the heat out of a portfolio which had become extremely controversial under his predecessor.

---

[70] Minister for Education, Gemma Hussey, address at the John Marcus O'Sullivan Memorial Lecture, Tralee, 25 January 1986.
[71] *Irish Independent*, 13 March 1986.

OECD proposals 1991

The issue of regionalisation was revived in 1991 by the Organisation for Economic Co-operation and Development (OECD) in a review of national education policies in Ireland.[72] The examiners sought to identify and discuss in general rather then technical terms the present and emerging issues and problems that appeared to be facing Irish education. The report suggested, *inter alia,* that

> The department is concerned with such minor matters because there is no administrative layer interposed between it and individual institutions. The question arises, therefore, whether it would not be desirable to devolve some of the department's routine functions to regionally based administrative units. This could serve the double purpose of improving overall efficiency and freeing the department to address substantive matters designed to serve ministers in the development and implementation of policies.[73]

An earlier unpublished draft of this report went further in recommending some form of intermediate structure.[74] This suggested that there was a lack of consistency in implementing government decisions about education. It noted, for instance, that Gemma Hussey's Green Paper had not been implemented nor had a promise that responsibility for the examinations would be transferred to the National Council for Curriculum and Assessment. It went on to deal with some of the benefits of a regional education authority. It made the point that post-primary school amalgamations required local and community backing and added that it would be odd if only vocational schools could benefit from already having in place a flexible intermediary managerial structure able to cope with the development of new functions and services. It stated that in view of current school needs in the fields of management, leadership and accountability, a regional authority could also be the place where such issues as

---

[72] OECD, *Review of National Policies for Education, Ireland,* Paris, OECD, 1991.
[73] Ibid, p. 41.
[74] John Walshe, 'The Urgency of Making Sense (The OECD Report)', in *Decision Maker,* No 2, Association of Chief Executive Officers of VECs, Winter 1990, p. 8.

1 the managerial needs of the several types of secondary schools
   could be reviewed and alternative solutions sought, including
   lay people on school boards and related structures
2 various modes of educational evaluation could be worked out
   so as to help schools cope with an open scheme of accountability, based on the formulation and implementation of a school
   plan
3 the preparation of a plan of in-service education for teachers
   could be discussed and steps taken to co-ordinate its implementation.[75]

Minister Mary O'Rourke had, of course, been given a copy of this
earlier draft. The examiners anticipated the inevitable arguments
that the country had a small population inhabiting a small geographic
area and that the department had established over the years intimate
contacts with local interests and institutions and that, therefore, to
add another administrative level was quite superfluous. The arguments they expected were indeed presented at a review meeting
that took place in Paris on 30 November 1989 which was attended
by the examiners, by the OECD Education Committee, and by the
Irish delegation led by Minister O'Rourke. The discussion ranged
over many of the issues raised by the examiners, including their
suggestion for an intermediate tier. However, an intermediate
structure was opposed by the minister, who pointed out that the
department had a total personnel of 830, of which 240 were
professional or technical staff. She said that the department served
an education system of around 900,000 full-time participants and
over 40,000 teachers, and administered a budget of some £1.3b.
The salary bill for the department itself represented only about
1.25 per cent of the total budget. She said that she was among
those who believed that the country was too small to have a regional
layer of administration imposed between local institutions and central
government.[76]

---

[75] Ibid.
[76] OECD, *Review of National Policies for Education, Ireland,* pp. 119-120.

County Committees of Education proposed and dropped

Yet two years later Mary O'Rourke's own draft Green Paper on education stated that the establishment of an intermediate support structure for educational services, between the Department of Education and the individual schools, would seem to be both desirable and timely.[77] Without any trace of irony the draft quoted the OECD report to buttress the case for an intermediate structure. Her draft Green Paper proposed the establishment of County Committees of Education which would have a mainly supportive and co-ordinating role in respect of the activities of all primary and post-primary schools.

> What is being proposed is to develop a new and more embracing body to replace the existing VECs, with responsibility for the provision of a range of services initially to all second-level schools, and, later, to all primary schools within the county, as well as providing a range of other services.[78]

So why did she change her mind? According to Professor Coolahan, who was involved in the preparation of her draft Green Paper, the minister came around to the idea in discussions on the Paper's contents in October 1991.[79] In an interview with the author she agreed that initially she did not see the need for intermediate structures.[80] However, she said that her attitude changed as the discussions on her draft Green Paper developed. She had favoured a commonality of post-primary school types and wanted to bring about rationalisation:

> The only way you could do that was under an umbrella structure and that was to be the County Committees of Education. I did not want to call them local committees. That was our starting point on that. Then we looked at whether or not we would eventually put in primary under it. We put in a teaser that we would look at other structures later.

[77] *Draft Green Paper on Education*, 25 October 1991, unpublished.
[78] Ibid.
[79] John Coolahan, address to the Society for Management in Irish Education, TCD, 17 October 1998.
[80] Mary O'Rourke, interview with author, 16 November 1995.

She added that later that autumn the bishops, under Bishop Thomas McKiernan, chairman of the Episcopal Commission on Education, asked to meet her:

> We had a long meeting. Margaret Walsh (her adviser), the Secretary (Noel Lindsay) and myself met them for two hours.[81] I was quite frank with them about what I was proposing to put in the Green Paper. They were worried about what these county committees would do to their special place. I did my best to reassure them that I would not be prescriptive. I would have county committees that would have a loose arrangement of perhaps funding for the schools' libraries. They were mollified by John Coolahan being in the process.[82] I saw that in time the county committees could adapt to primary schools. It tied in imaginatively with several things such as commonality and it tied in with giving autonomy to primary schools.

As already stated, Mary O'Rourke's draft was never officially published. She was succeeded for a brief period as minister by Noel Davern who retained proposals for county committees and who, in turn, was followed by Séamus Brennan. A final version of the Green Paper was published by Brennan in June 1992 but the section proposing county committees had been deleted entirely.[83] Brennan, initially, feared that the county committees would become an enlarged version of Vocational Education Committees; unlike many Fianna Fáil party colleagues he did not come across as a firm advocate and defender of the VEC system. His Green Paper envisaged instead the devolution of powers to school boards of management and to executive agencies such as a payroll agency, an educational property management agency, and a school psychological agency.

There was, as we have seen in an earlier chapter, an astonishing reaction to the Green Paper in terms of the quality and quantity of responses, with over 1,000 written submissions to the department and innumerable meetings all over the country. There was considerable criticism of the absence of any intermediate tier. For instance

---

[81] Margaret Walsh is a former president of the ASTI.
[82] Prof Coolahan is Professor of Education at what was then a recognised college of the National University of Ireland, and the national seminary for the training of priests, St Patrick's College, Maynooth.
[83] Department of Education, *Education For A Changing World,* Dublin, Stationery Office, 25 June 1992.

Dr Garret FitzGerald, former Fine Gael education spokesperson and former Taoiseach, noted the absence of any proposal for co-ordination of education at local or regional level. He wrote that

> Any proposal for a local or regional co-ordination mechanism is, of course, bound to evoke howls from a whole range of vested interests; I don't need to name them! But any talk of devolution of power from the Department of Education is quite meaningless when there is apparently to be no regional or local body with a co-ordinating function. In these circumstances all the key decisions will remain with the department. This is thoroughly disappointing – indeed alarming. One can only hope that recovery of nerve will take place before this Green Paper turns white.[84]

It did and even before he left office Séamus Brennan was coming round to the idea of some form of local education authority: he said that he had taken the county committees out of the Green Paper partly to hear the arguments for their justification and had since taken those on board.[85]

Catholic Church views on regionalisation

An interesting debate was also taking place within the Catholic Church on the issue. The Bishop of Cork and Ross, Dr Murphy, suggested that a regional layer of management, representing all the schools in an area, could improve efficiency. He said that Brennan's proposals for executive agencies might be realistic if they were to exist at regional level. At national level they would prove as unwieldy as the Board of Works in its handling of national school construction and maintenance, suggested Dr Murphy.[86] Given the hierarchy's opposition to regionalisation a decade earlier his views were very significant and he was thought to have been the first Catholic bishop to openly favour regionalisation in some form.

However, the bishops were no longer the force they once were, nor were they the only Catholic Church voice in education. One

[84] Garret FitzGerald, 'The Future of Irish Education', in *Decision Maker*, No 6, Autumn 1992, Association of Chief Executive Officers of VECs, p. 8.
[85] Séamus Brennan, interview with author, April 1997.
[86] *The Irish Times*, 19 October 1992.

reason was the erosion of their perceived authority generally, because of a succession of Church scandals. Another was the increasing assertion of their own authority by both the Conference of Major Religious Superiors (later the Conference of Religious of Ireland) and the secondary school managers.

The CMRS came out in favour of regionalisation, stating that Local Education Committees would respond to a series of challenges facing the Irish education system.[87] In its document published in January 1993 it listed the benefits of such committees. For instance they could moderate the undesirable consequences of competition between schools; allow for more participation in decision-making; lead to more co-operation between the various sectors; and allow for greater responsiveness to the needs of the local area, especially in relation to adult and community education. The CMRS envisaged a total membership of not more than twenty on each council, drawn from elected representatives, community based organisations, business, parents, teachers, school providers, adult and community education, and co-opted members.

The CMRS proposal sparked off an extraordinary reaction, little of which spilled over into the public arena. The Secretariat of Secondary Schools, which represents the school managers, reported in its February 1993 newsletter that its office had received 'many protests' from principals and management about the recent document and press statement from the CMRS.[88] The newsletter contained a copy of a letter sent to Sr Bernadette McMahon DC, chairperson of the CMRS Education Commission by Br. Declan Duffy, General Secretary, Council of Managers of Catholic Secondary Schools (CMCSS). Because of its significance it is worth quoting in full.

Dear Sr Bernadette

Re: Document on Local Education Committees

The Council of Management of Catholic Secondary Schools at its meeting on Friday, 15th January 1993 had before it the above document after it had been released to the Press. The Council expressed

---

[87] CMRS Education Commission, *Local Education Committees, A Case for their Establishment and a Tentative Proposal,* January 1993.
[88] Secretariat of Secondary Schools, *Newsletter,* February 1993.

surprise and disappointment at the context in which the document was made public. CMCSS asked me to write to your Commission in the following terms.

1. CMCSS has no difficulty with the fact that the Education Commission holds a different view from itself on the issue of intermediate educational structures.

2. However, they feel it was insensitive to seek publicity at this time for a view which runs contrary to *all* the other partners in Catholic primary and secondary education, especially in the context of CMRS's evocation of the need for partnership and consultation among the various interests in education.

3. CMCSS is consequently astonished – in view of the position adopted by all the other partners in Catholic education – that CMRS Education Commission should in the final sentence of their document pledge the resources of the CMRS to the development of a local education structure: 'we are deeply committed to developing such an educational system and pledge the resources of CMRS to this end'. p. 19.

There are many problems to be faced by all partners (religious, clerical and lay) who are involved in Catholic education. These problems are now aggravated by the alienation of most of these partners from CMRS on the delicate issue of intermediate educational structures. This most recent example of public dissonance between Trustees and all others, repeats the problems and the pain which occurred in the release of the CMRS Education Commission document 'Inequality in Schools in Ireland – 1989'.

We would appeal for greater sensitivity by the CMRS Education Commission towards those struggling in Catholic education at the grass roots.

The language in the letter is extraordinary, with its references to alienation and public dissonance and its appeal for greater sensitivity. It also confirmed what had long been suspected, namely that the managers were still smarting over a 1989 document from the CMRS which had recommended ending the use of selective entrance exams.[89] As one managerial source commented: 'if they (the CMRS)

---

[89] CMRS Education Commission, *Inequality in Schooling in Ireland: The Role of Selective Entry and Placement,* September 1989.

felt so strongly about this issue why didn't they do something about it, instead of attacking us in public. After all they represent the Trustees of the schools'.[90] As in many areas of life, personality issues came into play as much as policy and there was known to have been little love lost between the Secretariat and the Commission. The Secretariat had long and successfully defended secondary school management interests but it was perceived as somewhat conservative compared with the more 'progressive', if not left-wing, CMRS. The CMRS was also seen as much more proactive in leading or influencing the debate, not just on educational issues but on other social justice issues such as unemployment and the disadvantaged in society.

The CMRS education secretariat was headed by Sr Teresa McCormack, a Presentation nun whose Provincial Superior, Sr Imelda Wickham, responded by writing to all the order's school principals and chairpersons. She welcomed the CMRS document and expressed the concern that delegating authority to individual schools without the safeguard of a local co-ordinating structure would have negative consequences for schools in disadvantaged areas.[91] Her letter added:

> In view of this, we were disappointed to read a letter from Br. Declan Duffy which was published in the February issue of the Secretariat Newsletter. We accept and welcome Br. Declan's differing views, but we are concerned that some of his statements re. the CMRS publication were inaccurate, and that our position as trustees in relation to intermediate structures was not adequately represented. We have written to Br. Declan on this matter.[92]

The Secretariat agreed to a request from the CMRS to publish a lengthy reply with its newsletter the following month. This reply described as absurd the suggestion that the CMRS was willing to finance local education structures and claimed that this was a misreading of the CMRS's proposals. It also rejected the claim that all the other partners in Catholic primary and secondary schools were opposed to local education structures and quoted the CMCSS's

---

[90] Off-the-record source.
[91] Presentation Provincialite, *Letter to Principals and Chairpersons*, 15 February 1993.
[92] Ibid.

own submission on the Green Paper which recognised that 'it may be desirable to establish a co-ordinating agency for a geographic area with a very specific remit'. The reply stated that the intention of the Commission to publish its views had been made clear at a number of meetings at which the CMCSS was represented. The CMRS had taken the view that all of the different organisations should make and publish their own responses. The letter rather pointedly went on:

> We further felt that positive reform of the education system would be best served by a full, frank and open exchange of views among all those involved in education. We are aware that you expressed a different view at the meeting convened by the Joint Education Commission (of the Hierarchy and CMRS) in September 1992 when you stated that you felt that more progress would be made in private discussions and negotiations. We respect your opinion in this matter.[93]

Certainly the model of private discussions and negotiations had served the Catholic Church well in the past, but the CMRS's commitment to open dialogue was more in keeping with the political instincts of Brennan's successor, Niamh Bhreathnach, and the tempo of the times summed up in the phrase 'inclusive talks'. Coming from the CMRS, the proposals for local education structures were in many ways a generous and significant contribution and it has been argued that they made it easier for the government to favour such a policy.[94] Indeed Pat Keating, the minister's programme manager, has confirmed that the CMRS document was seen as a key contribution by policy advisers at that time.[95]

Position paper from the minister on Regional Education Councils, 1994

By the mid-nineties there seemed to be an almost unstoppable momentum towards some form of intermediate or regionalised structures, even though reservations continued to be expressed by

---

[93] Letter from CMRS Education Commission to CMCSS, in *Newsletter*, Secretariat of Secondary Schools, March 1993.
[94] Imelda Bonel-Elliott, *Administration*, p. 54.
[95] Pat Keating, interview with author, October 1998.

some groups such as the ASTI. There was thus no surprise that a commitment to 'democratic intermediate structures for the management of first- and second-level education' was contained in the government programme of January 1993.[96]

Towards the end of 1993 the National Economic and Social Council, which represented the social partners, issued two reports, both of which came out in favour of local education structures. The first noted that much of the debate on this issue had centred around the changed distribution of power in a development of this kind. The Council decided to support such structures 'not in terms of any particular reallocation of power, but rather on the basis of more effective service provision and more efficient use of available resources'.[97] The second report recommended that such structures should cover both primary and post-primary levels.[98] The organisation of specialist services on an area basis would allow for more efficient use of resources across a range of schools and services, it argued.

The issue was discussed at some length at the National Education Convention held in October of that year. The report of the Convention suggested that there had been a considerable change of attitude towards local education structures since Gemma Hussey published the Green Paper in 1985.[99] This change might have been influenced by the declared intention of the department to disengage from day-to-day involvement with schooling issues, but it might also have been affected by changing social attitudes, demographic trends and economic circumstances.[100] The report acknowledged concerns that new structures might be too costly or too intrusive or too politicised but stated that there was also a realisation of the need for greater professional support services to schools.[101]

---

[96] *Programme For a Partnership Government,* January 1993.
[97] National Economic and Social Council, *Education and Training Policies for Economic and Social Development,* NESC, October 1993, p. 220.
[98] National Economic and Social Council, *A Strategy for Competitiveness, Growth and Employment,* NESC, November 1993, p. 495.
[99] John Coolahan (Ed.), *Report on the National Education Convention,* Dublin, National Education Convention Secretariat, 1994.
[100] Ibid, p. 18.
[101] Ibid, p. 19.

In her closing speech to the NEC the minister undertook to publish a paper on regionalisation. The paper was published in March 1994 and proposed the introduction of eight Regional Education Councils.[102] It outlined proposed functions, powers and duties for new intermediate education structures: they would have statutory planning, co-ordinating, support and service roles for all educational activity and continuing education, excluding third-level education, in their jurisdiction. Schools would continue to have their own boards of management and would be responsible for their own internal governance, including the appointment of teachers. It was envisaged that eventually wages and salaries would be paid by the RECs but the staff selection process would be the responsibility of the individual school in accordance with selection procedures determined by the minister following consultation with the partners in education, including the trustees and patrons. The composition of selection boards would include one nominee of the REC and one non-voting nominee of the chief executive officer of the REC in the case of larger schools. The RECs themselves would comprise owners/trustees/patrons/governors, parents, teachers, locally elected represententatives and ministerial nominees. The support services to be provided by the RECs could include management services (e.g. training for general management, budgeting and financial management); industrial relations/legal services and teacher welfare services; curriculum support and staff advisory services; psychological services; library and media services; school transport services; and building maintenance services.

It was not envisaged that the establishment of RECs should substantially alter the current arrangements for school property. However, it was proposed to confer powers on the RECs to own new school buildings for leasing to different groups, including patrons and trustees, in order to provide for the specified educational needs of the areas. This, it was argued, would help in particular the small multi-denominational school sector, which had encountered difficulties in acquiring school buildings in different areas.

The paper sought to build on the consensus formed to some extent at the NEC and through subsequent documents. However, it

---

[102] Department of Education, *Position Paper on Regional Education Councils*, 11 March 1994.

contained one curious proposal which had obviously not been thought through fully. The paper envisaged that the trusteeship of schools currently vested in VECs would be transferred to the relevant local authorities, who could form sub-committees to deal with matters relating to the trusteeship of their schools and membership of the boards of management. The ownership of the buildings would be transferred to the RECs.[103] This, of course, raised the spectre of the RECs giving preferential treatment to their own schools over and above the private primary and secondary schools. Such a possibility was acknowledged by the Irish Vocational Education Association, which stated that it would be inappropriate for an education authority to be involved in the direct management of a school. 'To do otherwise would call into question the impartial status of the education authority, which is paramount'.[104]

The Association, of course, had a vested interest in ensuring the survival of the VEC system, which was threatened by the proposals in the document. The VECs are statutory committees in their own right, not, as sometimes thought, sub-committees of the local authorities. As statutory bodies they have legally binding contractual obligations, for instance to provide certain educational services. There would have been considerable legal logistics involved in dismantling the sector, even if there was the political will to do so. The Association campaigned hard behind-the-scenes with the politicians and achieved considerable success with Fianna Fáil backbenchers who raised the issue at parliamentary party level. As time went by, it became obvious that the VECs would be retained, although they faced the probability of some form of rationalisation.

Multilateral discussions among the concerned interests were held in Dublin Castle in April and May 1994. On the morning they began, *The Irish Times* reported that the VECs were to remain in existence. According to a source at the discussions, from which the media were excluded, the minister did not refer to the newspaper account which, suggested the source, had the effect of killing off whatever prospects there were of agreement on regionalisation.[105] However,

---

[103] Ibid, p. 16.
[104] Irish Vocational Education Association, *Response to Minister's Position Paper on Regional Education Councils*, April 1994.
[105] Off-the-record source.

a report prepared on the round-table discussions was somewhat more optimistic and indicated that there was a fair measure of support for the idea of local education structures, with reservations about some of the proposals in the minister's document.[106] It reported considerable concern at the danger of an over-prescriptive department controlling many areas of policy with tight accountability, from the RECs upwards to the department. 'The danger is that decentralisation may only shift from the Centre to the Regions, and even that would be limited'. Opinion was divided on the proposal that nominees of RECs should act on selection boards. The geographic remit received a great deal of attention in the discussions.[107] One view was that the proposal to have eight regions was not acceptable because the regions would be 'unmanageable, too remote from local communities, and would have no local involvement': this view expressed a preference for a county structure, with clusters of counties combining for some specialist services. A second view, that of the majority of participants, expressed general support for the proposals but with reservations about only one REC for all the border counties and the view that Dublin should be divided into two regions – one north and the other south of the Liffey. As subsequent events showed, however, the general support for local education structures was less secure than the report indicated and ebbed away once the political climate changed.

White Paper, *Charting our Education Future,* 1995

The consultative process that Breathnach had engaged in was a very useful prelude to the publication of the White Paper.[108] Apart from helping to form a consensus, admittedly fragile at times, it meant that there would be few surprises when the government's decisions were announced. There was a long delay from the Convention in October 1993 to the White Paper in April 1995,

---

[106] John Coolahan and Séamus McGuinness (Eds), *Report on the Round-table Discussions in Dublin Castle on the Minister for Education's Position Paper on Regional Education Councils,* June 1994.

[107] Ibid, p. 18.

[108] Department of Education, *Charting our Education Future,* Dublin, Stationery Office, 1995.

perhaps too long, because it slowed down the impetus to change. The White Paper announced, *inter alia*, that

- legislation will be presented to the Oireachtas providing for the establishment of ten Education Boards, which will also set out their functions and composition
- following enactment of the legislation there will be a phased transfer of functions to the Education Boards
- after a period of five years there will be a full independent evaluation of the effectiveness of the boards.[109]

It is worth noting that the word Regional had been dropped from the designation Education Boards and that the minister had decided to increase the number of such boards from eight to ten.

The Paper confirmed what had already been clear for some time, namely that the VEC system would be retained within the new Education Board structure. This, it concluded, would necessitate changes to the legislation under which the VECs operated.[110] The amending legislation would provide for the retention of VECs 'with a substantial local authority involvement' as statutory committees with responsibility for

- the second-level schools currently under their remit
- ownership of the schools
- employment of staff
- appointment of boards of management in their schools
- vocational education and training, including PLC courses
- adult and continuing education
- out-centres
- the arts in education
- operation of outdoor education centres.

However, the White Paper also stated that there would be rationalisation of VECs. A penultimate draft of the White Paper is known to have actually listed the committees due for rationalisation. But it was decided that if this information was published the ensuing row would overshadow the anticipated positive response to the White Paper. Instead it was agreed that the issue would be a priority

---

[109] Ibid, p. 166.
[110] Ibid, p. 177.

one for a promised Commission on School Accommodation Needs.[111]

The VECs again mounted a rear-guard action to protect their interests and sought support from various quarters. The General Council of County Councils requested each member council to pass a motion expressing grave concern over the White Paper proposals to '(a) rationalise VECs, (b) strip VECs of their powers and functions, (c) establish Regional Education Boards and (d) effectively abolish all VECs'.[112]

Draft education legislation

The preparation of the draft heads of the Education Bill took longer than expected and they were finally presented to the cabinet in March 1996.[113] The Universities' Bill had been given priority and the department's own legal expert, Tom Boland, was working on both, which meant that the Education Bill was delayed. An earlier draft of the Education Bill that went before cabinet ran to 120 pages and contained over 50 heads which set out, *inter alia*, the composition of the education boards, their objectives and functions, staffing arrangements including the inspectorate, and powers over the recognition of schools.[114] These issues relating to the education boards were dealt with in the first section of the draft Bill while the second section dealt with boards of management of schools, the patrons, school year and school day, the curriculum, ethos etc.

The section on Education Boards did not differ very much from what was already in the public domain. A core board was to be appointed comprising equal numbers of nominees of the patrons/ trustees/owners/governors/VECs, parents, teachers, local elected representatives and ministerial nominees. Once appointed they would put forward additional agreed nominees from the wider community. The draft document stated that 'in co-opting, boards are required to have regard to local educational needs and to the

---

[111] Off-the-record sources.

[112] General Council of County Councils, *Letter to each Member Council*, 27 October 1995.

[113] *The Irish Times* and *Irish Independent*, 13 March 1996.

[114] Draft Heads, *The Education (Education Boards and Boards of Management) Bill 1995*, unpublished.

desirability of bringing minorities, disadvantaged groups and people with special expertise on the board'.

Among the general functions of the boards would be the channelling of Exchequer funding to providers of educational services, be they in schools at first and second levels or in other centres providing adult and continuing education, vocational education and training or outdoor education. The boards too would have responsibility for co-ordinating the provision of youth and sport activities which were funded under the Department of Education Vote in the budget. Support services to be provided by the boards included services in relation to

- advice on and training in school management for members of boards of management
- industrial relations matters
- teacher welfare
- school transport
- school maintenance, and such other services as are specified by the Act or considered appropriate by the board.

A further section of the Bill provided for the transfer of staff from the Department of Education and from VECs to the boards. It is interesting to note that there was some union disquiet within the department over the possibility of transfer of staff. This was expressed at a briefing session which the Secretary, Dr Thornhill, had with the staff, some of whom complained about what they saw as the lack of consultation on this issue.[115] Draft head fourteen set out budgetary provisions and contained powers to enable the minister to exert control in order to ensure that the programmes the boards adopted did not lead to unexpected demands on public finances.

A sub-head provided that the boards would have a gender balance as determined by the minister. An explanatory note to this sub-head explained that 'the difficulties in ensuring such balance in bodies established by other statutes is recognised as is the desirability that each nominating group should carry equal responsibility'. Sub-head (6) provided that the minister may require the

---

[115] Off-the-record sources.

nominating bodies to provide a gender balance in their nominees. The note added that

> This provision is intended as an encouragement to the bodies to seek a gender balance at the outset. Experience in the case of the Regional Technical Colleges, where the 1992 Act required the nominating Vocational Education Committees to have regard to gender balance, was that this was ignored until, by an amending Act, the minister was effectively given power to impose a gender balance. As a result, the many arguments which previously were put forward as to why a balance could not be achieved were no longer advanced and balance was achieved with little difficulty. This sub-head seeks to achieve this position from the outset.

This particular explanatory note was subsequently disputed at the annual congress of the Irish Vocational Education Association in Newcastle, Co. Down, held from 22-25 April 1996. The General Secretary of the Association, Joe Rooney, described the above note as 'an appalling abuse of the truth'. However, the VECs did indeed have some difficulties in meeting the gender balance. The General Secretary produced a copy of the supposedly confidential draft Bill which, he told delegates, he had been given without his having asked for it. Pointing to the draft Education Bill he added the comment that 'even the dogs in the street seem to have seen this'.[116]

The fact that the IVEA was furnished with a copy of the draft Bill is of some significance. If information is power, than certainly the Association had a fair idea of what was in store for its sector. It is not clear who furnished the IVEA with its copy but is assumed to have been some official, or semi-official, source. It is known that Pat Keating, the minister's programme manager, had consulted the IVEA and some other groups but they were given access only to some edited heads – certainly they were not given the controversial explanatory notes. However, the full heads of the Bill had gone to all government departments in the normal way. The document could have been leaked from political sources in other departments or possibly by officials in the Department of Education who did so in a 'political' way. To the author's knowledge, the Catholic Church interests were not accommodated by the same source.

---

[116] Author's notes from IVEA Congress, and *The Irish Times,* 25 April 1996.

Rationalisation of VECs

While the parliamentary drafting office was working on the Education Bill the future of the VECs was being examined by the Technical Working Group on School Accommodation Needs, which reported in June 1996.[117] The report contained an unanswerable case for rationalisation pointing out, for instance, that twelve of the thirty-eight VECs had three or fewer schools each. The reduction in the school-going population would undoubtedly mean a reduction in the number of schools, thus calling into question the viability of some committees. After examining the range of services provided the Technical Working Group concluded that the existing arrangement was an expensive administrative system.

The group suggested that the number of committees be rationalised to eighteen, a figure which was somewhat lower than had been expected. Of equal significance was the proposal that the membership of VECs be radically altered. Instead of being dominated by members of political parties or their nominees, it proposed that, in future, committees would have twenty members. A maximum of ten would be public representatives and the remainder would comprise parents, staff, one ICTU and one IBEC nominee, two nominated by organisations representative of agriculture, industry, commerce, the professions and other appropriate interests, and one or two from the arts/voluntary community groups in the vocational education area.

The report prompted a walk-out from the much larger Steering Group by the Irish Vocational Education Association, which had clearly been appraised in advance of its contents because it had alerted RTE to send a camera crew to record the protest.[118] The following week the CEOs Association left the Steering Group. In July both the IVEA and the CEOs' Association rejected requests from the minister to rejoin the commission. The CEOs' Association informed her that it considered it inappropriate to be on a commission deciding the number of bosses that its members would have. Its letter to the minister also referred to low morale among

---

[117] Commission on School Accommodation Needs, *Report of the Technical Working Group, Rationalisation of Vocational Education Committees,* June 1996.
[118] RTE News, 27 June 1996.

chief executive officers. This was a reference to the fact that a large number of CEOs had been appointed in an acting capacity since 1985: Breathnach had, however, begun to redress this by making permanent appointments to those VECs which were certain to survive. Its letter stated that the Association was opposed to a double layer of intermediate bodies – i.e. VECs and Regional Boards.[119] Around this time it emerged that the department had floated the possibility of retaining all thirty-eight committees at least until after the next local elections on the basis that the main savings would be made from merging the administrative offices of committees; this was seen as an attempt to quell political unease among government supporters over the proposed merging of so many committees.[120] The Steering Group issued it own agreed report in October in which it recommended a reduction in the number of VECs from thirty-eight to twenty-one.

The IVEA kept up its unrelenting campaign of opposition to the proposals but its case was undermined by a succession of inquiries into the financial affairs and reported irregularities of several committees by the Comptroller and Auditor General. The most damaging was Co. Westmeath where the minister had commissioned a separate report to find out how the VEC had gone so deeply into the red and why it had entered into a controversial lease purchase agreement on property in Montbard in France without departmental approval.[121] VEC sources responded by leaking two letters, one from the minister in which she regretted that due to a 'very large number of commitments' she was unable to perform the official opening of the Montbard centre in May 1994.[122] A second letter from the minister's programme manager, Pat Keating, was potentially more embarrassing for the government. In it Keating congratulated the VEC on 'such an enlightened initiative' and suggested that an alternative arrangement might allow the minister to travel to

---

[119] Interview with representative of CEOs Association, 31 July 1996.
[120] Off-the-record interviews with VEC representatives.
[121] *Westmeath VEC, Report of the Inspector appointed Pursuant to Section 11 of the Vocational Education Act 1930,* Department of Education, September 1994.
[122] Minister for Education, *Letter to Acting CEO, Co. Westmeath VEC,* 27 April, 1994.

Montbard after the summer.[123] It should, in fairness, be pointed out that similar letters are sent out daily, turning down invitations to various events, and that at the time of the two letters the full details of the Montbard property were not established. The leaking of the letters may have caused some embarrassment to the minister and her advisors but much more serious damage had been done to the VEC sector by inquiries such as that into the Co. Westmeath committee.

A neighbouring scheme also ran into difficulties when the Comptroller and Auditor General reported that the acting CEO of Co. Longford VEC had claimed travel and subsistence expenses for travelling from his home in Ballymahon to Longford town for over nine years. The report said it was estimated that under this arrangment payments of the order of £4,500 were made to the acting CEO in respect of 1994.[124] A number of other reports from the same source added to the obstacles facing the IVEA's public case for the retention of all thirty-eight VECs.

The minister eventually announced the first phase of the rationalisation process with a decision to amalgamate five town-VECs into their respective counties.[125] The five were Bray, Wexford, Tralee, Sligo and Drogheda. As had already been signalled the committee members were to stay in place until after the next local elections – this was an important political consideration that helped explain the lack of any real protest to what was then the inevitable.

In many respects picking off the five town-VECs was the easiest part of the VEC rationalisation process because future amalgamations would require amending the 1930 Vocational Education Act. It had the virtue of allowing the minister to argue that she had started a process that would eventually lead to savings and that would facilitate the transfer of staff to her planned Education Boards.

[123] Advisor to Minister, *Letter to Acting CEO, Co. Westmeath VEC,* April 1994, published in the *Irish Independent,* 11 October 1996.
[124] *County Longford Vocational Education Committee, Report of the Comptroller and Auditor General,* Dublin, Stationery Office, 1996.
[125] Minister for Education, *Press Release,* 21 February 1997.

84   A New Partnership in Education

Conclusions

Almost a century after Chief Secretary Wyndham first proposed local education structures an Irish minister was able to build on the work of her predecessors, of various reports from at home and abroad, and form a fair degree of consensus around the idea of regional boards. Her Education Bill was published in early January. There was little new in it about the education boards from what had already been long signalled.

The minister's case for intermediate structures was strengthened by a further report from the OECD which pointed to the centralised nature of decision-making in Irish education. The report acknowledged that Irish schools had a large degree of autonomy but adverted to the lack of decision-making at intermediate level.[126]

The consensus that she had fought so hard to secure became increasingly fragile shortly after the Education Bill was published and the traditional sceptical attitude of the Catholic bishops to intermediate structures resurfaced. In a statement the hierarchy warned that the Education Boards would exercise 'excessive control' over Church-linked schools. It pointed out that no costings had been published for the operation of these boards and added that 'while schools are still very inadequately funded, we would question the value of setting up another, perhaps costly, layer of bureaucracy'.[127] The ASTI reiterated its misgivings on a number of occasions, drawing attention in particular to the cost implications of the proposed boards. It expressed concerns that the autonomy of schools and thus their flexibility of response would be inhibited by regulations from Education Boards.[128]

One of the surprising features of the debate on the Education Boards was that it took so long to undertake a detailed study into their cost. This left the minister open to the charge that she was setting up a new bureaucratic structure without costing it in advance, a charge that had some justification. The Secretary of the Department, Dr Don Thornhill, defended the delay by stating that there was little point in hiring the consultants until the exact functions of the

[126] OECD, *Decision-Making in 14 OECD Education Systems,* Paris, OECD, 1995.
[127] Irish Bishops' Conference, *Spring Meeting of Irish Bishops' Conference, Statement on Education Bill,* 12 March 1997.
[128] ASTI, *Briefing and Position Paper on the Education Bill, 1997.*

boards were known, because these had evolved from the original position paper through to the round-table discussions and to the Education Bill.[129]

As time went by the minister was becoming more and more vulnerable to the easy political charge that she was planning to set up structures whose costings were unknown. Shortly before the end of 1996 the firm of Deloitte and Touche was hired at a cost of £112,000 with the following terms of reference: (a) to review the organisation and structure of the Department of Education, (b) to make recommendations on its future organisation and structure, and (c) to make recommendations regarding (1) the operational planning and (2) the possible administrative structures of the proposed ten Education Boards.[130]

However, by then political events were taking on a momentum of their own with talk of a general election in the air. The education spokesperson for the main, Fianna Fáil, opposition party, Micheál Martin, criticised the Education Boards and promised to disband any that the minister set up once Fianna Fáil got into government.[131] Other party members also criticised the idea of the boards and committed themselves instead to a county committee system that would be established on a voluntary basis – however, there was a vagueness about precisely how the system would work.

The rest, as they say, is history. Niamh Bhreathnach did not get her Bill through before she left office at the end of June 1997. Her successor, Micheál Martin, went ahead with his threat to drop plans for Education Boards and his revamped Education Bill contained provision for executive agencies, along the lines that Séamus Brennan had first proposed. The moves were welcomed by the IVEA, which said that the boards would have been 'an unwieldy, costly, bureaucratic nightmare which would probably have stifled innovation and educational development'.[132] The response of Catholic Church bodies was mixed. In a letter to the minister, Sr Eileen Randles said 'we welcome the exclusion of the Regional Education Boards. CPSMA had not been convinced of the value or

---

[129] Briefing for education journalists, 24 January 1997.
[130] Information supplied by Department of Education.
[131] *Irish Independent*, 8 January 1997.
[132] IVEA, *Press Release*, 3 January 1998.

usefulness of such boards.'[133] However, CORI criticised the decision, saying that the administration of education would remain 'excessively centralised' and provision would continue to be fragmented.[134]

The likely cost of the boards proved to be a matter of political contention when Micheál Martin became minister. On a number of occasions he said he had discovered that a 1995 estimate prepared in the department had indicated that the Education Boards could cost up to £40m, a claim that was challenged by the Labour Party's education spokesperson, Brian O'Shea, in the Dáil on 14 May 1998. In response to the challenge the minister laid a document in the Oireachtas Library for consultation by members of the Oireachtas. This contained finance estimates for a number of proposals including the Education Boards. The projections were quite brief and not explained in any detail; they indicated that if VECs were fully abolished and savings transferred to the Education Boards (as originally envisaged) the cost would be approximately £35/£40m.[135]

Intermediate bodies would have been expensive but they could have allowed the central department to prioritise its activities instead of trying to cover so many different areas – the immediate often drives out the important and leaves little time or room for long-term strategic thinking. Opponents of regionalisation would claim, however, that executive agencies would achieve the same result for less. But it could be argued also that such agencies would not allow for the same sense of democracy and ownership as region-alised bodies might have done.

Ironically, the new minister announced two important initiatives in 1998 which, some would argue, would have been ideally suited to a regionalised structure, namely the introduction of a national educational psychological welfare service and a national educational welfare service. There was a further irony in the autumn of 1998 when the government decided to divide the country into two regions for purposes of securing on-going structural funds from the EU. One suspects that the idea of intermediate structures in education will resurface early in the twenty-first century.

---

[133] CPSMA, *Letter to Minister for Education and Science*, 20 January 1998.

[134] *Irish Independent*, 13 December, 1997.

[135] Department of Education estimates prepared in March 1995 and laid in the Oireachtas library in May 1998.

CHAPTER 4

The Governance of Schools

I rish schools were slower in broadening the base of management to include parents and teachers than those in many other developed countries. The *Investment in Education* report in 1965 revealed, according to one educational historian 'a dismal Irish educational landscape, a landscape in which parents had no noticeable place'.[1] This was in spite of the fact that Article 42 of the constitution proclaims that 'the state acknowledges that the primary and natural educator of the child is the family'. It was not until the early seventies that parents were invited to join school boards of management and it was not until 1996 that draft legislation was put to cabinet which would, *inter alia*, give parents statutory rights to sit on boards of management.[2] Coolahan has argued that the establishment of boards in Irish schools has been notable more for the jockeying for power by interested parties than for the quality of the debate concerning what constitutes good management. This chapter will track the change from a single managerial system to boards of management. As in the case of the previous chapter on regionalisation it will seek to put these into their historical context. It will also examine Coolahan's observation that the progress to a more broadly based democratic mode of management has been a halting one, accompanied by some bitter debate.[3]

Primary schools

At primary level, from the setting up of the national school system in 1831, each individual school was run by a manager. By the mid-

---

[1] John Coolahan, address to the National Parents' Council (Primary) Annual Conference, Waterford, 21 April, 1995.

[2] Department of Education, *Draft Heads of the Education (Education Boards and Boards of Management) Bill, 1996,* unpublished.

[3] John Coolahan, *Irish Education: history and structure*, Dublin, Institute of Public Administration, 1981, pp. 145-146.

twentieth century virtually all schools were under denominational patronage and the manager – appointed by the Patron – was invariably the local clergyman, either Catholic or Protestant.[4] However, after the Second Vatican Council in the 1960s the Catholic Church became more responsive to the suggestion of greater lay involvement in the running of the schools.[5]

In June 1973 the Secretary of the Department of Education, Sean O'Connor, addressed the Catholic Primary School Managers' Association annual conference in Athlone and put forward a proposal for a new management structure.[6] He suggested that it was time for the managers to consider sharing some of the authority with the people who were part of the school – namely parents. O'Connor, an influential thinker on educational development, told the managers that they were fast becoming 'the autocrats at the breakfast table'.[7] He suggested that committees be set up in each school comprising two clergy, two parents and possibly the principal. The response was positive and the Association's Standing Committee issued a statement saying that the proposal appeared to be a development of the policy recommended by the bishops in 1969 in which they encouraged the managers to associate the parents with the work of the school.[8] The Bishop of Ardagh and Clonmacnoise, Dr Cahal Daly, who was attending the meeting said afterwards that he thought the bishops would be eager to get the new structures off the ground at the earliest possible date.[9] The INTO President, Sean O'Brien, said that his organisation had always supported the existing managerial structure but if the clergy felt that the proposed change would result in a better flow of money to the schools then the organisation would be happy with the change.[10]

The proposal was discussed for some considerable time by the various interests involved. The following Easter, the Minister for

---

[4] Áine Hyland and Kenneth Milne, *Irish Educational Documents Volume II,* Church of Ireland College of Education, 1987, p. 150.
[5] Ibid.
[6] *Irish Independent,* 13 June 1973.
[7] Ibid.
[8] *The Irish Press,* 14 June 1973.
[9] Ibid.
[10] Ibid.

Education, Richard Burke, elaborated on official thinking when he addressed the annual congress of the INTO.

> In this country, as far as the primary school is concerned, we have deluded ourselves into believing that correlation of the work of the parent as educator and that of the teacher was achieved by the system of clerical management which exists in relation to virtually all our national schools. We regarded the clerical manager as the person who ensured that the rights, and the inalienable duties, of the parents were being properly served by the teachers and the schools. This, I submit, was an attitude that was potentially unfair to all interests concerned: managers, teachers and parents. I say advisedly, potentially unfair; because in fact we all know and must acknowledge that by and large the system of school management which has existed since the establishment of our national school system has worked remarkably well, though no one could say that it has not its faults.[11]

The minister went on to state that the intention of the proposed changes was not to discard the system of parochial management, but to expand and develop it by having parents of children resident in the parish in effective co-operation with the parochial authorities in school management.[12] A few months later the minister confirmed that there would be a financial incentive to set up boards of management when he announced a 'Scheme of Capitation Grants towards operating costs of National Schools in which Committees of Management have been established'.[13] The official statement said that a full grant of £6 per pupil would be paid to those schools in which committees of management on the lines proposed by the minister had been established. Each committee would comprise six members, four of whom would be persons appointed by and representative of the Patron of the school and the remaining two would be parents (one being a mother of children enrolled in the school elected by the general body of parents of children attending the school).[14] To allow for the promised increase in capitation grants, provisions in the Estimates were increased from £997,500 (expressed

---

[11] Minister for Education Richard Burke, address to INTO Congress, 16 April 1974.
[12] Ibid.
[13] Department of Education, *Press Release*, 17 October 1974.
[14] Ibid.

on an annual basis) in 1974 to £3,231,000 for 1975.

Initially teachers were excluded from membership of the committee of management although the principal could act as secretary in a non-voting capacity. The INTO was unhappy at this and campaigned for teacher representation. Discussions were held on 1 December 1975 and 23 February 1976 between the minister, his officials, representatives of the Patrons and of the managerial authorities and the INTO, with the result that a revised circular was issued which provided for teacher representation for the first time.[15] In schools with six or fewer teachers the principal would become a full voting member. In large schools there would be a ten member board comprising six nominees of the Patron, two parents, the principal and an elected teacher.[16] However, the INTO was still dissatisfied with the preponderant number of Patron nominees on the boards and in 1978 when the boards were up for reelection they withdrew from participation pending a more satisfactory restructuring.[17] The INTO executive claimed that the mandate given by an INTO special congress in 1975 authorising the involvement in the new system of management was for one term of office which expired at the end of September 1978. That authorisation was given by the special congress on condition that the system would be reviewed before the second term of office commenced.[18] In 1980 the Churches agreed to reduce the number of Patrons' nominees from six to four in the large schools and from four to three in the small schools, leaving the Churches with 50 per cent of the representation and parents and teachers with 25 per cent each.[19] The Churches retained the right to appoint the chairperson of the board, who would have a second or casting vote.

White Paper 1980

That same year a White Paper was published by the new Fianna Fáil Minister for Education, John Wilson, which noted that parental

[15] Department of Education, *Circular Letter* 16/76, April 1976.
[16] Ibid.
[17] Coolahan, p. 175.
[18] *Irish Independent,* 7 September 1978.
[19] Coolahan, p. 175.

representation on boards of management had undoubtedly engendered a closer relationship between home and school. It added that the question arose, however, whether such representation was in itself sufficient to achieve the full involvement of all parents in the life and activities of the school and whether measures should not be taken by school authorities to promote an increasing parental involvement.[20] Around the same time a Fine Gael policy document on education was issued by the party's spokesperson on education, Edward Collins, which argued that the matter of control and management of schools should be seen as a partnership between the major interests involved: community/VEC; parents; religious authorities and teachers. It added that the composition should be such as to allow for effective participation by each group, but the document did not put forward any specific proposals for changing the composition of the boards.[21] There was no reference at all to the boards in the subsequent *Programme for Action* which was laid before the Houses of the Oireachtas in January 1984 by the Fine Gael Minister for Education, Gemma Hussey.[22]

Four years later, in February 1988, Hussey's successor Mary O'Rourke set up a Primary Education Review Body chaired by Dr Tom Murphy, former president of UCD. The Secretary to the Review Body was a rising young inspector, John Dennehy, later to become Secretary General of the department. The Review Body reported in December 1990 and made a number of recommendations aimed at improving the quality of education in primary schools, for example increased capitation grants, better in-service provision, an agreed procedure for dealing with complaints, the establishment of a structured psychological service, additional inspectors, and an immediate reduction in the pupil teacher ratio. It noted criticism presented to the Review Body of the management of primary schools:

---

[20] Department of Education, *White Paper on Educational Development*, Dublin, Stationery Office, December 1980.

[21] Fine Gael policy document, *Action Programme for Education in the 80s*, November 1980.

[22] Department of Education, *Programme for Action in Education 1984-1987*, Dublin, Stationery Office, 1984.

It has been stated that the management board is little more than a minor maintenance committee and that all major functions of management are controlled by some other authority. For example, the Department of Education controls the curriculum, makes the rules and decides all major matters of policy, while the Patron plays a central role in the appointment of the Board, its Chairperson, the Principal and Assistant Teachers; and many agreements entered into between trade unions, the Department of Education and/or management bodies limit further the autonomy of boards of management.[23]

The report recommended that the functions of the board be strengthened to ensure that it played a more meaningful role in the management of schools. For instance the boards should be given greater autonomy in relation to many matters which required departmental approval. They should also be given the necessary finance to carry out such delegated functions as minor building works, the purchase of furniture and equipment and the funding of in-service education suited to local needs. The report recommended no change in the composition of the boards. It did, however, note that the chairperson was usually the local clergyman and suggested that not all clergymen were suited to this role, nor indeed did some of them wish to assume this responsibility.[24] This point was picked up by the minister when she addressed the annual meeting of the Catholic Primary School Managers' Association the following year. She said that the matter was given added weight by the statement in the Association's annual report for 1991 that 'priests are into questioning their role as chairmen of boards, a role which on occasions may come into conflict with their pastoral functions.[25]

Post-Primary schools

At second level, progress was very uneven. The breakthrough came in the early seventies with the establishment of community schools which had boards of management with parental representation

---

[23] *Report of the Primary Education Review Body,* Dublin, Stationery Office, 1980, p. 36.
[24] Ibid, p. 37.
[25] Minister for Education, Mary O'Rourke, address to CPSMA Annual Conference, 19 May 1991.

from the very beginning. Community schools were seen as drawing together the traditions of the separate vocational and secondary school sectors, and while their establishment was dogged by various rows the question of parental representation on community school boards was never really an issue.[26] Progress was slower in other types of post-primary schools. In 1974 Minister Dick Burke issued a circular to Vocational Education Committees suggesting that they should avail of powers under Section 21 of the Vocational Education Act 1930 to set up sub-committees that would act as boards of management for vocational schools.[27] Owing to the fact that community schools had no statutory basis for operation, vocational schools were thus the first schools to set up boards that operated under a clear legal framework.[28] Each board was to consist of four members of the VEC and two parents. The circular specifically stated that 'no person employed for the purposes of the school shall be a member of the board of the school'. However, some VECs were much more cautious than others in responding to the suggestion. In 1994, a survey carried out by the Irish Vocational Education Association revealed that almost half of the thirty-eight VECs still had not established boards in their schools. A confidential letter sent by the IVEA's General Secretary, Joe Rooney, to the chief executive officers of the VECs expressed alarm at the findings.

> Clearly we are extremely vulnerable and at risk while that situation continues to exist. Our claim to local democratic structures rings hallow and our commitment to school autonomy is hypocritical. Should our minister ever become aware of the true situation, our system would be in deep trouble, White Paper or not. At the moment, CEOS and VECs have the power to set up boards tailor-made to fit their local situations. As things stand we are inviting a minister to impose his/her solution on all VECs.[29]

Progress continued to be slow and even in 1996, six of the thirty-eight VECs still had no boards of management in their schools –

---

[26] Louis O'Flaherty, *Management and Control in Irish Education: the Post-Primary Experience,* Dublin, Drumcondra Teachers' Centre, 1992.

[27] Department of Education, *Circular Letter,* 15 July 1974.

[28] John Coolahan (Ed.), *Report on the National Education Convention,* Dublin, National Education Convention Secretariat, 1994, p. 27.

[29] Irish Vocational Education Association, confidential letter to VECs, 21 October 1994.

Co. Carlow, Co. Leitrim, Co. Roscommon, Town of Sligo, Town of Wexford and Co. Wicklow.[30]

It took much longer to establish boards in Catholic voluntary secondary schools, where the initial attempts to do so were unsuccessful. A proposal for boards of management was put forward in a report entitled *Future Involvement of Religious in Education* which was prepared by a working party set up at the request of the hierarchy and the Education Commission of Major Religious Superiors.[31] The report argued that boards would broaden the basis of support for Catholic schools by sharing with 'competent and influential laymen' the religious and managerial control of the school. The ownership of the school, and the appointment of the managerial board, and whatever other powers were thought necessary to retain, would remain in the hands of the present trustees. The report went on as follows:

> Two developments in particular lend urgency and importance to this move; first, the fundamental changes which are being planned and executed by the Civil Service in the structure of Irish post-primary education; and secondly the rapidly declining strength and bargaining power of clerical and religious managers, due to the changing proportion which religious teachers constitute in the whole teaching force. The decline can be summarised:
>
> • in 1965-66, religious and priests constituted 50 per cent of post-primary teachers
> • in 1968-69, religious and priests constituted 45 per cent of post-primary teachers
> • in 1969-70, religious and priests constituted 38 per cent of post-primary teachers
> • in 1970-71, religious and priests constituted 34 per cent of post-primary teachers.

The Education Commission of the Conference of Major Religious Superiors adopted articles of management and announced that the first boards would be set up in 1976.[32] This announcement proved

[30] Department of Education, statistical data submitted to Commission on School Accommodation Needs, 21 May 1996.

[31] Working Party on the Future Role of the Religious in Education, *The Future Involvement of Religious in Education* (the 'Fire Report'), February 1973, unpublished.

[32] Conference of Major Religious Superiors, *Press Release*, 11 February 1976.

to be premature. The articles provided for ten-member school boards, comprising six nominees of the trustees, two elected parents, one full-time teacher elected by the full-time teaching staff and one additional person chosen by these nine. The school principal would act as non-voting secretary to the board. What is interesting in the light of later events is that the trustees did not insist on the right to appoint the chair at this stage, presumably on the basis that it was expected that one of their six nominees would be elected chairperson anyway. The articles simply said that 'the first business of the board upon coming into operation of these articles and thereafter at its first meeting in each school year shall be the election of the following officers: a chairman and a deputy chairman'.

Bro. Declan Duffy, who was involved in the CMRS at that time, explained that the articles were drawn up in response to a demand from the ASTI for 'open', i.e. lay, principalships. 'We felt we could not have open principalships unless we had boards of management'.[33] However, the ASTI rejected the proposals, describing the boards as a 'democratic sham'.[34] Its Standing Committee met in October 1976 and unanimously passed a resolution directing its members not to co-operate with or participate in any form of board of management until agreement had been reached.[35] It decided that where an attempt was made to impose a board of management then the union would direct its members

- not to seek representation on any board of management established in accordance with the CMRS Articles of Management
- not to attend any meetings at which proposals to establish such boards would be discussed
- to cease all forms of voluntary contribution in the running of the school
- not to carry out any voluntary, unpaid work or duties.

Negotiations took place between the CMRS and the ASTI resulting in agreement by the religious authorities that the co-opted person on the board would be a teacher, thus giving teachers two seats on

[33] Interview with author, 30 May 1996.
[34] *Times Educational Supplement,* 14 October 1977.
[35] *ASTI Letter to each CMCSS School,* 9 November 1976.

the board. But this still did not satisfy the union, which was angered by the setting up of a board in a Dublin school.[36] It proceeded to ban voluntary co-operation at St Paul's secondary school, Greenhills, Walkinstown, Dublin.[37] Plans were confirmed at that time for the setting up of other boards 'fairly soon'[38] but these did not materialise for some years. The Greenhills board effectively ceased to function and it was not until the mid-eighties that agreement was finally reached on the introduction of boards. This was done in the context of a package of proposals which was voted on by the ASTI. Long before the package was put to the union the managers had agreed to further modify the composition of the boards.[39] Draft articles provided for boards comprising eight members, four nominees of the trustees, two elected parents and two elected teachers. The trustees would appoint the chairperson. This formula was repeated in the subsequent documentation that went to the union. The other elements of the package included moves to lift a union ban on parent teacher meetings and negotiations on a redeployment deal for secondary teachers.[40] The proposals for boards of management were accepted in a vote of ASTI members by 55 per cent to 44.5 per cent in a ballot concluded in September 1985.[41] Boards were gradually introduced into the sector over the following few years, again with the trustees having a voting majority through the appointment of the chairperson, who would have a second or casting vote. O'Flaherty has suggested that initially the ASTI was not in favour of boards of management but it later realised that they might help to prevent the redundancy of lay teachers. O'Flaherty, a former president of the ASTI, has suggested that this fear of redundancy was exploited by the Council of Managers of Catholic Secondary Schools.[42]

---

[36] *Times Educational Supplement,* 14 October 1977.
[37] *Irish Independent,* 4 October 1977.
[38] Ibid.
[39] Council of Managers of Catholic Secondary Schools, *Draft Articles of Management,* September 1981.
[40] O'Flaherty, p. 109.
[41] *Irish Independent,* 28 September 1985.
[42] O'Flaherty, p. 110.

National Parents' Council

Politicians also began to play much greater attention to the role of parents in education around this time. A Fine Gael-Labour coalition government headed by Dr Garret FitzGerald came to power after a general election in November 1982. Its *Programme for Government* contained a short section on education which included the following commitment: 'A National Parents' Council, through which parents' views on policy matters can be expressed, will be established'.[43] The Council was set up three years later by the Fine Gael Minister for Education, Gemma Hussey. The importance of the Council was noted by the OECD in its review of Irish education. It suggested that it was only when the Council was established in 1985 that people began to speak of the need for local parents' associations as well, and that, in general, the idea began to be entertained that parents should be actually, and not merely constitutionally, partners in the educational process.[44]

Mention should also be made of the Labour Party, which issued a policy document in early 1985. It put forward the proposal that boards of management should comprise one-third parents' representatives, one-third teachers' representatives and one-third representation from school owners.[45] This was certainly a radical notion at the time and it is interesting that more than a decade later the party's first Minister for Education, Niamh Bhreathnach, would be in a position to see if such a proposal could be implemented.

Draft Green Papers

During her ministry from March 1987 to November 1991 Mary O'Rourke also played particular attention to the parents' 'constituency' and made a point of attending their annual conferences. Her draft Green Paper referred to the partnership in education approach that she (and subsequent ministers) adopted. It contained

---

[43] Fine Gael/Labour coalition, *Programme for Government* 1982, December 1982.
[44] OECD, *Reviews of National Policies for Education, Ireland,* Paris, OECD, 1991, p. 59.
[45] Labour Party, *Socialist Principles in Education Policy: A Discussion Document,* February 1985.

a number of proposals that were to cause difficulties for her successors. One condition for state funding was that schools would be required to establish a representative board of management with the necessary authority to manage.[46]

The draft put forward the following suggested composition of boards of management. At primary level in schools with six teachers or less it suggested three nominees of the trustees/owners, two elected by the parents, and the principal as a voting member. In primary schools with seven or more teachers it suggested four nominees of the owners/trustees, two parents, two elected teachers, and the principal as a non-voting member.

At post-primary level where a school was the sole provider it suggested a board as follows: three nominated by the County Education Committee; three nominees of the religious authorities, two elected by parents, two elected by teachers, and the principal as a non-voting member. In existing secondary schools five would be nominated by the trustee/owners, one by the County Education Committee and there would again be two parents, two teachers, and the principal as a non-voting member. In vocational, community and comprehensive schools the board would comprise five nominees of the County Education Committees, one nominee of the religious authorities, two parents, two teachers, and the principal as non-voting member. It is interesting to note that the draft envisaged only one situation where the principal would be a voting member of any board and that was in the case of primary schools with six teachers or less.

The draft stressed the importance at all levels, and particularly at the second level, of forging strong links with the community, with particular reference to the relationship between the school and the world of work. 'For this reason, it is seen as highly desirable that one, at least, of the nominees of the proposed County Education Committee and/or religious authorities should be from the local business community'. This particular proposal was to cause an amount of controversy when the Green Paper was eventually published. O'Rourke was succeeded by Noel Davern, who held

[46] Department of Education, *Draft Green Paper,* 29 January 1992, unpublished.

the office briefly from November 1991 to February 1992. Davern appears to have made no change in the section of the Green Paper dealing with school governance; his main change to the draft dealt with the area of vocational education and training.

Green Paper, *Education for a Changing World,* 1992

Mary O'Rourke's draft had suggested that the chairperson be elected annually from among the members of the board, but she was careful to give school owners the same representation on boards as parents and teachers would jointly have. A very much amended Green Paper was published on 25 June by Davern's successor, Séamus Brennan.[47] It also proposed that the representation of school owners would equal that of parents and teachers combined, but in a slightly different format to that put forward by O'Rourke.

For primary schools with four teachers or less it suggested the following composition: three nominees of the trustees/owners, two elected parents, one co-option from the local community, and the principal as a voting member. In schools of five teachers or more it suggested five nominees of the trustees/owners, two elected parents, two elected teachers, the principal as a voting member and one co-option from the local community, preferably a representative of local business. In secondary schools it suggested the following: five nominated by the trustees/owners, two elected parents, two elected teachers, one co-option from the local business community, and the principal as a voting member. It would be open to smaller schools, within the one or adjacent catchment area, to come together to form a common board of management.

The proposals meant that school owners would have a minority of members on the boards, something they were hardly likely to agree to at that stage. What is interesting is that an unpublished draft prepared by Brennan a fortnight previously had a different version. This earlier version would have meant two co-options from the local community in the case of primary schools with five teachers or more and in the case of all secondary schools.[48] In the

---

[47] Department of Education, *Education for a Changing World,* Green Paper, Dublin, Stationery Office, 1992.
[48] Department of Education, *Draft Green Paper,* 8 June 1992, unpublished.

case of the primary schools one of the co-options would preferably come from the local business community while in the case of the secondary schools the two co-options would have come from the local business community. The number of nominees of the owners/ trustees would have been four instead of five as appeared in the final document. It is not known why the minister changed his mind and increased the balance of representation by the time he published the Green Paper a fortnight later: it may well be that he correctly anticipated objections from school owners/trustees to their having minority representation on the boards of their own schools.

Reaction to the Green Paper

There was, as we have seen in chapter 2, a considerable response to the Green Paper. The widespread reaction to the perceived utilitarian approach in the Paper influenced the views of many organisations in regard to individual proposals in the document. The INTO insisted that, while it was not opposed to the concept of devolution in principle, it rejected the market-led model envisaged in the Green Paper. In particular it rejected the emphasis on the chief executive model of leadership envisaged for principals. Instead it proposed a more organic form of school organisation, one in which the principal was head of a team of teachers sharing responsibility for collaborative planning and evaluation in the school.[49] It called for equal representation of teachers, parents and owners/trustees on the board of management.

The Church of Ireland viewed with 'grave concern' the proposal for a reduction in the proportional representation of the Patron in the structures outlined for primary schools.[50] It pointed out that Church of Ireland primary schools had traditionally accepted on their rolls varying numbers of children whose parents were not members of that Church. The schools had done so on the basis that there existed in the management structure, by virtue of the Patron's representatives' voting majority, a safeguard for the long-

---

[49] INTO, *The INTO Response to the Green Paper,* January 1993.
[50] Church of Ireland Board of Education, *Response to the Green Paper,* November 1992.

term preservation of the school and its ethos: 'We believe strongly that a further reduction in the proportion of Patron's representatives on boards of management would remove that safeguard and thereby represent a potential threat to the denominational character and in some cases, the very survival of some of our schools'.[51]

The Church of Ireland was equally apprehensive about the proposals for secondary schools, pointing out that the majority of Protestant schools were run by boards of governors that allowed for a broad representation of interests and expertise. It argued that the universal establishment of one particular board model for every school in the country, regardless of size, origin, tradition or ethos, would be inappropriate. 'We further believe that to put such a model into legislation would be a very grave error'. It called for a more flexible approach to be taken, with allowance for variation to suit particular conditions.[52]

The Catholic Primary School Managers' Association was not convinced that there was any intrinsic merit in enlarging the boards of management at primary level.[53] The Association noted that the Primary Review Body had recommended no change in the current size and composition of boards. Its position was that the Patron would require as of right that his representatives on the board of management constituted an effective majority.[54] The chairperson of the Association, Rev. Ray Brady PP, issued a very strong denunciation of the Green Paper proposals for primary education. He alleged that under the Green Paper the bishops as owners/ trustees would have a momentary say – a moment literally every three years – of nominating a minority of each board of management. 'Thereafter there would be no foreseen role for the Churches except in the reserved area of religious education', he claimed.[55] Fr Brady also suggested that the 'silent revolutionary character' of the Green Paper proposals was nowhere more significant than in its proposed abolition of the Patron system of management.

---

[51] Ibid.
[52] Ibid.
[53] CPSMA, *Response to Education for a Changing World,* December 1992.
[54] Ibid.
[55] Rev. Ray Brady PP, *Observations on the Green Paper, Education for a Changing World,* 29 August 1992.

> This has been central to education policy for a century and a half
> – undenominational education under denominational management,
> actively supervised and progressively underwritten by the state.
> Here is where we come to the dog that does not bark. There is a
> total and deliberate omission from the Green Paper of any mention
> by name or title of the cornerstone of the primary school
> management system since the Stanley Education Act (sic) of 1832.[56]

Bishop Thomas Flynn, chairman of the Episcopal Commission on
Education, took a somewhat similar line when he told a seminar in
Sligo later in the same year that to exclude the Patron from a role
in the primary school system would be seen as an attempt to push
the Church out of education.[57] However, a Department of Education
note prepared in November 1992 suggested that these particular
fears seemed to have been based on a misunderstanding. It stated
that in order to allay any concerns the minister had no hesitation in
extending the use of the word owner to read 'Owner or Trustee or
Patron'. The note added that in the course of further consultation
on the Green Paper it might be possible to come up with a word
such as sponsor or promoter in lieu of the word Patron which,
'while capturing the meaning, would be more in tune with modern-
day terminology'. The same briefing note confirmed that the school's
philosophy of education would be embodied in articles of management, or a school charter, to be approved by the minister in
accordance with legislation.[58] If this had been made much clearer
earlier it might have taken some of the heat out of the very controversial debate.

National Education Convention

The Fianna Fáil/Labour *Programme for a Partnership Government*
promised that the White Paper would be published by the end of
1993 and a new Education Act would be published shortly
thereafter.[59] However, the new minister, Niamh Bhreathnach, opted

[56] Ibid.
[57] Bishop Thomas Flynn, address to seminar on Green Paper, Sligo, 6 November
1992.
[58] Department of Education, *Briefing Note,* 20 November 1992.
[59] Fianna Fáil and Labour Party, *Programme for a Partnership Government 1993-
1997.*

instead for a long consultative process before issuing a White Paper. A National Education Convention was held in Dublin Castle from 11 to 21 October that brought together forty-two organisations – educational bodies, the social partners, and the Department of Education – to engage in structured and sustained discussions on key issues of educational policy in Ireland. One of these key issues was that of school governance. Substantial clarification of the roles of the Patrons, trustees and owners of schools emerged during the discussions.[60]

The National Parents' Council (Primary) made a very strong case for equal representation with other partners on the boards. Representatives of post-primary parents favoured the same, though not insisting on it in all cases.[61] All the teacher unions made a case for equal representation with trustee nominees on the boards. New models for the composition of boards were tabled by the Educate Together movement and Gaelscoileanna, in keeping with their aims. Gaelscoileanna unambigiously supported the idea of the Patron system because it guaranteed the maintenance of the all-Irish ethos of their schools. Educate Together which spoke for the eleven multi-denominational primary schools supported equal partnership for its schools. At that time each of the eleven schools had a limited company as its Patron. Each had an elected chairperson based on the four (Patron's nominees), two (parents) and two (teachers) model. Educate Together supported the general policy that Patrons who opted for equal representation on boards of management should be allowed by the Department of Education to do so.[62]

The Church bodies initially took a very hard line, warning of strong resistance to any attempt by the state to interfere with either the composition of boards or with their various functions. The Catholic Church and the Church of Ireland bodies in particular supported each other's position. Bishop Flynn said that it would be unconstitutional if the state insisted on a management structure which prevented the Catholic Chuch from being able to guarantee the religious character of its schools. It would also be against the

---

[60] *Report on The National Education Convention*, 1994.
[61] Ibid.
[62] Ibid.

wishes of the overwhelming majority of the citizens of the state, he added. Bro. Declan Duffy, General Secretary of the Secretariat of Secondary Schools, warned that 'We would resist any attempt by the State to interfere with the composition of boards of management which would result in minority trustee representation being unable to implement their policy on substantive issues, especially ethos, teacher appointments and property decisions'.

Brian Duffy, Vice-Chairman of the Secondary Education Committee, said that the Green Paper had not once acknowledged that there might be certain issues which needed extra sensitivity because of the Protestant minority. He said that the existing governors must have a determining influence in the management of each Protestant school. 'This we do not regard as negotiable', he added.[63]

The convention attracted considerable attention in the media, which reported what was seen as a generally hard line by the main Churches. Some of the Church participants were known to be concerned at the impression that they were holding up progress on reforming board structures and a certain softening of the hard line began to emerge as the convention developed and went into private session for two days. By the end of the convention there were definite signs that the Churches were willing, at least, to consider 'alternative effective mechanisms' to board majorities, which would still protect the religious ethos of their schools.[64] The Catholic bishops and the Conference of Major Religious Superiors indicated that board majorities were the 'currently preferred means' of ensuring the maintenance of the religious ethos and social mission of their schools but they also indicated that they were open to discussions. The Protestant representatives said, however, that they felt that the Patron's right to nominate the majority on boards was essential to maintain the ethos of their schools.[65]

The Secretariat for the National Education Convention prepared a detailed report of the proceedings and put forward some recommendations. It stated that the rights and authority of Trustees/ Patrons in Irish educational provision for all types of school needed

---

[63] *The Irish Times,* 12 October 1993.
[64] Ibid, 22 October 1993.
[65] Ibid.

to be much more clearly articulated in state documents.[66] Agreed deeds of trust and articles of management should be drawn up, within the ambit of which the board of management would operate and departures from which could lead to its being called to account. The report opted for the model of boards that would be equally representative of Patrons, teachers and parents and that could co-opt individuals from the local community.

The Catholic Church's unease resurfaced at the following Spring meeting of the hierarchy in Maynooth. Dr Thomas Flynn told reporters afterwards that the bishops had taken legal advice on the options of charters or deeds. He said that: 'Because the ethos of a school is a living reality incorporating the Gospel response to the issues of life, the bishops are not convinced that either alternative on its own is capable of guaranteeing the Catholic character of schools into the future'.[67]

In response to reporters' questions about why the bishops had conceded majority control on boards in Northern Ireland he responded: 'if we got the deal our counterparts have in the North, we'd take it in the morning'. In return for 100 per cent funding the schools in Northern Ireland had ceded to the North's Department of Education or local education authority the right to appoint up to three members of the board of management. But these were selected from a list of names submitted by the bishops, thereby preserving an effective Church majority.

Position paper on the governance of schools

In July 1994 the minister, Niamh Bhreathnach, sought to progress the issue by publishing a position paper on the governance of schools.[68] The paper provided for boards of management in all publicly funded primary and post-primary schools – indeed the receipt of state funding by a school would be conditional on putting in place a board consistent with the approach and criteria outlined

[66] *Report on The National Education Convention,* 1994, pp. 23-30.
[67] *The Irish Times,* 10 March 1994.
[68] Department of Education, *Position Paper on the Governance of Schools,* July 1994.

in the position paper. The paper cautioned that the management structures in schools should reflect the reality that the state paid most of the capital and current costs of recognised schools. The composition of boards should reflect the increasing desire for participation and partnership in the running of schools on the part of teachers and parents but the paper agreed that a single model was not satisfactory. It indicated that the minister noted the reservations expressed about proposals in the 1992 Green Paper for involving the school principals as voting members of boards. The minister proposed that, at a minimum, principals would be ex officio, non-voting members of boards but that the question of whether or not the principal would be a voting member was one to be determined by the choice of model of school board.

The Green Paper had also proposed the co-option of persons from the local community, particularly the local business community. But Breathnach did not consider that it would be appropriate that such persons should be voting members of boards of management. She proposed an equivalence of membership on the part of parents and teachers on the boards. This would be achieved through a formula which required trustees to include in their nomination parents of pupils in the schools and teachers, so that there would be equivalent membership of parents, teachers and others on the board. A number of illustrative possibilities were quoted in the document. For instance a board with eight members could have two elected teacher representatives, two elected parent representatives and four trustee nominees one of whom would be a parent of a child or children in that school and another would be a teacher. The chairperson would have a second or casting vote. The other models offered slight variations of this formula. Whatever model was chosen would have to conform with government policies on gender balance.

Round-table discussions

The minister's proposals would allow the trustees to retain their majority on the boards and she might have assumed that her position paper would prove acceptable to the Churches. She organised a meeting of school owners, parents and teachers in Dublin Castle on 12 and 13 September 1994 to discuss the paper. Sixteen groups were represented and the minister told them that the conference was the final stage of her extensive consultation process prior to the publication of the White Paper.[69] She said that she did not expect the participants to agree on every detail of the management board proposals but that the discussion should help her in deciding the final White Paper position. She was indeed correct in anticipating lack of full agreement.

The teacher unions again favoured equal representation as between parents, teachers and Patrons, as did Educate Together. The INTO submission claimed the minister's document attempted to fudge some of the core issues by allowing the Patrons' nominees to spill over into the teacher and parent representatives.[70] The Irish Vocational Education Association and the Association of Community and Comprehensive Schools, representing school management in the public sector, were largely supportive of the minister's proposals. The Church representatives had, however, many concerns and the Catholic spokesperson, Bishop Thomas Flynn, made quite an astonishing attack on the minister.

> We find within the documents on the governance of schools and on the Regional Education Councils the bricks of a secularist agenda and a bid to control the schools to such an extent as to undermine the principle of subsidiarity. The ideology behind some of these proposals is seen by some bishops as an attempt by the state to push the Church out of education.[71]

Bishop Flynn added:

> We do not look for secret deals: our cards are already on the table but there is no structure here to facilitate negotiation. Presenting papers and positions is not very helpful and there are some who see this process in a more hostile light. None of us wants this very worthwhile undertaking to end up in recrimination: we can save it from that by talking to one another rather than at one another. Perhaps it is still not too late for the minister and her department

[69] Department of Education, *Press Release*, 12 September 1994.
[70] INTO, *Presentation to Round-Table Discussions*, Dublin Castle, 12 September 1994.
[71] Catholic bishops, *Presentation to Round-Table Discussions*, Dublin Castle, 12 September 1994.

officials to begin talking to all parties responsible for education and to be sensitive to the difficulties which many of them have.[72]

Bishop Flynn referred to some of the constitutional issues arising from the position paper published by the minister where it was stated that the receipt of state funding would be conditional on putting in place a board of management consistent with the approach and criteria outlined in the paper.

> Apart from the fact that this would cut across a right based on the natural expectations of a school, our legal advice tells us that it would be unconstitutional for the state to impose conditions which require the Churches or Religious Orders to lose control of their schools as a condition of obtaining grants. And this is the issue here. The state has a right and an obligation to see that money paid to schools is well spent. But there is a big difference between making a school accountable for its use of state grants and interfering with the running of the school. A delicate balance must be maintained between state assistance and state interference.[73]

Bishop Flynn's comments were all the more surprising given the previous indication at the National Education Convention that the Church was at least willing to consider alternative mechanisms for ensuring the ethos of its schools. The bishop was chairman of the Episcopal Commission on Education at that time and, according to one Church source, had not advised the Commission of the detailed comments he had intended to make. Nevertheless, his comments were echoed by other Church representatives. The General Secretary of the Catholic Primary School Managers' Association, Sr Eileen Randles, was equally forthright in her views. She began by querying the appropriateness and usefulness of the forum: 'I'm sure we'll have a pleasant day listening to our friends. But what more?' she asked. Sr Eileen pointed out that the minister's document was silent about the management structures of vocational schools in the future and she asked 'why, then, should representatives of that sector be expected to comment on and influence the affairs of Catholic primary schools?'.[74]

---

[72] Ibid.
[73] Ibid.
[74] CPSMA, *Presentation to Round-Table Discussions,* Dublin Castle, 12 September 1994.

A strong line was also taken by the Association of Management for Catholic Secondary Schools, which criticised the 'heavy-handed threat to withdraw funding from those schools which refuse to bow their stubborn knee before the altar of equivalence',[75] and by the Federation of Catholic Lay Secondary Schools, which warned that it would take legal action if any further steps were taken by the minister to force its schools to implement boards along the lines proposed.[76] The Education Commission of the Conference of Religious of Ireland was the most conciliatory of the Catholic groups represented. Its submission stated that the position paper had a number of very positive features although failing to address adequately many issues related to the governance of schools.[77]

The Protestant Church representatives were not quite as trenchant in their views as the majority of Catholic groups but they were also unhappy at the basic thrust of the minister's proposals. The Church of Ireland submission included the following:

> We have recognised the increased desire for participation and partnership in the running of schools on the part of parents and teachers. We have never been convinced, nor do we accept, that this desire should lead to an equality of representation for parents and teachers. It would be unusual, to say the least, for the owners, workers and representatives of the consumers to be represented in equal numbers in the management of any enterprise and we would seek a more comprehensive debate on this issue than has been held heretofore.[78]

Brian Duffy from the Secondary Education Committee spoke on behalf of the Protestant Churches. He said that they considered it essential that there should be a majority at all times in school management structures for the owners of the school. They accepted that parents and teachers had a legitimate right to be involved in

---

[75] AMCSS, *Presentation to Round-Table Discussions*, Dublin Castle, 12 September 1994.

[76] Federation of Catholic Lay Secondary Schools, *Presentation to Round-Table Discussions*, Dublin Castle, 12 September 1994.

[77] CORI Education Commission, *Presentation to Round-Table Discussions*, Dublin Castle, 12 September 1994.

[78] Church of Ireland Board of Education, *Presentation to Round-Table Discussions*, Dublin Castle, 12 September 1994.

the management structures of schools but saw no convincing argument for the need for equality of representation with the owners of
the schools. He also issued a warning that 'for schools to be com-
pelled to alter their management structures as a condition of the
receipt of future state funding would seem to us to be open to
legal challenge'.[79] The Irish Schoolmasters' Association, representing
managers/principals of the secondary and comprehensive schools
under Protestant management in the Republic, similarly voiced
concerns about the possibility of having equal representation for
parents, teachers and owners.[80]

Progress in facilitation talks

The two days of discussions were an obvious setback but not a
complete disaster for the minister. The National Parents' Council
(Primary) reiterated proposals for equal representation of owners/
trustees, parents and teachers, who would together nominate two
further members – and it was agreed that these would form the
basis for discussions that started quickly under an independent
facilitator, Dr Tom McCarthy of TCD. There was a certain irony in
the talks going back behind closed doors, because the minister
had sought greater openness in negotiating change and wanted to
move away from the culture of closed meetings. There was of
course a difference, in that in the past the talks that took place
behind closed doors between department officials and the Catholic
Church representatives saw the Church in a favoured position –
the phrase 'Staighre na nEaspaig' (the bishops' stairs) was a term
used to indicate the easy access the bishops had to the department.
Later the unions joined these behind-the-scenes talks. In the case
of the facilitation talks the participants were the Churches, the unions
and the parents representatives. The department was not represented
– the facilitator Dr McCarthy briefed the minister when the deal
was done.

A softening of the Churches' opposition to giving up majority

---

[79] Secondary Education Committee, *Presentation to Round-Table Discussions*,
Dublin Castle, 12 September 1994.
[80] Irish Schoolmasters' Association, *Presentation to Round-Table Discussions*,
Dublin Castle, 12 September 1994.

control began to emerge from these talks. Despite earlier doubts, the Churches shifted towards a view that written legal guarantees could protect the ethos of their schools. Around this time the Catholic Primary School Managers' Association requested that the government give a commitment to abolishing the local contribution for primary schools. The local contribution at that time amounted to a quarter of the state grant and as the state grant kept increasing so, obviously, did the amount sought by way of local contribution which, in the case of Roman Catholic schools, came from the individual parishes. In the past the Catholic Church had always insisted on some element of local funding, lest its primary schools be regarded as state schools. In the 1996 budget the government agreed to freeze the local contribution at the 1995 level for designated disadvantaged schools and the minister agreed to examine the possibility of phasing out the local contribution entirely.

There were some false dawns before agreement was reached. For instance, at the annual meeting of the CPSMA in Emmaus Centre, Swords, Co. Dublin on Friday 26 April the General Secretary, Sr. Eileen Randles, announced in her annual report that following legal advice and consideration of all aspects of the question the Patrons had accepted the proposed new structure for boards – two nominees of the Patron, two elected parents, two teachers and two co-opted members. She reiterated that this was conditional on the provision of a legal guarantee of the status of Catholic primary schools and added that 'the terms of this legal instrument have been agreed between the bishops and the Minister for Education'.[81] However, her statement provoked some surprise. A Department of Education spokesperson said that while the talks were well advanced the minister had still not received the final report of the facilitator.[82] The Church of Ireland education spokesperson, David Meredith, said that it was still examining the drafting of the legal instrument and added that a final decision on a new board structure would not be taken until the Church had seen and was satisfied with the forthcoming legislation.[83]

---

[81] CPSMA, *General Secretary's Report*, Annual Conference, Emmaus Centre, Swords, Co. Dublin, 26 April 1996.
[82] *Irish Independent* and *The Irish Times*, 27 April 1996.
[83] *The Irish Times*, 27 April 1996.

The talks continued for much longer than expected and had still not concluded by the end of September 1996. The CPSMA requested the minister to extend the mandate of the existing boards and she agreed to do so. She said that an extension of up to three months would allow sufficient time to put the arrangements for the appointment of the new governance structures in place, prior to the reopening of the schools after the Christmas holidays.

Eventually the minister was able to announce, in November 1996, what she correctly referred to as 'historic agreement' on the composition of boards.[84] That agreement was the result of two years of negotiations and discussion among the education partners under the facilitation of Dr McCarthy. Instead of an inbuilt voting majority for the owners of schools it allowed for equal representation for parents, teachers, owners and the wider community. The change was in return for statements guaranteeing the ethos of schools.[85]

The INTO raised doubts about aspects of the agreement which seemed to empower the Church of Ireland to refuse access to pupils of other religions or none.[86] The impression was given initially by the minister that all was well with the governance document but three weeks later she announced that as part of the process of consideration she had referred the agreement to the Attorney General for advice on its 'format, constitutionality and general legality, prior to submitting the agreement to government for approval'.[87] This, of course, caused some confusion and led to further delays in establishing boards of management in primary schools. Inevitably, it took longer than expected to get the advice from the overworked office of the Attorney General and in the meantime the political clock was ticking away. Indeed, by the time the word came through from the Attorney General's office that the agreement was generally in order it was too late for the minister to make much political capital from it and she indicated that she was recommending that the new elections be held in the Autumn of

[84] Minister for Education, *Press Release – A New and Stronger Partnership in the Running of Our Schools,* 28 November 1996.
[85] Ibid.
[86] *Irish Independent* and *The Irish Times,* 29 November 1996.
[87] Minister for Education, *Press Release – Governance of Primary Schools,* 11 December 1996.

1997. She also indicated that the matter would not be going back to cabinet until the Supreme Court had ruled on the Equal Status Bill. This was because of fears that the court might rule it unconstitutional, as it had done with parts of the Employment Equality Bill.[88]

Difficult as the talks were at primary level they were expected to be even more difficult at post-primary level, partly because of the variety of structures across the various types of schools. The majority of post-primary schools have boards, but some do not, especially the small, lay, Catholic-owned voluntary schools. Niamh Bhreathnach's intention was to wait until the primary boards were agreed before turning her attention to the post-primary sector. Nevertheless she had made it clear in her governance of schools document that she wanted equivalence for parents, teachers and school owners/trustees on the boards at post-primary level as well. Her successor, Micheál Martin, also favoured changes in the governance of post-primary schools although he did not favour a legal obligation on schools to establish boards of management – in fact his own Education Bill removed the compulsion aspect and instead stated that schools had a duty to establish boards where feasible.

A possible indication of the difficulties Niamh Bhreathnach might have faced was given by Bro. Declan Duffy in his valedictory address as General Secretary of the Association of Management of Catholic Secondary Schools' at the annual conference in Galway.[89] Bro. Duffy referred to the shared management structure for secondary schools that involved representatives of trustees, parents and teachers. The feedback from these groups attested, he said, to the wisdom and effectiveness of the articles of management. 'Therefore, we shall not readily or easily depart from this structure which has been tried and tested, and which guarantees the ability of the trustees to carry out their objectives and secure the stability of the school'.[90]

However, his views have to be set against a background of the obviously strained relations between the Churches and the minister, Niamh Bhreathnach. These were not helped by the leaking of a

---

[88] Minister for Education, briefing for education journalists, 18 May 1997.
[89] Bro. Declan Duffy, *General Secretary's Report*, AMCSS Annual Conference, Galway, 3 May 1996.
[90] Ibid.

provision in her draft Education Bill which contained a legal obligation on all schools in receipt of state aid to establish representative boards of management. Failure to establish boards would have resulted in a 'freezing' of state grants at current levels.[91] Chapter six will examine the draft Bill in more detail.

Her successor, Micheál Martin, indicated on a number of occasions that he intended to facilitate talks to allow for the establishment of boards in all second-level schools. In the 1997-8 school year about 170 out of 762 second-level schools still did not have boards of management. He pointed out that Section 14 of the Education (No 2) Bill 1997 made provision for the establishment and membership of boards of management, in line with his policy that all post-primary schools had such structures. To this end, it was his intention to facilitate agreements between the revelant partner groups similar to the agreement reached in 1997 at primary level.[92] His Bill did not place an obligation on schools to establish boards, however, a change that prompted a threat of industrial action by the ASTI, whose general secretary Charlie Lennon said it was preparing a campaign of action – including industrial action – to pursue the establishment of boards in all schools. Lennon said that boards were the key to promoting partnership between teachers, parents and school owners. The minister responded that he did not believe in coercion and expressed confidence that his promised facilitation process would have the desired result of boards in all schools.[93]

Commentary

Despite the setbacks and delays much has changed in the management and governance of primary and post-primary schools over the past twenty-five years, and further changes are likely. Parents in particular are benefiting from these changes. While the unions have been open to broadening the base of management, some union sources are suspicious of the official commitment to partnership and see in it an attempt to weaken their power. There

[91] Department of Education, *Draft Heads of the Education (Education Boards and Boards of Management) Bill, 1996*, unpublished.
[92] Minister for Education, reply to Dáil question, 20 October 1998.
[93] *Irish Independent,* 13 December 1998.

is no doubting the strength of the Irish teacher unions, which are much more influential than their counterparts in the UK or in America. They have used their considerable bargaining strength to further the interests of their members over the past few decades and succeeded in gaining improvements in salaries and conditions of work which put Irish teachers in a better position than teachers in many other developed countries. According to the 1998 *Education at a Glance* publication from the OECD, Irish primary teachers with fifteen years teaching experience are the fourth highest paid in OECD countries while second-level teachers are the sixth highest paid.[94] Some union leaders believe that the department would like to see their powers curtailed or at least sufficiently curtailed to accept more change in schools. They cite the appointment of several working groups – such as those on bullying and the initial group on relationships and sexuality education – without direct union representation as an indication of official thinking. They believe that the deliberate cultivation of parent power is another example of efforts to curtail the power of the unions by building up another power base in the education arena.[95]

The strengthening of the position of parents may indeed have as much to do with educational politics as it has to do with education but the schools and ultimately the pupils should be the main beneficiaries.

As a result of the Education Act 1998

- statutory recognition is given to the National Parents' Council
- parents have a statutory right to establish parents' associations in schools
- parents' representatives have a statutory right to participate in boards of management
- parents are entitled to receive copies of any reports on the operation and performance of the school produced by the board of management and have access to the school accounts on the same basis as the minister
- parents will be involved in the preparation of the school plan, copies of which will also be circulated to them
- parents will have a right of access to their children's school records

---

[94] OECD, *Education at a Glance: OECD Indicators*, Paris, OECD, 1998.
[95] Off-the-record discussions with union leaders.

- parents will be consulted in relation to the assessment of the psychological needs of their children and will be advised by the psychologists concerned in relation to the education and psychological development of the children
- parents have the right to appeal to the board of management against a decision of a teacher or member of staff of the school and to the Secretary General of the Department of Education and Science against certain actions taken by the board of management.

In addition, other promised legislative reforms will mean that parents have a statutory right to representation on Vocational Education Committees. There is also a promise that they will be consulted in each area on the provision of new school buildings and specialist facilities.

These changes do not amount to the full realisation of the equal partnership that successive ministers have promised. Indeed not all schools have yet embraced the notion of partnership articulated in the White Paper – some schools still do not have boards of management and some are reluctant to encourage parents' associations. At times, also, the partnership between the teachers and parents can become strained. In 1998, for instance, a joint campaign by the teachers and parents was launched to secure improved staffing and funding but the NPC was annoyed when the INTO decided to initiate a series of one-day stoppages without the Council's backing. The NPC also believed that Micheál Martin's Education Act was somewhat less parent-friendly than Niamh Bhreathnach's Education Bill, watering down in particular provisions for dealing with disputes in schools. It is true that the unions were happier with Martin's Bill but ministerial sources argued that the minister was simply restoring a balance in his Bill. Despite these reservations, the changes over the years represent considerable progress and put parents in a stronger position in Irish education than in many other developed countries. This was noted in a 1997 OECD report, entitled *Parents as Partners in Schooling*, which suggested that the various measures then proposed would mean that Ireland was about to have one of the most 'parent-participative' education systems in the world.[96]

---

[96] OECD/CERI, *Parents as Partners in Schooling,* Paris, OECD, 1997.

CHAPTER 5

Higher Education

The number of full-time undergraduate and post-graduate students in third-level colleges grew dramatically in Ireland over three decades, rising from 18,693 in the 1965-6 academic year to 88,193 in 1993-4 and to around 106,000 in the 1998-9 academic year.[1] A further 22,097 students were on one-year Post-Leaving Certificate (PLC) courses, 3,411 were on two-year and 293 were on three-year PLC courses in 1998-9. The increase reflected demographic trends, better retention rates at second level, growing transfer rates to third level and better opportunities for third-level award recipients. Ireland very quickly moved from a situation where a relatively small elite went into higher education to something approaching mass higher education.

The growth was across all sectors of higher education. For instance in 1965-6 there were only 1,007 full-time students in the Regional Technical College/Dublin Institute of Technology sector, but by 1993-4 this had grown to 34,673. The growth was greater in the university sector which had responded to the increasing demand for higher education by providing extra places with limited additional capital investment. The university growth took place mainly in the seventies and nineties and full-time enrolments rose from 16,007 in the 1965-6 academic year to 52,300 in 1993-4.[2]

In 1980 a fifth of the age cohort progressed to third level and this proportion had more than doubled by the time the government's White Paper on Education was published in 1995. Ireland, of course, was not unique in expanding its higher education numbers – other OECD countries did as well, paying greater attention than Ireland did to catering for part-time and mature students. Expenditure on higher education in Ireland, as a proportion of total government

---

[1] Department of Education and Science figures.
[2] *Report of the Steering Committee on the Future Development of Higher Education,* Dublin, Higher Education Authority, 1995 p. 105.

spending on education, increased steadily from 18 per cent in 1980 to 24 per cent in 1993.[3] There was an increasing reliance on tuition fees to fund expansion in that period, with fees constituting 33 per cent of total university income in 1993 as against 12 per cent in 1980. However, there was also a substantial increase in student support schemes over the same period.[4]

This chapter will review some of the more recent developments in higher education such as the Green and White Papers on education, the socioeconomic background of students, the abolition of tuition fees, the introduction of university legislation, and the upgrading of the technological college sector. It will seek to put some of the more important decisions in their historical context.

Green Paper on education, 1992

Ó Buachalla has referred to the transformation of higher education policy from one of expansion based upon an ideological base of social demand to one based upon 'vocationalism' and the demands of the market.[5] The policy shift was accompanied by more intrusion by the state, he suggested, and his analysis is reflected in various official documents. For instance, a White Paper on education published in 1980 referred to conversion courses that had been introduced to boost the supply of highly qualified and skilled craft, technician, engineering and computer manpower in manufacturing and service industries.[6] The courses were provided in response to serious shortages which had been identified by a Manpower Consultative Committee. The White Paper also referred to the 'pronounced bias' towards the professions that had been manifested, in the past, by third-level education.[7] It predicted that the extent of the provisions

---

[3] Department of Education, *Charting our Education Future*, White Paper on Education, Dublin, Stationery Office, 1995.

[4] *Report of the Steering Committee on the Future Development of Higher Education.*

[5] Séamas Ó Buachalla, 'Self-regulation and the Emergence of the Evaluative State in Irish Higher Education Policy 1987-1992', in *European Journal of Education*, Vol. 27, Nos. 1/2, 1992.

[6] Department of Education, *White Paper on Educational Development*, Dublin, Stationery Office, 1980, pp. 70-84.

[7] Ibid.

in the future to be made for students desiring professional qualifications would be influenced increasingly by consideration of
employment demand.

Over the next decade and a half successive governments progressively sought to influence not only the type of courses provided
but also the manner in which the universities were governed and
run. The *Programme for Action in Education 1984-87* stated that
priority would be given to courses geared to the developments of
modern society to ensure that graduates were kept abreast of rapidly
changing technology and could compete with graduates of other
countries.[8] It also promised an 'urgent examination' of the anomalous
situation whereby degree courses in some institutions were of four
years duration while similar courses in other institutions were
provided over three years.[9] Nowhere, however, was the transformation referred to by Ó Buachalla more clearly illustrated than
in the Green Paper published in 1992 by Séamus Brennan when
he was Minister for Education.[10] Brennan's Paper stated that it was
necessary to strengthen the executive role of college presidents
and that there was a need to rationalise the composition and
functions of governing bodies. It indicated that legislation would
be brought forward that would be more compatible with the role,
function and operation of universities in modern society. The
minister also promised to create four constituent universities within
a federal National University of Ireland structure.[11]

The Paper referred to the need for quality assurance in higher
education and stated that the approach to be adopted would be a
combination of the development of performance indicators and of
internal quality review procedures within the colleges, together
with appropriate monitoring and assistance through a proposed
academic audit unit within the HEA.[12] It suggested that the role of
the HEA should be reviewed and it listed some of the Authority's
possible enlarged functions:

---

[8] Department of Education, *Programme for Action in Education 1984-1987*,
Dublin, Stationery Office, 1984.
[9] Ibid.
[10] Department of Education, *Education for a Changing World*, Green Paper on
Education, Dublin, Stationery Office, 1992.
[11] Ibid, pp. 154-155.
[12] Ibid, pp. 144-145.

- overall co-ordination of the two sectors – university and non-university – and the elimination of unnecessary duplication and overlap
- ensuring a balance of level, type and variety of programmes across the two sectors
- ensuring an appropriate overall balance between certificate, diploma, degree and postgraduate work
- ensuring cost-effectiveness throughout the two sectors
- ensuring that quality assurance procedures are put in place in all institutions
- monitoring quality assurance through an academic audit unit
- monitoring and promoting links between colleges and industry
- the development of a comprehensive database for the entire higher education sector
- receiving annual reports from each of the third-level institutions and preparing a subsequent yearly report on the performance of the third-level sector generally.[13]

The Green Paper added that these proposals would require a change in the composition of the Authority through larger representation of business and industrial interests and of the non-university colleges sector.

The socioeconomic background of students

Increasing attention was paid in the 80s and 90s to the social composition of the college intake. Dr Pat Clancy, a sociologist at UCD, tracked changes in the social composition of higher education students over the course of three national surveys of entrants to college in 1980, 1986 and 1992. In the 1992 study five socioeconomic groups were 'over-represented' in proportion to their numbers in the population at large. In descending order these were: higher professional, employers and managers, salaried employees, lower professional and farmers. The degree of underrepresentation of the semiskilled manual workers' group was almost as great as that of the unskilled. Three other groups were significantly 'under-represented': other agricultural occupations, skilled manual and other non-manual. The intermediate non-manual group was

[13] Ibid, p. 151.

marginally 'underrepresented' with a participation rate of 0.91.[14]

With the expansion in higher education numbers, it is no surprise that with one exception (salaried employees) all social groups experienced an increase in the proportion going on to higher eduation. Clancy's third study confirmed that there had been some decline in inequality between 1980 and 1992. Even still, the disparities between the various social groups was striking. For four groups, the proportion of young people who enrolled in 1992 was over half and in the case of farmers it doubled to just below half. In the case of the higher professional group, it was an impressive 89 per cent, which was probably at saturation point given ability and motivational thresholds. In the second highest group, employers and managers, it was estimated that their rate of admission exceeded two-thirds of the relevant age group. Three of the lower white-collar groups had not shown the same proportionate increase in enrolment as had the other groups. In the case of skilled manual and other non-manual workers, it increased from 9 to 26 per cent and from 3 to 13 per cent for children of unskilled manual workers.[15]

The expansion of the RTC (now the Institute of Technology) sector had an impact on improving participation rates among lower socioeconomic groups. Dr Clancy pointed out that the degree of inequality was significantly less in the RTCs than in the other sectors. All of the manual socioeconomic groups had their highest represen-tation in this sector. Within the universities, the higher professional groups had their strongest representation while students from working-class backgrounds had their lowest representation. There was further differentiation within the university sector with the higher professional group being especially represented within the faculties of architecture, medicine and law while semiskilled and unskilled manual groups had their highest proportionate representation in education and social science.[16] While his report did not make recom-mendations Dr Clancy drew attention to the danger that the more prestigious programmes, which were usually of longer duration,

---

[14] Patrick Clancy, *Access to College: Patterns of Continuity and Change*, Dublin, Higher Education Authority, 1995, pp. 51-54.
[15] Ibid, p. 55.
[16] Ibid, p. 155.

would remain the 'cultural possession' of traditionally advantaged groups.

Disadvantaged Irish adults have a much lower chance of getting into higher education than adults in other OECD countries. Very little of the increase in third-level numbers could be attributed to mature students, who accounted for only 3.4 per cent of full-time entrants into state-aided colleges in 1993-4.[17] A study published in 1998 showed that only around 5 per cent of those who had left school before the Leaving Certificate returned to get higher education qualifications in the six years following their finishing school. The sudy showed that the higher the level of initial education completed, the greater the chance of subsequently improving that level.[18] However, there is a growing recognition of the need for greater education opportunities for adults, particularly those who are disadvangated. This is reflecterd in the Green Paper on adult education published in 1998 and in the brief for the Institute of Technology at Blanchardstown which included provision for a one-third intake of students with non-standard qualifications.[19]

The White Paper on education, 1995

In recent years the universities have been developing access programmes for second-level students from disadvantaged backgrounds through measures such as the BITE initiative, which helps prepare students in selected schools for entry to DCU.[20] The 1995 White Paper encouraged further developments of this type and set out a target of an annual increase of 500 students from lower socioeconomic groups at third level over the following five years.[21] It

[17] *Report of the Steering Committee on the Future Development of Higher Education.*

[18] Damian Hannan, Breeda McCabe and Selina McCabe, *Trading Qualifications for Jobs – Overeducation and the Irish Youth Labour Market,* Dublin, Oak Tree Press in association with the ESRI, 1998.

[19] Department of Education and Science, Green Paper, *Adult Education in an Era of Lifelong Learning,* Dublin, Stationery Office, November 1998.

[20] For a description and critique of the BITE and similar programmes see Kathleen Lynch and Claire O'Riordan, *Social Class, Inequality and Higher Education,* Dublin, Equality Studies Centre, UCD, 1996.

[21] White Paper 1995, p. 100.

promised that the HEA would be given a key role in advising on the most appropriate and effective means of achieving this target. The HEA was also to be made responsible for monitoring gender-equality policies.[22] All colleges would be asked to develop and publish policies in this area to include

- policies for the promotion of equal opportunities and associated action programmes, including procedures for preventing the sexual harassment of students and employees
- strategies to encourage increased participation by women students in faculties and courses of study in which they have been traditionally underrepresented, including liaison with second-level schools and the preparation and distribution of suitable promotional materials
- appropriate gender balance on all staff selection boards
- encouraging and facilitating women to apply for senior academic and administrative positions
- the putting in place of arrangements to assist students with young children.[23]

The White Paper added that, in accordance with government policy, new education legislation would provide for an appropriate gender balance on all governing bodies where it did not apply already. Legislation would be built upon the 1994 Regional Technical Colleges and Dublin Institute of Technology Amendment Acts which had given these institutions a large measure of autonomy and removed them from direct control by local Vocational Education Committees.

Niamh Bhreathnach shed much of Brennan's business-type approach to educational reform, especially at first and second level, but she retained references to the need for quality assurance at third level. She was known to have been influenced by the secrecy of the institutions, particularly about their drop-out and failure rates in various faculties. She also reportedly had doubts about the cost-effectiveness of some of the universities.[24] Her White Paper quoted the agreement recorded in the NEC report on the need for quality assurance but also referred to the complexities of the matter. The White Paper added that the rationale for public accountability arose

---

[22] Ibid, p. 100.
[23] Ibid, p. 102.
[24] Off-the-record sources.

from the large investment of state funds in educational institutions, the pervasive social and economic impact of third-level education and the extended remit of the Comptroller and Auditor General. Building on the NEC report the Paper proposed that public policy in relation to quality assurance in third-level institutions would be guided by a number of considerations, specifically

- recognition of the respective rights and responsibilities of the institutions and the state
- recognition of the primary responsibility of the institutions themselves for putting procedures in place
- an emphasis on rigorous peer review procedures
- a recognition of the need for public accountability in relation to quality and value for money
- the need to ensure that mechanisms in place are adequate for their purpose.[25]

The White Paper stated that university legislation would be introduced in relation to governing bodies in 1995. It reiterated the Green Paper's commitment that amending legislation would be introduced to the National University of Ireland Act under which the existing constituent colleges at Galway, Cork and Dublin and the recognised college at Maynooth would become constituent universities of the NUI. More comprehensive legislation for the university sector as a whole would also be introduced, it stated.[26]

Thus nobody directly concerned should have been unaware that legislation was planned. But what was surprising was the extraordinary debate that took place over the following year and a half even before the promised Bill was introduced into the Oireachtas. At one stage it seemed that the issue of university legislation would lead to an embarrassing defeat for the government in Seanad Éireann (see below).

University funding and free third-level tuition, 1994

Before reviewing the debate on legislation it is worth looking at the relations between the minister and the universities around this time. Relations could be described as fraught, for two main reasons.

---

[25] White Paper 1995, pp. 103-104.
[26] Ibid, pp. 105-106.

One was the attitude of the academic community to the minister's plans to abolish undergraduate tuition fees and the other was the very public campaign for additional resources by the universities.

The abolition of fees was one of the most important and controversial decisions affecting higher education taken in Ireland during the nineties. It came at a time when other countries whose students had enjoyed free higher education, such as the UK, were considering the introduction of fees to meet the rising cost of higher education. The minister's thinking was disclosed, prematurely from her point of view, in a newspaper report on 26 July 1994 and confirmed by her later that day on television.[27] At that stage the cabinet had not formally considered the proposals and some Fianna Fáil ministers were known to have been unhappy about it. Although Séamus Brennan had earlier flagged it as a possibility, senior party sources say it was not seriously considered by Fianna Fáil because of the arguments about cost and equity. However, once the idea had got into the public domain it began to take on a life of its own and a group called the Campaign for Free Third-Level Education kept up the pressure for its introduction. For some time no other senior Labour politician came out to support Niamh Bhreathnach until two months later when the proposal secured the public backing of party leader Dick Spring.[28] The proposal was subsequently written into the agreement on the formation of a new government involving Fine Gael, Labour and Democratic Left in December 1994.

Despite this agreement, Democratic Left continued to express strong reservations when the issue came to government in January 1995. It arose in the context of discussions on a report from the Advisory Group on Third-Level Student Support.[29] The Group opposed the notion of free fees for all. Its report recommended the phased abolition of income tax relief for covenants and the application of the revenue to increase direct expenditure under the student support schemes. Niamh Bhreathnach, however, proposed in a memorandum to government to use the savings to cover the introduction of free fees. The observations of some of her ministerial

---

[27] *Irish Independent*, 26 July 1994.
[28] Ibid, 17 October 1994.
[29] *Report of the Advisory Committee on Third-Level Student Support*, Dublin, Stationery Office, 1993.

colleagues are revealing. The Minister for Equality and Law Reform, Mervyn Taylor, said he would like to see heavy emphasis on the grant/support structures for those on lower incomes and in particular on the threshold limits. He said also that it was necessary to provide adequate child-care/child-minding facilities to enable students with children to benefit from the abolition of fees initiative. The Minister for Agriculture, Food and Forestry, Ivan Yates, raised some queries about the effects of the measures proposed. He said that if the net costs of the proposals were substantially in excess of what was indicated by Ms Bhreathnach the overall effect could be regressive in social terms, involving, in general, a transfer of income from lower to higher socioeconomic sectors in society.

The Minister for Social Welfare, Prionnsias De Rossa, leader of Democratic Left, said he had concerns and reservations about what was proposed. There was abundant research to indicate that lower income groups were very under-represented at third level. In the most recent ESRI report on poverty it was shown that while 40 per cent of heads of households who had a professional/managerial background had third-level qualifications, only 3 per cent of those from lower working-class backgrounds had such qualifications.

> In the minister's view, it is this participation issue that needs to be addressed. Arguably the existing means tested grants scheme should be changed to permit a higher income limit to bring in the lower income middle-class groups referred to in the memorandum or alternatively the savings from abolition of covenants could be directed at a child benefit supplement to lower income households. Otherwise the abolition of tuition fees for all students will have regressive effects favouring many higher income households directly. It is worth noting that the direct cashflow advantage to the higher income parent is of more benefit than the more elaborate covenant arrangement.

In short, the concerns about the proposed approach are:

- it is regressive
- it does nothing for real lower income groups
- it defers tackling the inequalities in the means test for grants, in particular the proposals re. assessment of capital.[30]

---

[30] Observations of ministers on Third-Level Student Support, January 1995, unpublilshed.

The views of the Department of Finance provoked a strong reaction from the Department of Education which accused it of 'gross exaggeration and scaremongering' in one of its arguments and, in response to another observation, a strong denial that it was Education's intention to provide places on demand. Finance, somewhat unexpectedly expressed concern that the quality of university education could be endangered if fees were abolished. It referred to the position of local authorities following the abolition of rates and their increased dependence on exchequer funding. It warned that in the event of a tight budgetary situation the universities might be tempted to take in more non-EU students to generate income but at the expense of places for Irish students. It also warned that the decision would increase the demand for places from middle-income families and from those who might otherwise have gone to the UK.

Finance accepted the proposal to abolish income tax relief on covenants (other than for the elderly and incapacitated) on the grounds that the cost was escalating and the system was subject to abuse. However, in an *aide memoire* it said that this would give rise to 'losers' who would not necessarily be the same people as the 'winners' from the free fees proposal. The main losers would be

- post graduate students (about 7,000 full time) and students in private colleges (estimated at 4,500)
- students on ESF grants (about 30,000 – a significant proportion of whom would have covenants to subsidise their maintenance)
- students studying abroad – these students (estimated at 4,500) are in a similar position to ESF students above
- others having covenants. Apart from the elderly and the incapacitated, all others having covenants will lose their tax relief as a result of the proposal. While this will include many who are using covenants for tax planning purposes or to enhance significant gifts, it will also include others who may well consider themselves more deserving than third-level students.[31]

Finance added that the position of the losers could not be alleviated by retaining covenants for them as there were constitutional limits

---

[31] *Aide Memoire* on Third-Level Student Support. Comments of the Department of Finance, January 1995, unpublished.

to allowing covenants to some students while withdrawing them from others in similar circumstances. Any other proposal to replace the lost funds to those students who lost would quickly eliminate the savings from the covenant proposal, it stated.

The proposal to abolish fees did not attract any public backing from the academic community. The Provost of Trinity College Dublin, Dr Tom Mitchell, was one of the most outspoken critics of the decision. He said that the funding of universities in order to provide more places, especially for the disadvantaged, was a greater priority than abolishing fees.[32] Later Dr Mitchell said

> I can see no reason, social or educational, why those who will receive lifelong benefits – personal, professional and financial – from their university education and who have the capacity to make at least some contribution towards the high cost of that education, should not make some form of payment. I believe it is untenable that benefits of such magnitude should be given at taxpayers' expense to the better-off sections of society when the system is so starved of resources that it can satisfy only a fraction of the demand and must constantly struggle to maintain its standards.[33]

Official sources at the time indicated that the revenue forgone through tax relief would have shortly overtaken the full amount earned by the colleges in tuition fees. The tax relief was about to be abolished anyway and Breathnach saw it as an opportunity to link it to the abolition of tuition fees. It could be argued that if tax relief was withdrawn from parents who used covenants to send their children to college and nothing was put in its place there would have been political uproar. The minister insisted that the abolition of fees was a separate issue from that of assisting the disadvantaged to get into higher education but this cut little ice with many critics of the plan. Although the middle and upper income groups benefited from the decision to abolish fees, the minister and the Labour Party earned few political kudos for it. Far from gaining from the decision, it could be argued that Education lost out because some of the increases in its budget for the following two years went towards meeting the cost of the free fees initiative.

---

[32] *The Irish Times*, 27 July 1994.
[33] *Irish Independent*, 23 October 1995.

The issue was highlighted again three years later in a report edited by a team from the Economic and Social Research Institute which stated that the decision was unfair on taxpayers. It said that the gains from pursuing third-level education accrued mainly to the private individual. It was therefore appropriate that students should pay some of the costs through fees while pursuing their courses or, alternatively, later by means of loans. The report, *National Investment Priorities 2000-2006* was commissioned by the Department of Finance to form the basis of the next National Development Plan.[34] Fine Gael immediately rejected the notion[35] and politically it would have been difficult for the government to reintroduce fees so soon after their abolition.

Relations with the universities were not helped either by a very public campaign by them for extra resources to cater for the additional students they had accommodated over the previous two decades. The minister was not over-sympathetic to their pleas for extra funds because she believed that they were generously funded relative to primary education, especially by international OECD comparison.[36] She saw also that there was scope for economies, a perception borne out in a report from the Comptroller and Auditor General into their purchasing policies. The report found wide variations in the prices paid for items and said that significant savings could be achieved by better procurement policies.[37] For instance, in a study of nine categories of goods and services which collectively accounted for over £17m annually, it discovered that

- cleaning costs per square metre varied from £4.87 to £8.73
- security costs per square metre varied from £2.20 to £5.69
- discount on books purchased varied from nil to 10 per cent, depending on the supplier and the university
- the prices for chemicals varied widely. Acetone ranged in price from £0.97 to £12.00; Ethanol ranged from £2.15 to £26.00 (prices based on units of 2.5 litres).

[34] *Irish Independent*, 22 February, 1999
[35] RTE news, 22 February 1999.
[36] OECD, *Education at a Glance*, Paris, OECD, 1995.
[37] Report of the Comptroller and Auditor General, *Procurement in Universities*, Dublin, Stationery Office, 1996.

When she released the report, the minister acknowledged that the universities were autonomous, independent bodies and as such the first responsibility was for each university to review its own practices and procedures in the light of the findings. She said that she was asking the HEA to liaise with the universities to ensure that every opportunity to achieve savings identified in the report was fully explored.[38]

The campaign for additional funding by the universities was unrelenting. Dr Mitchell stated on a number of occasions that capital funding had fallen from £22,000 per additional student in 1982 to £1,950 in 1993 (figures adjusted for inflation). He said that Ireland was accommodating only 18 per cent of its school leavers in university and predicted that this figure would worsen because of rising demand. He added that 'this figure is far below the EU average of about 30 per cent and over the long term must weaken our ability to maintain competitiveness within an increasingly knowledge-driven European economy'.[39]

It is known that the minister was unhappy at the campaign and in particular at an article written by Dr Mitchell in *The Times Higher Education Supplement* which drew attention to the issue.[40] The minister pointed out on a number of occasions that the universities were not the only providers of third-level education. The campaign did, however, meet with some success and on 13 September 1995 she announced the creation of 6,200 additional places in the university sector at a cost of £60m.[41] Dr Mitchell acknowledged the programme, but said that it would only dent the problem and that it could be implemented only if the universities could raise £30m from private sources – no small task.[42] According to political sources, it was the universities themselves who came up with the idea of funding the expansion in this way. The same sources also indicated that the 50:50 split was the only way the idea could have been sold to the Department of Finance. Indeed, the generally

[38] Minister for Education, *Press Release,* 17 January 1997.
[39] Dr Tom Mitchell, address to a conference on the White Paper, organised by the Irish Federation of University Teachers, 21 October 1995.
[40] Dr Tom Mitchell, *The Times Higher Education Supplement,* December 1994.
[41] Department of Education, *Press Release,* 13 September 1995.
[42] *Irish Independent,* 14 September 1995.

sceptical attitude of that department towards expansion in higher
education numbers was confirmed in a government memorandum
which was, unexpectedly, released under the Freedom of Information Act three years later in 1998. The memo dealt with an
application from the Minister for Education, Micheál Martin, for
cabinet approval for a new institute of technology in Blanchardstown, Co. Dublin. This was opposed by the Minister for Finance,
Charlie McCreevy, who said that the number of eighteen year olds
in Ireland would drop by 22,000 or one-third in the year 1998. He
stated that existing and planned provision was for 114,000 places
in higher education – if that were exceeded the liklihood was that
there would be considerable wasted investment in hugely expensive
third-level places. 'Despite prospective increases in participation
rates, the required numbers of qualified students are unlikely to be
available to fill the additional places', he said. The minister did
accept that there were demands to meet anticipated skill shortages
but argued that these could be provided by substitution within
existing places.[43] It should be noted that the objections of the Minister
for Finance were overruled and the government gave the green
light to the Blanchardstown project.[44]

Position paper on university legislation, 1995

Returning to Niamh Bhreathnach and 1995, the Department of
Education issued a confidential position paper to university heads
on university legislation and it initiated discussions with the college
presidents.[45] Before examining the paper it is worthwhile sketching
in the immediate background to its preparation. One element in
that background was the report of the NEC which quoted NUI
spokespersons as urging the early implementation of legislation to

---

[43] *Department of Education and Science, Summary of Memorandum for
Government: New Third-Level Institution at Blanchardstown*, 29 June 1998,
obtained by Joan Burton, vice-chairperson of the Labour Party, under the
Freedom of Information Act.

[44] Minister for Education, *Press Release re. Blanchardstown Institute of Technology*,
30 September 1998.

[45] Department of Education, *Position Paper on University Legislation*, July 1995,
unpublished.

amend the Irish Universities Act 1908 to give independence to the three constituent colleges at UCD, UCG and UCC and the recognised college at Maynooth.[46] Another was the preparation of the White Paper, which dealt with legislation as well as with issues of accountability and quality assurance.[47] Niamh Bhreathnach told the author that pressures from the former president of St Patrick's College, Maynooth, Mgr Michael Ledwith, was one of the factors that gave impetus to the legislation. There were also pressures for changes in the composition of the governing bodies. For instance, the Union of Students in Ireland wanted statutory representation for students on all governing bodies. There was, in addition, a government commitment to gender balance on state boards and other boards funded by the state. Breathnach wanted to achieve a minimum 40 per cent representation of females on the governing boards of the universities and thought that this could be done in the context of legislative changes for the institutions.[48]

The paper was issued in the summer and was a surprise for a number of reasons. One was that it came a few days after the CHIU met senior department officials for discussions about university legislation who apparently gave no indication of its imminent release. Another was the input from a committee whose existence was not known to most people in the university community, including some university heads. The committee's membership included Noel Lindsay, then chairperson of the Higher Education Authority, John Hayden, Secretary to the HEA, and Dr Tom Murphy, former president of UCD. The committee also included a number of middle-ranking department officials. (This committee was effectively sidelined and wound up shortly afterwards.) The third reason for surprise lay in the contents.

The document was awkwardly phrased in parts and its approach could be described as heavy-handed. It reaffirmed the long-standing commitment of successive governments to give constituent university status to four NUI colleges – UCG, UCC, UCD and Maynooth. It contained three other proposals, two of which were to cause serious

---

[46] John Coolahan (Ed.), *Report on the National Education Convention*, Dublin, Stationery Office, 1994, p. 95.

[47] White Paper on Education 1995, pp. 103-105.

[48] Niamh Bhreathnach, interview with author, 30 November 1998.

political problems for the minister over the next year and a half. One dealt with the future of the NUI itself as an institution. The second dealt with proposed changes in the governance of the universities, and the third dealt with powers proposed for the minister and the Higher Education Authority over financial affairs and staffing matters of the institutions. The latter two issues were to prove much more intractable than the first.

The matter of the possible dissolution of the NUI to form separate universities had long been on the agenda. Osborne and Fisher, from the Centre for Policy Research in Northern Ireland, have noted that many assumed that this process was inevitable and that some in the NUI had campaigned for it.[49] They went on to point out the following, however:

> During the 1989-91 period, when the issue was once more to the fore, the debate within the NUI was coloured by the new developments on funding, which were perceived as threatening to the traditional institutions, but also by the state's perceived desire to intervene in university autonomy, as represented by the arrangements for the two new universities (DCU and UL). Caution, it was argued, should be exercised in giving any opportunity to the state through a major new Universities Bill.

The upshot was that in 1991 the NUI wrote to the then minister Mary O'Rourke, setting out the views of the three constituent colleges, of St Patrick's College, Maynooth, and of the Senate of the university as follows: 'Despite differences as to the extent and degree of change desired, it is the common preference of the four colleges to remain constituent elements of an NUI system but each with the status and title of a university and a significant redistribution in its favour of powers and functions'.[50]

O'Rourke's unpublished draft Green Paper stated that she had agreed to sponsor legislation to amend the 1908 (Irish University) Act, on the basis of proposals put forward by the Senate of the

[49] R.D. Osborne and N.A. Fisher, *Recent Developments in Third-Level Education in the Republic of Ireland,* Research Paper No 4, Centre for Policy Research, Northern Ireland, June 1992.
[50] National University of Ireland, *Letter to the Minister for Education, Mary O'Rourke,* 5 March 1991.

NUI, aimed at creating four constituent universities within a federal NUI structure[51] and a similar promise was contained in Brennan's published Green Paper.[52] Thus, it is easy to understand why the NUI colleges were taken aback at the unexpected suggestion that the NUI be dissolved which was contained in the document they received in mid-1995. The document commented that

> The legislation proposed by the Senate of the NUI provides for the retention of the NUI as envisaged by them. However, the proposals made by the NUI Senate do not provide for any real residual functions to be retained by the NUI. The effect of the proposals would be to transfer the real powers of a university to the colleges, and to dilute the powers of the NUI to a stage where it would become largely redundant, with a nominal co-ordinating role (and a cost per year estimated to be in excess of £1m).[53]

The Paper added that it would be difficult for the NUI to enforce standards when the universities themselves were designing the courses and setting their own standards and examinations. The suggested dissolution of the NUI infuriated the university authorities, whose Chancellor Dr T.K. Whitaker wrote in very forceful tones to the minister. She had not involved herself directly in the discussions but she quickly gave a written assurance to the NUI that it would be retained if and when the four colleges obtained constituent university status.[54]

It was obvious to the parties directly concerned that the attempt to reach early agreement had got off on the wrong foot by the issuing of the document. The university heads, who had taken initiatives to promote quality assurance in their institutions, felt disappointed and they had serious concerns about the degree of financial control proposed for the HEA. They also had concerns about possible restrictions on the appointment of senior staff and about the proposed composition of the governing structures. They were worried about the proposal in the document that the post of President/Provost/Master be publicly advertised and the appoint-

---

[51] Department of Education, *Draft Green Paper on Education*, October 1991, p. 120, unpublished.

[52] *Education for a Changing World*, p. 155.

[53] *Position Paper on University Legislation*, p. 8.

[54] *Irish Independent*, 27 September 1995.

ment made in accordance with procedures approved by the minister. The document proposed that a selection board, of the appropriate level and with appropriate gender balance and outside interests, should be established by the university. It was intended that the person appointed should be the chief officer and the accounting officer of the university and should report to the governing authority. The approval of the minister would be necessary for the creation of posts at the level of senior lecturer or higher, or posts with comparable remuneration. The procedures for filling permanant posts would also be subject to the minister's approval. The universities saw these provisions as constituting unwarranted interference in their traditional autonomy.

The initial public controversy, however, arose over the provisions for governing structures. The model proposed would have given academic staff (junior and senior), non-academic staff and students statutory representation on all governing bodies, with an additional provision for the trustees to be represented in the case of Maynooth. The balance of the membership would come from business; industrial and agricultural interests; the professions; employers; trade unions; local authorities; regional education boards and minister's nominees. Co-option of up to two members was also provided for. A minimum and maximum level of representation from each staff constituency and from the local authority/local education sector was also recommended in the document. One issue that was to cause some confusion subsequently related to the chairperson of the governing authority. The document was quite clear on this.

> The chairperson should be appointed by the minister from a group of three persons nominated by the governing authority, at least one of whom shall be a woman and one a man. The person so appointed should not be from the staff of the university, or already be a member of the governing authority. Essentially, the governing authority itself would decide on the short list from which the chairperson should be chosen. It is anticipated that the independent chairperson should be a person of well-established reputation and high standing in the community. Each university shall choose the title by which the governing authority shall be known, e.g. Chancellor, etc.

For some reason the minister was subsequently to deny that it was her intention to appoint the chairperson (see below).

The document acknowledged that the authorities at Trinity College Dublin which, it agreed, had 'virtually total independence' might be apprehensive about increased regulation of their affairs. It argued that because Trinity would receive in excess of 90 per cent of its operating income from state funds then the same legislative provisions should apply to all the publicly funded universities. Its predictions of apprehension within Trinity were borne out by subsequent events.

Public reaction to the proposals for university legislation

The manner in which details of the position paper became public is worth recording because the premature disclosure of its contents was to have a significant effect on the course of the debate. As Education Editor with the *Irish Independent,* the author was approached at a function by a university official. The official appraised the author of the contents of the paper and expressed concern over what was proposed; some days later the author obtained a copy of the paper from a separate source. The publication led directly to a strong campaign of opposition. The first critical public reaction came from a lecturer in economics at TCD, Dr Sean Barrett, who expressed alarm at the proposals. In a Sunday newspaper article he defended the autonomy of TCD which, he claimed, was under threat.[55] He suggested that newspaper leaks (of the discussion document) 'were an attempt to soften up public opinion for changing Trinity College Dublin from an autonomous college to a Labour Party quango'. He warned that 'the nationalisation of the college will be fought tooth and nail by those who are loyal to a college which has served this country well'. While his reaction was overstated, it had the effect of helping to galvanise opposition within the college.

Discussions with the Department of Education were confidential, which meant that the university heads were unable to comment directly on the specific proposals. They did, however, refer in general to the principles of university autonomy and related issues. The President of UCC, Dr Michael Mortell, for instance, told a conferring

---

[55] *Sunday Independent,* 15 October 1995.

ceremony that the university 'must have the freedom to maintain a
certain critical distance from prevailing political, ecclesiastical and
market imperatives'.[56] He quoted Edmund Burke's warning that
the university could not be 'a weathercock on top of an edifice,
exalted for its levity and versatility, and of no use but to indicate
the shiftings of every fashionable gale'. The Provost of TCD, Dr
Mitchell, said that it was difficult to justify any greater level of
interference by the state in the workings of a university. 'Many of
the additional modes of regulation commonly mooted would be
counter-productive and, in some instances, seriously destructive',
he said.[57] UCD president, Dr Art Cosgrove, assured graduates at a
conferring ceremony that the college's history and traditions were
not about to be abandoned. 'The preservation of our autonomy is
seen as essential so that we may continue to provide for the community the higher education and leadership which it deserves', he
added.[58]

Minister's briefing note for senators, 1995

While these comments were being made publicly, there were still
no official proposals in the public domain. The first document to
have an official circulation outside those directly involved in the
discussions was a briefing note for members of Seanad Éireann at
the end of October 1995.[59] This set out legislative principles and
proposals. It sought to reassure critics that there was no attempt to
impose a uniform representative structure for each governing body
and insisted that the Heads of the Bill as drafted did not confer any
power on the minister to become involved in the day-to-day running
of the universities. It went on:

> As a further acknowledgement of autonomy, governing bodies will
> themselves be allowed to decide whether they should be chaired
> by the President/Provost or a person from outside the university.
> Press reports that the minister would appoint all chairpersons are
> inaccurate.

---

[56] Dr Michael Mortell, speech at conferring ceremony, UCC, 25 October 1995.
[57] Dr Tom Mitchell, IFUT seminar, 21 October 1995.
[58] Dr Art Cosgrove, speech at conferring ceremony, 25 October 1995.
[59] Minister for Education Niamh Bhreathnach, *Briefing Note for Senators*,
31 October 1995.

Why the minister would choose to deny that she would appoint the chairpersons is not entirely clear because we have seen earlier that the original proposals had indicated that the chairperson would be chosen by the minister from a group of three persons nominated by the governing authority of each institution. One likely explanation is that by then the original proposals had been modified in the discussions with the Conference of Heads of Irish Universities.

Leaving that issue aside, the minister's briefing note indicated some change in the proposed membership of governing authorities. The universities themselves would determine which outside bodies would be represented on the governing authorities. In addition, provision would be made for the continued appointment of county councillors in the case of the NUI and of Fellows in the case of TCD. The only constituency over which the universities would not have the power of selection would be a small number of ministerial nominees. The universities would also be obliged to ensure gender balance in making their selections.

The briefing note reiterated that the governing bodies would be required to prepare a five-year strategic plan, set up procedures for evaluating academic standards and prepare a statement of its policies relating to access to the university. It asserted that the government could dissolve a governing body for stated reasons and for a period not longer than one year, a provision that was bound to cause difficulties. The briefing note was prepared on foot of a motion tabled by John Dardis and Cathy Honan of the Progressive Democrats which read: 'That Seanad Éireann rejects any attempt by the government and the Minister for Education to interfere with the governance and charter of Trinity College Dublin or to weaken the autonomy of the colleges of the National University of Ireland'.[60]

Senator Shane Ross, who represented the graduates of the University of Dublin constituency, made little secret of his willingness to defy the Fine Gael party whip over the issue and two independent members of the House, Senator Joe Lee and Senator David Norris, also elected by university graduates, were known to be unhappy at the reported provisions in the initial document. If the other university

---

[60] Senators John Dardis and Cathy Honan, *Motion tabled in Seanad Éireann*, 1 November 1995.

senators and Fianna Fáil members rowed in behind the PD motion then a government defeat was possible.

Intervention by the Taoiseach, 1995

The Taoiseach, John Bruton, was sufficiently exercised about the potential defeat to seek an additional briefing document from the Minister for Education.[61] This went over much of the same ground as was covered in the note for senators but it also contained some fascinating insights into Department of Education thinking at that time. In particular it showed how the department saw the main opposition as coming from Trinity. The note referred to the resolution of potential areas of disagreement through the consultation process with university heads. It then went on to refer to the concern of TCD's Provost, Dr Mitchell, that the proposals would be seen as encroaching unduly upon TCD's historic autonomy and self-governing status. It added:

> In particular, the proposal to have representative outside bodies and ministerial nominees on the board (TCD's Governing Body) is viewed as undermining its self-governing status. Dr Mitchell indicates that he personally would be receptive to proposals for changes in the composition of TCD's board; but any change must be made with the agreement of TCD, and should still leave the Trinity community with a majority on the board. The department's proposals meet this objective but are still not satisfactory to the Provost.

The note went on to confirm that the effect of the proposals at that time was that a thirty-member Governing Board could contain up to twenty members from within the TCD community, comprising Fellows (6), senior officers (3), senior academic staff (5), junior academic staff (2), non-academic staff (2), and students (2). Of the other 10 members, four would be chosen by the Provost from among representative bodies which in the view of the Board deserved representation, one would be a graduate, the local Education Board would have one representative and the remaining

---

[61] Department of Education, *Confidential Note for the Taoiseach*, 31 October 1995, unpublished.

four members would be appointed by the minister. It argued that this structure preserved the elements of self-governance while ensuring meaningful representation of other interested parties. It added that 'further discussions with Dr Mitchell are planned when he returns from a visit to the US on 8 November'. The lengthy note to the Taoiseach cautioned against the dangers of allowing Trinity to opt out of any legislation.

> The TCD position appears to be that they want legislation which will deal with the college in a manner fundamentally different from the other universities – ideally, probably no change from the current position where the Board is dominated by Fellows of the college. Diversity in universities and in their internal operations is a quality which will be promoted in the Bill. However, such diversity should accord with broad principles. In the case of governing bodies the principle at the centre is that various stake holders in the universities should have a meaningful voice at that level. Allowing TCD to opt out from that principle on the basis of an ancient charter will undermine the principle itself. It should be noted, in passing, that the present structure of Trinity's Board dates from 1911, whereas, the structure of the NUI colleges dates from 1908. Thus it can be seen how the tradition argument could cause the entire legislation to unravel.

The minister of the day, Niamh Bhreathnach, later told the author that she had come under a lot of pressure to exclude Trinity from the legislative framework but felt 'as a Dub' that she could not, especially as the university was getting so much money from the taxpayers. She also believed that her stance was one of the smaller factors that helped contribute to her own electoral defeat subsequently in the Dunlaogaire-Rathdown constituency in the 1997 general election. 'It came up on the doorstep in a number of cases – little old dears asking me what was I trying to do to Trinity'.[62]

New position paper, 1995

Fortunately from the government's point of view the Seanad agreed to postpone a vote on the PD motion for some weeks. This gave the minister time to issue a revised position paper, which she did

---

[62] Niamh Bhreathnach, interview with author, 30 November 1998.

on 28 November.[63] There was little new in this document but it was the first departmental publication on the issue of university legislation to be given wide circulation. Had it been issued much earlier the debate might well have taken a different turn. It expanded on what was already known and it put forward various models for the composition of governing bodies. Significantly, around this time two university presidents, Dr Danny O'Hare from Dublin City University and Dr Edward Walsh from the University of Limerick, wrote newspaper articles about the legislation that were sympathetic to what the minister was proposing.[64] Both institutions would have benefited from the legislation because all of their governing bodies had heretofore being appointed by the minister of the day.

The vote in the Seanad was taken on 30 November. Senator Ross met the Taoiseach immediately before the vote and told the House that he had received certain assurances from Mr Bruton and on the basis of these he had agreed to move an amendment on behalf of the government. However, he reiterated his threat to resign the party whip if the subsequent legislation were unacceptable to Trinity. The amendment welcomed the intention of the Minister for Education to bring forward legislative proposals for the universities and it called on the minister to ensure that these proposals

- preserve the academic freedom and ethos of individual universities and university colleges
- give university status to the individual colleges of the National University of Ireland, including the recognised college at Maynooth
- broaden the composition of the governing bodies to make them more representative of the university communities and to involve the wider community which they serve, and do so in a way which best allows the universities achieve their particular mission
- ensure accountability and transparency in the use of state funds.

Many members of the House contributed to the debate. Breathnach, who was present, told the senators that the minister would be required to consult with the President or Provost of a university

[63] Department of Education, *Position Paper on University Legislation*, November 1995.
[64] *Irish Independent*, 25 November 1995 and *The Irish Times*, 28 November 1995.

before appointing any ministerial nominee. She said that guidelines would be issued by the HEA on the appropriate distribution of funds but these would not be mandatory. The government amendment was carried.

Universities' Bill, July 1996

The issue largely disappeared from public fora until the minister published the Universities Bill on 30 July 1996, completing what she described as a lengthy process of consultation and dialogue between the Department of Education and all the interested parties.[65] The degree of consultation was quite unusual because the university presidents were, according to one source, given sight of the Heads of the Bill which were to form the basis of the draft legislation. They were able to negotiate changes in the Heads and assumed that they had 'a done deal' when the negotiations concluded before the Bill was published. They were seriously mistaken.

As expected the Bill dealt with the structure of the governing authorities for all seven university institutions, the reconstitution of the NUI, as well as with new transparency and accountability procedures for the universities. The Bill would allow the minister to appoint a maximum of four representatives to any governing authority, following consultation with the head of the university. Up to four other members would be chosen by the governing authority from nominations made by outside bodies, such as industrial bodies and trade unions.

There seems to have been a belief at that time in the Department of Education that the Bill would prove to be relatively uncontroversial. It was apparently felt that Trinity would accept the minimum number of outsiders on its governing structure as proposed in the Bill and that this acceptance would signal the end of the major opposition to the Bill. The basic premise was probably correct, because Trinity would most likely accept a minimum of outsiders on its governing board, but it was an error to assume this was the end of the controversy over university legislation. Indeed, the department seems to have failed to anticipate the extraordinary

[65] *Universities' Bill 1996.*

reaction to the specific provisions which were aimed at ensuring greater accountability and transparency.

Because the Bill was published during the summer holidays it did not generate much public comment immediately. That was to change once the academic year got underway. The most reasoned and well-argued criticism came from the former Taoiseach, Dr Garret FitzGerald, who wrote two articles in *The Irish Times*.[66] In the first he dissected the complex provisions for the governing structures of the universities. While welcoming the fact that there was no attempt at uniformity he argued that the academic representation on the governing bodies of the NUI colleges would be reduced from half or more to – at most – between one-third and two-fifths. The University of Dublin would have an academic majority of over two-thirds while Maynooth would have a governing authority half of whose members would be academic.

The second article was much more damning. It demonstrated that the Bill contained eight sections which, between them, proposed to hand over de facto control of key aspects of the universities to the government-appointed Higher Education Authority. These included provisions for issuing strategic development plans, annual reports and evaluative material on the performance of the universities to the Authority. The universities would not be allowed to borrow without the consent of the Ministers for Education and Finance, and then only on such conditions as the HEA might determine. Guidelines were to be issued by the HEA dealing with the proportion of the university budget to be applied to different activities and guidelines were also to be issued on matters relating to the number and grades of employees. If the universities failed to comply with a requirement the HEA could report the matter to the minister who would publish any such report in *Iris Oifigiúil*, the government's official gazette. Having listed the contentious sections, Dr FitzGerald then asked: 'How has our Oireachtas come to be presented with such an extraordinarily authoritarian, indeed Thatcherite, Bill – a measure profoundly contrary to, and openly dismissive of, our highly successful university system?'

This was strong stuff indeed and bound to carry weight. FitzGerald

---

[66] Dr Garret FitzGerald, *The Irish Times*, 23-24 September 1996.

was, of course, an *engagé* party long associated with UCD and later to become Chancellor of the NUI. It is known that FitzGerald spoke with the minister's programme manager, Pat Keating, and the department's Assistant Secretary, Oliver Cussen, before the articles appeared.[67] Whatever arguments he was offered were clearly insufficient to prevent him castigating the Bill – but worse was to come, from the minister's point of view, in terms of determined opposition from some of the university institutions and, surprisingly, from the HEA.

Reaction from the universities

The most trenchant criticism came from UCC and UCG. In UCC the Academic Council at a special meeting on 4 October established a group to analyse the strategic options open to UCC and to report on these with recommendations to a further special meeting which was fixed for Wednesday 16 October.[68] The group met on three occasions and concluded that the Bill had gone much further than had been requested by UCC in seeking university status for the college. It claimed that provision was made for specific powers for the HEA, the Ministers for Education and Finance 'which would cause a loss of public and international confidence in the integrity of the university system in Ireland'.[69] The document listed many areas of concern, covering much the same ground as Dr FitzGerald had done. The group considered broad strategic options which could be adopted by UCC: namely to reject the Bill outright, to delay the Bill with a view to dealing with a future government which might produce better legislation, or to facilitate the then government in improving the Bill by seeking significant and substantial amendments to it, as well as sufficient time to prepare them. It suggested opting for the latter but urged the college to prepare 'contingency plans for possible outcomes' of the committee stage in the Dáil. Obviously, if all the college's proposed amend-

---

[67] Off-the-record sources.
[68] *Report of the Academic Council Group,* October 1996, unpublished.
[69] Ibid.

ments were agreed the legislation would be acceptable from its point of view but if none of them was accepted the document suggested that there might be need for a 'strategy for further Dáil/ Seanad opposition and public action on the Bill'. Quite what public action the group had in mind was not spelt out in the document but the fact that such a possibility was even considered by a group chaired by the college's vice-president, Dr D.I.F. Lucey, indicates the concern at high levels in the college over the Bill.

The UCC governing body held a special meeting on 31 October and issued a lengthy statement which welcomed the minister's intention to continue dialogue on possible amendments to the Bill.[70] However, it also commented that the Bill as introduced into the Oireachtas involved controls which the long, untroubled history of the university sector had shown to be unnecessary and bureaucratic – that there was a grave danger that some of the provisions would stifle initiative and retard the future contributions which the college wanted to make to Irish society. The statement contained a warning:

> The Academic Council and Governing Body believe that, without significant and substantial amendment, the Bill is unsafe and not in the public interest. Some of the provisions would curtail the powers which UCC has under its 1908 Charter to such an extent as to be open to constitutional challenge.

The public statement from UCG was even stronger, with references to the 'heavy-handed and bureaucratically stifling' nature of the detailed regulations, the 'excessive regulatory role' proposed for the HEA, the 'paralysing and utterly unnecessary bureaucratic machinery of regulation, decision-making and management' proposed in the Bill which would 'disable the universities in discharging their fundamental role in society'.[71] According to some sources, UCG did not play any meaningful part in the discussions but that did not deter it from issuing its very strong statement which went on:

---

[70] 'Statement of UCC Governing Body', in *Eolas*, the magazine for staff and students, UCC, No 218, Nov. 11-17 1996.
[71] *Statement of the UCG Governing Body*, October 1996.

There is no evidence that their stewardship of public moneys has given cause for concern or serious complaint. It is all the more disappointing, therefore, that the Bill seems pervasively suspicious of, and frequently hostile to, the universities and that its provisions reflect a lack of trust in the universities' objectives, effectiveness and sense of responsibility.

The college submitted its own amendments to and detailed comments on the Bill. Referring to the composition of the governing body it agreed that representation of the public interest was legitimate and must be accommodated. The configuration of that representation in the Bill was, however, 'grossly skewed against the uniquely collegiate nature of the institution'. It added that it was wholly unacceptable that only TCD should enjoy the provision for, in practice, an extra six academic staff. The college also made the interesting observation that 'the privileging of the business/industry interest over all other interests is socially divisive, anachronistic and unacceptable'. Referring to Section 16 (2) of the Bill, which dealt with the development of interview and other procedures to ensure high quality candidates for employment, the college said this 'insulting' sub-section illustrated once again the 'extent to which the Bill is grounded in an obsessive quest for regimentation'.

It was particularly scathing about Section 17 of the Bill, which dealt with Visitation, saying that the section purported to enable the Minister for Education to submit her/his grievance concerning the conduct of the university to the Visitor of the university for adjudication. In the long history of the concept and operation of the Visitorial jurisdiction there was no legal authority for that proposal. It also criticised the next section, which would have allowed the suspension of the governing authority if its functions were not duly and effectively performed. 'It is quite astonishing in any case, apart from the legal lack of standing of a government minister in relation to availing of the Visitorial jurisdiction, that a provision so flawed in basic natural justice could seriously be promulgated in a Bill whose proponents profess to take some regard of the concept of university autonomy'.

The biggest institution, UCD, was more restrained in its public comments. At a conferring ceremony the college president, Dr Art Cosgrove, welcomed earlier statements from the minister that neither she, nor the government, had any desire to run the universities and that the legislation would strengthen academic freedom.[72] He said that 'the key issue now is that the text of the Bill should accurately reflect the principles enunciated. For it is the actual wording of the Bill rather than expressed intentions which will affect the universities'.

The college obtained opinion from a senior counsel, Paul Gallagher, about aspects of the Bill. The opinion was that Sections 17 and 18 which dealt with Visitation and the power to suspend the governing authority gave extensive powers to the minister and ultimately to the government.[73]

> It would be very difficult as a matter of law to judicially review an opinion formed by the Minister pursuant to Section 17 (1), notwithstanding the requirement that the opinion be based on reasonable grounds. Similarly it would be very difficult to judicially review an opinion formed by the Minister in exercise of his powers under Section 18 of the Act or any subsequent order made by the Government.

There was no official public response from TCD but the Fellows, all senior academics, issued a statement that the Bill was unacceptable in its present form and that it was an unnecessary intrusion which undermined academic freedom and the autonomy of all Irish universities.[74] The statement went on: 'the Fellows support the Provost in his opposition to aspects of the Bill and in his determination to secure changes to those provisions which are repugnant to the good and efficient conduct of university affairs'.

The Higher Education Authority

At the end of October the HEA placed a totally unexpected advertisement in the newspapers. It is known that the HEA was disturbed by some of the comments made about its role, and in particular by a highly critical newspaper article by Ronan Fanning, Professor of Modern History at UCD, who suggested that the

---

[72] Dr Art Cosgrove, speech to conferring ceremony, 1 November 1996.
[73] Paul Gallagher SC, *Legal Opinion for UCD*, 21 October 1996, unpublished.
[74] *Statement from the TCD Fellows*, 30 October 1996.

Authority's 'appetite for power over the universities is insatiable'.[75] The advertisement, in the form of a statement, began:

> The public debate on the proposed legislation has been marked by a series of fundamentally erroneous conceptions, even bordering on the bizarre, about the role of the HEA and the nature of its interaction with the universities. These distortions, at times couched in deeply offensive language, do a great disservice to the debate, in that they deflect attention from the important and weighty issues which lie behind the legislation and which deserve thoughtful and considered analysis.[76]

The lengthy advertisement then went on to review the role that the Authority had pursued over a period of twenty-eight years 'in a spirit of collaboration and dialogue with colleges'. It pointed out that the HEA was an important element in maintaining that 'critical distance' between universities and the state that was a vital component of Irish democratic life. Its statutory role was to allocate funds made available by the government to the universities and to ensure that deficits were not incurred. This process had worked well according to the advertisement which added, significantly, that the HEA had not sought and would not wish that any change in this process would be reflected in the legislation.

The latter was a key sentence because the widespread assumption in the universities was that the HEA was the driving force behind many of the detailed provisions in the Bill. Further confirmation of the HEA's unease came with a newspaper disclosure of the fifty-six amendments submitted by the Authority to the minister.[77] Many of these were textual and relatively minor but some were very significant because they proposed the deletion of the very sections that Dr FitzGerald and others had identified as 'unacceptable', including those sections that would have given the HEA powers to draw up budgetary and staffing guidelines. The HEA also wanted the deletion of parts of Section 22 which would have given it powers to appoint an inspector to investigate cases where it was not satisfied with the information furnished by a university about its staffing

[75] Ronan Fanning, *Sunday Independent,* 29 September 1996.
[76] *The Irish Times,* 29 October 1996.
[77] *Irish Independent,* 11 November 1996.

structure. Sub-sections dealing with the publication of disputes in *Iris Oifigiúil* should also be deleted, it suggested. It described as 'unwarranted and too restrictive' subsections 34 (1) and (2) of the Bill which stated that the universities would need prior approval of the Ministers for Education and Finance before borrowing on terms determined by the HEA. At a minimum, the references to the ministers should be omitted, it argued.

The newspaper disclosure was a source of great embarrassment to the minister. It transpired that almost to the day that she was informing the Dáil that the guidelines would not be mandatory[78] the HEA was advising her to drop the guidelines altogether. The newspaper reports were published on the front page and an inside page in the *Irish Independent*. Unfortunately, a sub-editor mis-interpreted the substance of the accounts and wrote one heading which suggested that this was a Bill that nobody wanted. The heading was inaccurate and prompted statements of support from the Presidents of Dublin City University and the University of Limerick for the Bill.[79] Both of these institutions would benefit most because until then all of their governors were appointed by the minister. Maynooth, which would also benefit by becoming an independent university, came out in general support of the Bill[80], although like DCU it sought managerial freedom in relation to budgetary and staffing matters. The three statements of support, however, could be viewed as a damage limitation exercise in view of the very serious reservations expressed by the HEA. The suspicion that the statements were at least encouraged by the department was substantiated by the fact that the President of UL, Dr Edward Walsh, was in the US at the time and considerable efforts were made to contact him for his approval of the statement of support.[81]

The following month the minister published over one hundred amendments to the Universities' Bill.[82] It is not unusual to have quite a number of technical amendments to government Bills and

[78] Minister for Education, *Second Stage of Universities' Bill*, 30 October 1996.
[79] *Irish Independent*, 12 November 1996.
[80] Ibid, 15 November 1996.
[81] Off-the-record information from University of Limerick sources.
[82] *Amendments to Universities' Bill*, 18 December 1996.

the number in this instance was not exceptional. However, the fact that they took up sixteen pages certainly was unusual considering that this was more than half the length of the original Bill. Some amendments were indeed technical but the most significant fact was that they either removed or amended many of the controversial clauses identified by the critics of the original Bill. The Conference of Heads of Irish Universities issued a statement that afternoon stating that the amendments resulted in a greatly improved Bill. It commented that the Conference was prepared to advocate support in general terms for the Bill as amended but would, of course, continue to monitor its progress through the Oireachtas and would seek to have further improvements made to it.[83]

Prior to the publication of the amendments, there had been protracted negotiations between the CHIU and the department, particularly with Secretary Dr Don Thornhill and Assistant Secretary Oliver Cussen. The CHIU, then under the chairmanship of Dr Mortell from UCC, presented a united front during these discussions. This was not easy, given that there were tensions between some of the main players involved. For instance, there was a feeling among some that TCD was, as one source put it, 'getting away with it' by being so accommodated by the department in the discussions. There was also a feeling that DCU and UL were willing to accept less than the older universities wanted by way of amendment.[84]

The Universities' Bill went through the initial stages in the Dáil with relative ease and went to the Seanad in March 1997. During the debate Senator Shane Ross, who was elected in the University of Dublin (TCD) constituency, made it clear that he was still unhappy over aspects of the Bill and indicated that he might vote against it the following week.[85] He was contacted the next day by the leader of the House, Fine Gael Senator Maurice Manning, who asked what his concerns were.[86] Given the imminence of the general election the government could ill afford a defeat in the Seanad and any

[83] *Statement from the Conference of Heads of Irish Universities,* 18 December 1996.
[84] Off-the-record sources.
[85] *The Irish Times* and *Irish Independent,* 21 March 1997.
[86] Senator Ross, interview with author, 21 March 1997.

delay in approving the Bill would mean that the minister would be out of office before it could be enacted. Ross indicated that his main concern was to ensure that any ministerial appointee to the board of Trinity College would not be a party political person and that political considerations would not dictate which sections of society were seriously underrepresented in university. In the event Ross voted against the government on the second stage and resigned from the Fine Gael parliamentary party. The government won the initial vote but was helped by the fact that a number of Fianna Fáil members of the Seanad were absent that evening.[87]

The Bill went through the final stages in the Seanad the following month but only after what one newspaper called a 'dramatic intervention' by the Provost of TCD led to an eleventh hour amendment.[88] The House was adjourned briefly while the minister and her officials reworded a section of the Bill dealing with the composition of the academic councils of the universities – the Provost had objected that as worded it could have meant councils with up to eighty members. The amendment was carried and the Bill went back to the Dáil. The order initiating the Act was signed by the minister on Friday 13 June 1997 at Maynooth College which was renamed the National University of Ireland, Maynooth. UCG, UCC and UCD also became constituent universities of the National University of Ireland when the order was signed, and were renamed.[89]

Part of the arrangement was that there would be a separate Private Members' Bill for the University of Dublin to define a new board structure for the board of TCD. This was important to the university which had been founded by a Royal Charter in 1592. In November 1998 the Private Members' Bill passed the second stage during a debate which was much more low key than those heard on the main Universities' Bill. Shane Ross said that while the Bill's provisions were generous in many respects, the measures still provided for the nomination of a government appointee in consultation with the Provost of Trinity. This was a fig leaf, because

[87] *Irish Independent*, 28 March 1997.
[88] *The Irish Times*, 25 April 1997.
[89] *Irish Independent*, 14 June 1997.

at the end of the day the minister would decide who the nominee should be, he claimed. Senator David Norris said, however, that it was an important and historic day and that the Bill was 'generally welcomed by academics'.[90] This was certainly true as far as the university's leadership was concerned, because the Bill was a far cry from what was originally proposed.

Commentary on the Universities' Bill

The then Fianna Fáil education spokesperson, Micheál Martin, described the Universities' Bill as a textbook case of how not to deal with legislation.[91] Was he being fair? There are three fundamental questions about the whole process surrounding the preparation of the Bill. First, did something go badly wrong during the minister's consultation period? Second, why did she propose to give powers to the HEA which that institution said subsequently it did not seek. Third, why did the government allow the publication of a Bill which, without substantial amendments, faced probable defeat in the Seanad?

The minister wanted an Act that balanced autonomy with accountability. One Machiavellian theory is that what was offered initially was deliberately weighted in favour of strong controls and that this was done on the assumption that the subsequent consultations/discussions would restore the balance.

There is no doubt that the minister was committed to an extensive consultation process, but unless one accepts the Machiavellian theory then it is arguable that politically the process was not handled very well. Almost from the first newspaper disclosure of her confidential position paper to the university heads in September 1995 the minister seemed to be reacting to public comment rather than leading the debate. The process was not helped by the fact that the university heads felt constrained for a long time from commenting publicly on the grounds that the discussions with the department were confidential. Once her initial position paper was disclosed the public debate was taken over by people in Trinity who had very strong

---

[90] *The Irish Times*, 7 November 1998.
[91] Fianna Fáil, *Press Release*, 18 December 1996.

views and who narrowed the focus to issues of state interference and perceived threats to university autonomy. It was difficult for other and perhaps more moderate voices to join in publicly at that stage, because the paper was not officially published. The unbalanced nature of the debate made it easier for the Progressive Democrats' motion in the Seanad to be taken so seriously that it threatened a government defeat. By the time the minister did get around to publishing a modified position paper at the end of November 1995, she had lost a lot of ground to critics of her proposals.

The consultation process with the university heads did, however, allow for a large measure of agreement to be reached on the issue of the governing structures. According to one source the university presidents were given access to the Heads of the Bill and were able to negotiate changes in those heads – this was a unique form of consultation. The presidents were thus reasonably confident that their representations on the issues of accountability and transparency would also be taken into account in the Bill itself. There is no doubt that at least some of the university heads felt let down by the Bill published in July 1996. They had hoped that the points they had made earlier about the dangers of too much interference in the day-to-day running of their institutions had been taken on board and they were surprised by the prescriptive nature of the controls proposed for the HEA in the July Bill. As one commented, 'we felt betrayed after a year of negotiations'.[92] The published Bill probably undermined the position of the heads of TCD and the NUI constituent colleges and, even if they wanted to, made it more difficult for them to convince their colleges to accept the Bill without substantial amendments. It should be pointed out, however, that cabinet confidentiality would have prevented the Department of Education officials from showing the presidents the draft legislation.

It could be argued also that there was incomplete consultation with the HEA, because otherwise the Authority would not have felt it necessary to publish its advertisement and to submit as many amendments as it did at the end of October. However, as against that, the department was said to have been receiving what might

---

[92] Off-the-record discussions with university heads.

charitably be called 'mixed signals' from the HEA over what should and should not be in the Bill. Personality factors also came into play – it is known that there were tensions between senior officials in the department and some people in the HEA.

The case could be made also that the HEA in putting forward the amendments was simply minding its own 'patch' and that it was acting in a realistic fashion, because it did not have the staff to undertake the various extra duties proposed for it. Sources close to the minister have argued that what she was doing was, in effect, making a statement about the role of the HEA in terms of legislation and policy-making in much the same way as she had done in the context of the National Council for Curriculum and Assessment (NCCA). 'The HEA advises, the Minister decides', was how one source put it, pointing out that the minister had previously felt it necessary to remind the NCCA similarly that its function was to advise on curriculum and exam matters but that it was her's to take the decisions. Be that as it may, the end result was a Bill which sought to confer powers on the HEA that it clearly did not want.

Critics of the Bill argued that far too much power was proposed for the HEA, but sources close to the minister contended that what she was seeking to do was actually to limit, by definition, the powers of the Authority. The latter argued that the Authority had, under the 1971 HEA Act, almost unlimited powers of interference that would be limited by the new Bill. But this is to overlook the fact that the HEA has rarely used its sweeping powers to force decisions on the universities. Granted the HEA did introduce a unit-cost approach to funding some years earlier which upset some of the colleges but there had not been the interference in the day-to-day management of the institutions that they feared would result from the July Bill. The ministerial sources also argued that the initial provisions spelt out clear procedures for staffing, budgetary, quality control and reporting arrangements and that these introduced long overdue transparency and accountability. However, the procedures laid down were, perhaps, far too detailed and the idea that notices of disagreement with the universities would be published in *Iris Oigifiúil* was somewhat heavy-handed if not downright farcical.

There was in some official quarters a view that educational institutions in receipt of substantial public funds should be subjected to greater controls following various financial problems in a number of Vocational Education Committees and in the Letterkenny Regional Technical College, all of which problems had been the subject of official enquiries. These inquiries prompted pressures from the Department of Finance to seek detailed provisions in the Universities' Bill; indeed all the indications are that the Department of Finance pushed very hard for stringent controls over funding decisions.[93] Some improvements were certainly necessary, but perhaps they could have been worked out in discussions with the HEA and the universities rather than be set down in such detail in legislation.

This brings us to the third question – the reasons for publication of the Bill as drafted. As we have seen there were three objectives underlying the Bill – the restructuring of the NUI, revising governing structures and providing for greater accountability by universities to society generally. We have also seen that the minister ran into difficulties under all three headings. Her original discussion document recommended the abolition of the NUI, which was unacceptable; she had to modify her proposals to have ten of the thirty governors in Trinity coming from outside, and she had to introduce a raft of amendments under the heading of accountability. When she announced the details of her amendments the minister acknowledged that 'university legislation is complex. This means that a lot of detailed and painstaking work is necessary to achieve the best balance among often competing concerns and considerations'.[94]

Could it be that the minister and the government had not anticipated the reaction to what they regarded as a fairly non-contentious piece of legislation which was necessary to update the legislative base of the university system? Had they forgotten, perhaps, that academic politics can be much rougher than national politics, especially when that prized treasure – autonomy– is threatened?

University legislation everywhere is fraught with controversies, not least because it usually involves the most articulate and organised people in the community. While her consultation process might be faulted, the minister did achieve a balanced Bill in the end. This was acknowledged by Professor Joe Lee who said that her handling

---

[93] Off-the-record political sources.
[94] Minister for Education, *Press Release re. Universities' Bill,* 18 December 1996.

of the Bill in the Seanad had enhanced her reputation.[95] The Universities' Act brings about badly needed changes, particularly in the area of quality controls and assurance, the benefits of which will become clearer over the coming years. It balances accountability with autonomy in a manner that prevents too much state interference but at the same time ensures that public monies are expended in an accountable manner.

The Dublin Institute of Technology

The Dublin Institute of Technology waged a lengthy campaign for inclusion in the Universities' Bill. The demand came as a surprise initially because the idea had not featured in the earlier debate on university legislation; indeed it was seen as opportunism by some government sources. The Institute was in the throes of reorganising its academic structure on the basis of faculties and this was known to be causing some dissent among academic staff. The campaign for upgrading initially took the form of letter writing to the newspapers and to public representatives. It was tightly co-ordinated, as an internal memorandum sent to all staff in November 1996 confirmed.[96] This urged staff to lobby their TDs and it listed some of the arguments that could be used. The most salient was that an international review team, appointed by the Higher Education Authority at the request of the Minister for Education in 1995 to review quality assurance procedures in the DIT, had recommended that 'the relevant authorities should consider whether key features of the proposed universities legislation be extended to the DIT and its legislation amended in the light of such analysis'.[97] This particular sentence was inserted towards the end of the group's deliberations; it was unexpected because there had been little or no discussions of the matter until then within the group.[98]

[95] Joe Lee, *Sunday Tribune*, 27 April 1997.
[96] DIT, *Memorandum to all Staff,* issued by Declan Glynn, Director of External Affairs, 21 November 1996.
[97] Report of the International Review Team, *Review of Quality Assurance Procedures in the Dublin Institute of Technology,* June 1996, unpublished.
[98] Off-the-record sources.

The review team was headed by Dr Harry McGuigan, former Provost and Pro-Vice-Chancellor of the University of Ulster. Its main recommendation was that DIT be granted authority to award its own degrees, as provided for in the DIT Act of 1992. The report was to have been officially released but for some reason this never occured. Nevertheless, the DIT authorities made much play of the fact that it had recommended that consideration be given to extending key features of the university legislation to the Institute.[99] Far less attention, understandably, was drawn to some of the other findings such as the conclusion that corporate identity and co-operation were not yet fully established at all levels and that interaction between staff and students and feedback did not appear to be at an equal level across the Institute. The review team also felt that insufficient emphasis was given to the deployment and development of staff. It commented that the qualifications and profile of staff, particularly in some of the faculties, militated against the development of research and post-graduate work. It recommended that links at post-graduate research level with other third-level institutions should be retained and developed until such time as the DIT had developed sufficient expertise in each discipline area.

The campaign for upgrading the DIT to university status was unsuccessful at the initial stages when the Universities' Bill went before the Dáil. The 'Rainbow' coalition government's first response to the campaign was to agree to DIT being granted the power to award its own degrees and the announcement to that effect was made in December 1996.[100]

The DIT, or at least its leadership, was still not satisfied and continued its campaign for university status. It had hired a public relations firm run by Bill O'Herlihy to assist. O'Herlihy was well known as a television sports commentator and had been involved in handling various high profile client accounts, including those of government ministers from time to time. One of the lobbying techniques employed was a mass postcard campaign by the students. Ironically O'Herlihy's firm had earlier been hired by the Minister

---

[99] See, for instance, Dublin Institute of Technology, *The Case for University Status*, 1997.
[100] Dublin Institute of Technology, *News Update*, February 1997.

for Education, Niamh Bhreathnach, to advise on 'selling' the changes that would follow from the White Paper.[101] It is known that the minister was surprised when she was told that O'Herlihy's company was working for DIT. The campaign was to prove successful in securing promises from the opposition parties of Fianna Fáil and the Progresssive Democrats. Fianna Fáil sources have indicated that the party agreed to back the campaign on the recommendation of some Dublin-based TDs who argued that it was a good 'political' issue to champion. Eventually, and under pressure, the minister promised that when the Universities' Act came into law she would immediately request the government to appoint a review group to advise on whether, having regard to the objects and functions of a university, the DIT should be established as a university.[102] The review group, chaired by Dermot Nally, a former Secretary to the Government, comprised academics from Ireland and overseas as well as representatives of the business community. It reported towards the end of 1998, recommending significant further academic development before the Institute could become a university. It suggested that it could take three to five years before these developments were in place.[103] The DIT leadership interpreted the report positively and suggested it could meet the requirements in three years. The report suggested also that money be earmarked for the continuation of apprenticeship courses, diplomas and certificates as well as degrees – this would help ensure that DIT's unique place as a multi-level institution would be preserved.[104]

The Regional Technical Colleges

Quite separate from the demand by DIT for upgrading was a long-standing campaign for a university in the south-east of the country. As is increasingly happening in Irish education, political con-

---

[101] Off-the-record discussions with public relations consultants.

[102] Minister for Education, *Press Release re. Dublin Institute of Technology,* 10 April 1997.

[103] Report of the International Review Group to the HEA, *Review of the Application by the Dublin Institute of Technology for establishment as a university under Section 9 of the Universities' Act 1997,* Dublin, Stationery Office, November 1998.

[104] Ibid.

siderations came into play and in January 1997 the minister, Niamh Bhreathnach, announced that the Waterford RTC was to be upgraded to Institute status with the authority to issue its own awards within a national awards structure.[105] It was reported that the Taoiseach, John Bruton, who was due to visit Waterford had put pressure on the minister to take a decision.[106] It was widely assumed that the timing of the announcement was designed to take the heat out of the campaign in the region for a university and was not unrelated to the pending general election. As one political source put it, 'we didn't want another DIT campaign in Waterford'.

While nobody begrudged Waterford its success, the decision sparked off strong reaction elsewhere. A week of protests in Cork culminated in a demonstration in Dublin by over 2,500 Cork RTC students and staff on 27 January 1997[107] and there were fears that a Labour seat in Cork would be in jeopardy in the general election (Toddy O'Sullivan subsequently lost his Labour seat in the constituency).[108] More than 1,000 students and staff from the Athlone RTC[109] took part in a demonstration in the midlands town, also demanding an upgrading of their college. Other colleges were keeping an eye on events and certainly Galway RTC would have had a very good case if Cork were raised to Institute status with the power to issue its own awards. The Director of the Dundalk RTC, Dr Sean McDonagh, was quoted as calling for an upgrading of the status of his college.[110] Tralee RTC sought a similar upgrading but within a national framework to be known as the Irish Technological University.[111] The Council of Directors of RTCs issued a statement confirming its confidence in the quality, status and standing of national awards from all colleges. Rather pointedly, the statement did not refer to the role of the NCEA, which had awarded degrees, diplomas and certificates to the sector for more than two decades.[112]

---

[105] Department of Education, *Press Release*, 19 January 1997.
[106] Political sources.
[107] *Irish Independent* and *The Irish Times*, 29 January 1997.
[108] *Irish Independent*, 27 January 1997.
[109] *The Irish Times* and *Irish Independent*, 29 January 1997.
[110] *The Argus*, 24 January 1997.
[111] Tralee RTC, *Press Release*, 30 January 1997.
[112] Council of Directors of RTCs, *Press Release*, 30 January 1997.

The leader and the education spokesperson of the Progressive Democrats, Mary Harney and Helen Keogh, met the chairpersons of six of the RTCs and issued a statement commending for consideration a proposal that a National Institute of Technology be established embracing the country's eleven RTCs as constituent colleges.[113] Around the same time two Dublin national newspapers warned of the dangers of following down the UK route and ending up with too many degree awarding bodies in a relatively small country.[114] To ease the confusion and the growing political uncertainty the minister brought a proposal to government for the appointment of a high-level group that would draw up criteria for the redesignation of an RTC as an Institute of Technology and the most appropriate means whereby institutions would be independently evaluated in relation to such criteria.[115]

There was no official press release immediately after the government meeting and the stories that appeared the following day in the national newspapers came from what are commonly referred to as 'spin-doctors' who seek to present information in the best possible political light. It was no coincidence that the Cork-based *Examiner* newspaper went so far as to suggest that the Cork RTC would be the first to be upgraded once the group got down to business.[116] The official announcement of the terms of reference of the group and details of its membership were not announced for another few days when the minister said that she was inviting Professor Dervilla Donnelly, who had chaired the National Education Convention, to chair the new group.[117]

The setting up of the group and the manner in which details were leaked out was, once again, a belated effort to control events that should have been anticipated. Certainly the reaction of Cork RTC to the Waterford decision should have been foreseen because each institution had previously argued its case for upgrading. It could also be said that the timing of the Waterford announcement

---

[113] Progressive Democrats, *Press Release,* 30 January 1997.

[114] *Irish Independent,* 27 January 1997 and *The Irish Times,* 28 January 1997.

[115] *Irish Independent, The Examiner* and *The Irish Times,* 29 January 1997.

[116] *The Examiner,* 29 January 1997.

[117] Minister for Education, *Press Release re. High-level Group to advise on the Technological Sector,* 4 February 1997.

was misjudged not only because of the political impact elsewhere but because the minister was aware that yet another report was imminent that would seek to bring some coherence to the non-university awards systems.

TEASTAS

TEASTAS was established as an interim national certification authority by the minister on 18 September 1995. According to the cabinet memorandum that she had brought to government six months earlier the authority would 'weld the many existing certification systems into a coherent network: and by evaluation and validation of programmes, and assessment and certification of students, create routes by which students can gain access to and progress to further education'.[118]

Welding together very disparate systems was never going to be easy and whatever TEASTAS recommended was certain to lead to 'turf-wars' between the various organisations. Its first report suggested that a single awards body act on behalf of a consortium of RTCs which until then had received their awards from the National Council for Educational Awards (NCEA).[119] Predictably the NCEA reacted strongly and issued a statement in the name of its acting director, Séamus Puirséil, stating that the model proposed ignored the authority and value of the Council's validating role accumulated over twenty-five years.[120]

Puirséil had a valid point but the NCEA's own position had been weakened some months earlier by the disclosure in a newspaper report of a damning study prepared by a team of consultants appointed by the Higher Education Authority. The study, prepared by KPMG, claimed that the Council had 'lost its sense of purpose and sense of direction' and that it did not provide value for money.[121] The study covered the period immediately prior to Puirséil's appointment.

[118]Minister for Education, *Memorandum to Government*, 31 March 1995, unpublished.
[119]TEASTAS – The Irish National Certification Authority, *First Report*, January 1997.
[120]National Council for Educational Awards, *Press Release*, January 1997.
[121] *Irish Independent*, 29 August 1996.

The TEASTAS report recommended also that TEASTAS itself would
have powers to approve, review and audit the awards process not
only of a consortium of RTCs but also of the Dublin Institute of
Technology. Again, the reaction was predictable. The DIT President,
Dr Brendan Goldsmith, described the report as 'unacceptable'.[122]
Having recently secured the power to award its own degrees, the
DIT was understandably not enamoured of the idea that it would
have to submit these for approval to TEASTAS.

There was no official response from the other organisations
mentioned in the report, which had also recommended that the
National Council for Vocational Awards be incorporated into the
TEASTAS structure. The NCVA had been established to develop a
national certification system for vocational training programmes at
second level. The report suggested that steps be taken towards the
inclusion of the certification process and expert staffing of FÁS (the
National Training and Employment Authority), Teagasc (the Agriculture and Food Development Authority), and CERT/NTCB (bodies
providing and certifying courses for the hotel and tourism industry)
into the TEASTAS organisation.

It could be argued that the TEASTAS report was undermined by
the announcements and subsequent confusion arising from the
promises to upgrade both the DIT and the Waterford RTC. Instead
of bringing finality to the debate, the fact is that yet another report
had to be prepared to extricate the minister and the government
from the political difficulties that had been created in the RTC
sector. The high-level group reported very quickly. It recommended
the upgrading of all RTCs to Institute status and the creation of an
Irish National Institute of Technology (INIT) which would take
over the role of the NCEA in relation to the RTCs and which could
delegate awarding powers to individual colleges or consortia of
colleges. This was to be done within a national framework.[123]

The proposals made sense in so far as the RTC sector was concerned but what was not clear was what would happen to the non-
RTC colleges that received their awards from the NCEA. One group
was the private commercial colleges, whose presence in the NCEA

[122] *The Irish Times,* Education and Living Supplement, 28 January 1997.
[123] *Report of the High-level Group to advise on the Technological Sector,* presented
    to Minister for Education, 2 May 1997.

system was known to be a source of annoyance to the RTCs. Leaving aside this issue, it was not immediately clear who was, for example, to award degrees in religion to colleges such as St Patrick's College, Carlow – was it to be a rump of the NCEA, TEASTAS itself, or the proposed Irish National Institute of Technology?

Conclusion

Niamh Bhreatnach's successor, Micheál Martin, was left with the still difficult task of bringing coherence to the non-university sector. All of the RTCs were upgraded to Institute of Technology status – a politically popular decision but which still left a number of issues unresolved. There was considerable movement towards the end of 1998 with three separate reports and a draft Bill which pointed the way towards some resolution The draft legislation proposed a national qualifications framework for awards outside the university sector, with the emphasis on quality and progression.[124] A council for higher education was to oversee awards in the non-university sector of higher education while a council for vocational awards would look after all other vocational sectors outside higher education.

The universities were expected to come into the framework on a voluntary basis while the DIT was also to come in more formally. The fact that the DIT would not become a university for a few years at least helped take the heat out of a situation that a year and a half earlier looked like it was getting out of control. So too did two separate reports which looked at the applications by the Cork and Waterford Institutes of Technology to issue their own awards. The reports stated that awards should be made within a national qualifications framework in respect of all existing NCEA validated national certificate and diploma courses. After an appropriate period of time, following the delegation of qualification-awarding authority in respect of certificate and diploma courses, a review should take place which would have the potential to grant delegation in respect of degree courses.[125] The findings were strongly welcomed by the

---

[124] *Irish Independent*, 12 November 1998.
[125] Reports of Interim Review Group on Cork and Waterford Institutes of Technology, 1998.

Cork Institute which saw the recommendation as an endorsement of its programmes.[126] The minister spelt out his thinking on a number of occasions, such as in an address at UCD in December 1998 when he said that the importance of sub-degree qualifications had to be recognised just as much as that of degree-level qualifications. He said that he was absolutely determined that Ireland would not repeat the mistakes of other countries in bowing to the type of academic drift which could do so much damage. 'To borrow a phrase from another area of public debate: what we need in higher education is a partity of esteem not a uniformity of provision', he added.[127] The final pieces of a complicated jigsaw were starting to fall into place.

Much change has occured in the non-university sector of higher education and indeed in the further education sector where there has been extraordinary growth at the post-Leaving Certificate course level. These developments have opened up new opportunities for young people whose parents had a much more restricted number of educational outlets open to them. They have also acted as a spur to economic development in the regions, which have benefited from having a pool of highly skilled young people available locally. The 'binary' system of higher education, with its separate university and tecnological institute sectors, has served this country well.

---

[126] *Irish Independent*, 12 November 1998.
[127] Minister for Education and Science, Micheal Martin, UCD Charter Day Dinner, 4 December 1998.

CHAPTER 6

Draft Education Bill 1996

U ntil the enactment of the Education Bill in 1998, Ireland was unusual among developed countries in not having a comprehensive education Act or series of Acts that set out overall policy. Indeed, when she announced her plans for a discussion paper in 1990, Minister Mary O'Rourke said the whole intention was that the subsequent period of dialogue would lead to the introduction of such legislation.[1] She said that, while the legal basis for payments of grants by the state was not being challenged, concern had been expressed about

1   administrative procedures which permit a Minister for Education to issue important policy directives with a tenuous, if any, link to legislation

2   the multiplicity of rules and circulars which have their impact on and set various aspects of policy and

3   a variety of other sub-concerns including whether some of the current practices in relation to education conform with Article 42 of the constitution.[2]

Article 42 to which she referred reads as follows: 'The State acknowledges that the primary and natural educator of the child is the Family and guarantees to respect the inalienable right and duty of parents to provide, according to their means, for the religious and moral, intellectual, physical and social education of their children'.[3]

Much of the department's attention in the early 90s was devoted to the preparation of the Green and White Papers. However, once the consultative process was completed and the White Paper was

---

[1]   Mary O'Rourke, *Press Release on the Question of an Education Act*, 26 November 1990.

[2]   Ibid.

[3]   *Constitution of Ireland*, 1937, Article 42.1.

ready, department officials were able to spend more time on the draft legislation. This process was helped considerably by the appointment in 1993 of a legal expert to the department.[4] At least one version of a Bill was prepared in 1995[5] but it was not until March 1996 that the Draft Heads of The Education (Education Boards and Boards of Management) Bill 1996 were tabled at cabinet by the Tanaiste, Dick Spring, in the absence of the minister, Niamh Bhreathnach, who was ill at the time.[6] The document was approved by the cabinet and sent to the parliamentary drafting office for preparation, in the expectation that it would be published in the summer and introduced into the Oireachtas in the autumn of 1996.[7]

The draft Bill was not officially published but a copy was obtained by the author in April 1996. This chapter will examine the draft, it will also review what happened when the draft was leaked, and discuss some of the legal and denominational issues raised by the Bill.

The draft Bill

The lengthy draft Bill was divided into two sections: explanatory notes were provided after each head or sub-head.[8] The first section dealt with the establishment of the long-promised Education Boards (the word Regional had been dropped) and the other with school boards. There were more than fifty heads or divisions in the draft Bill, setting out the composition and functions of both the Education and school boards. The section on Education Boards dealt with issues such as the transfer of staff, co-operation between boards, programmes and budgets, inspection, committees, grants, reports, recognition of schools, annual school funding, the inspectorate and transfer of functions.

---

[4] Tom Boland, legal adviser appointed to Department of Education, November, 1993.

[5] Department of Education, *Draft Heads of The Education (Education Boards and Boards of Management) Bill 1995,* unpublished.

[6] *The Irish Times* and *Irish Independent,* 13 March 1996.

[7] Ibid.

[8] Department of Education, *Draft Heads of The Education (Education Boards and Boards of Management) Bill 1996,* unpublished.

The section on school boards covered areas such as school ethos, dissolution of a board by the Patron, provisions relating to staff, programmes and budgets, inspection, the school plan, the school year and the school day, parents' associations, appeals, curriculum, rules and regulations. The draft heads and explanatory notes were very detailed and precise in their language. This precision was later to prove to be of great assistance to the drafting office which sometimes has to frame Bills based on very general ministerial instructions.[9] Whatever about the precision of the wording of the sub-headings and the overall interpretation of the constitution and its impact on education the draft bill could be regarded as somewhat conservative in parts.

Details of the draft were reported in the *Irish Independent* in early April, just as the annual teachers' conferences were getting underway.[10] The newspaper account highlighted in particular the powers that it was proposed to give to Patrons to veto teacher appointments in certain circumstances. Sub-head 6 addressed what the document acknowledged was a particularly difficult and sensitive issue in the operation of schools, namely provisions relating to staff. The explanatory note to this particular sub-head repeated that the education system was largely a denominational one and as such had certain constitutional rights.

> A natural and reasonable corollary to the rights of parents to send their children to denominational schools and the rights of owners of schools to conduct them on denominational lines is the right of such owners to ensure that there is available to the school a cadre of staff who share the religious and moral beliefs of the owners and the parents who send their children to such schools because of those beliefs. The Attorney General's Office have (sic) advised that denominational schools have a right to hire persons of their own denomination only.[11]

---

[9] Off-the-record briefing with department officials, May 1996.
[10] *Irish Independent,* 9 April 1996.
[11] Draft Education Bill.

Advice from the Attorney General

The advice from the Attorney General's office was not entirely unexpected given that the Irish education system is basically a denominational one and has certain constitutional protections. What was somewhat unexpected was the proposal to give statutory powers to school Patrons to effectively block appointments of teachers where they believed such appointments could prejudice the ethos of their schools. Although the Church owners of schools had generally hired teachers of their particular religious beliefs it seems that they had not formally sought that this power be enshrined in law.[12] This particularly contentious part of the sub-head read as follows:

> The appointment or promotion of a member of the teaching or other staff of a school shall be carried out without reference to or consideration of the religion of the person to be so appointed or promoted, except where the Patron is satisfied, and so informs the board and the Education Board, that
> a) the religion of such person is an essential requirement for the post which is to be filled in view of the subject which such person will be required to teach, or
> b) that unless a person who professes the same religious values and beliefs as the religious values and beliefs which find expression in the ethos of the school is appointed or promoted the ethos of the school and the fundamental rights of students in the school to be educated in accordance with their religious and moral beliefs would be substantially prejudiced.[13]

The accompanying explanatory note claimed that the sub-head sought to find a balance between the rights of denominational schools and the rights of teachers and other staff to earn a livelihood and to be protected against invidious or other unreasonable discrimination. It suggested that the terms would apply overwhelmingly in the case of teachers of religion in second-level schools. However, it might equally be argued that sub-section a) was worded in such a way that it could, in theory, be used to block an appointment to

---

[12] *Irish Independent,* 8 May 1996.
[13] Draft Education Bill, p. 96.

a primary school on the basis that the integrated curriculum at primary level required teachers of a particular religion. Department of Education sources subsequently confirmed that this was indeed a possible interpretation but argued that the particular sub-head was necessary to protect small schools, particularly Protestant schools. They instanced the theoretical example of a three teacher primary school where two of the teachers might be Catholic and where the Protestant Church authorities could insist on the right to appoint a person of their own denomination in order to help maintain the ethos of their school. By the same token it could be argued that the appointment of a Catholic teacher might well be necessary to prepare pupils for religious services such as First Communion or Confirmation in schools where the other teachers might be non-practising Catholics. Similarly, it could be argued that the appointment of a Muslim was essential to ensure the ethos of the single Muslim school in Dublin or that committed Irish speakers were essential to ensure the ethos of the Gaelscoileanna, the all-Irish schools. The officials argued that the inclusion of this clause was a legal recognition of the constitutional situation and that if school Patrons blocked an appointment they would have to spell out their reasons for so doing. However, they also confirmed that they were aware of the possibility of a legal challenge to this particular section of the Bill if enacted and indicated that they had discussed the issue with their counterparts in the Department of Equality and Law Reform, which was in the process of preparing legislation to outlaw discrimination at work. They argued that the Education Bill and the Employment Equality Bill 1996 together would make it easier for teachers to take legal action if they were discriminated against in terms of appointments.

The explanatory note to the relevant Head in the Education Bill went into some detail on this issue. It pointed out that the Patron would be obliged to form a view that the denominational character of his school would be substantially prejudiced by the appointment of a person 'whose religion is other than that of the Patron'. The note added that

> The Patron will also be obliged to inform the board of management and the Education Board when he has reached the conclusion that religion should be a factor in filling a post. Consideration was given in drafting this provision to providing that the Education

Board should agree before religion could be a factor in these circumstances. This approach was not adopted, however, as it is likely
to amount to an excessive interference by a state body into an
essential aspect of denominational education and the constitutional
rights of children, parents and Patrons. Apart from providing
openness in respect of appointments on grounds of religion, the
obligation on a Patron to inform the boards will allow them to
exercise some, albeit informal, restraint on Patrons and to exert,
again informally, some influence and more formally to take action
where a Patron is considered to be overstepping the bounds of
reasonableness.[14]

Reaction to the draft Bill

The statement in the explanatory note that the particular sub-head
was an attempt to balance the rights of school Patrons and teachers
did nothing to prevent a very robust reaction from the teacher
unions to the newspaper's account. At the INTO congress in Belfast,
General Secretary Senator Joe O'Toole described the proposals as
'sectarian'. He said that the union would challenge, fight and resist
any attempts to restrict a teacher's right to apply for a job on the
basis of his or her religion. 'What is acceptable is that the ethos of
a school should be protected. Teachers can do that quite adequately
without being part of that ethos', he added.[15] The draft document
stated that the provisions of this particular section of the Bill would
not apply to vocational schools.[16] Nevertheless, the Teachers' Union
of Ireland, which represented teachers in the vocational sector,
passed an emergency motion on the final day of its congress in
Cork on 11 April noting with dismay a recent report that the minister
intended to give religious owners of schools 'the right to refuse to
employ a teacher of a different religion if they think it would
adversely affect the ethos of their school'.[17] The TUI motion remarked
that community schools had been defined as Catholic in a recent
High Court judgement. This was a reference to the ruling by

---

[14] Ibid, p. 97
[15] *The Irish Times,* 10 April 1996.
[16] Draft Education Bill, p. 96.
[17] *The Irish Times* and *Irish Independent,* 12 April 1996.

Mr Justice Declan Costello in the case taken by the Campaign to Separate Church and State over the appointment of teachers of religion to community schools in which he defined community schools as Catholic schools.[18]

There was also varied reaction on the political front. Michael McDowell from the minority Progressive Democrats party said that any legislation that did not offer denominational schools the right to hire teachers of a particular religion would be vulnerable to a constitutional challenge.[19] However, Micheál Martin, the education spokesperson for the main opposition party, Fianna Fáil, said that he was extremely concerned at the proposed provisions. He suggested that the proposed veto could lead to dishonesty and also to actions being taken against teachers on spurious grounds. It could be used as a pretext for settling old scores, he claimed.[20] The Minister for Social Welfare, Prionnsias De Rossa, put down an important marker about his party's attitude at a Democratic Left conference three days later.[21] He said that in the recent speculation about the proposed legislation there had been no recognition of the fact that Article 42 of the constitution accorded the right to Patrons to hire or not to hire a teacher on the basis of his or her religion:

> Until the people decide to amend Article 42 it is absolutely essential that the education legislation establishes clear limits on those powers. It might be appropriate, for example, to appoint a teacher of religion on the basis of their religion. I cannot think of other circumstances where religion would be a consideration.

Mr De Rossa elaborated on this when he responded to an article by Kate Cruise O'Brien in the *Irish Independent* which appeared on 16 April. He said that the point he had sought to make at the Limerick conference was that any government was constrained by the 1937 constitution as to what it might do with regard to the hiring of teachers on a denominational basis. He added that

[10] Mr Justice Declan Costello, *High Court Decision*, 17 January 1996, p.23.
[19] *The Irish Times*, 10 April 1996.
[20] Ibid.
[21] Minister for Social Welfare, Prionnsias De Rossa, address to Democratic Left Conference, Limerick, 13 April 1996.

The core of the matter is the balancing of individual and communal rights, and I hope that for the long term the Review Group on the Constitution can give the Oireachtas some guidance so that the Oireachtas parties can consider how best to address and reconcile those rights for the future. In any event, far from wishing to see untrammelled powers for Patrons enshrined in the proposed education legislation, my concern is that the legislation will effectively regulate those rights in accordance with other con-stitutional principles, e.g. freedom of conscience, freedom of expression and the right to privacy, so that any appointment would have to be justifiable to the relevant Education Board.[22]

Recognition and funding of schools

There were other parts of the draft Bill that were also potentially controversial. One section, in particular, dealt with the official recog-nition of schools. The structure of the education system in Ireland is unique among the countries of the European Union. At primary level nearly all schools are privately owned and publicly funded. At second level privately owned and managed secondary schools cater for 61 per cent of pupils, a further 26 per cent of pupils attend vocational schools which are administered by local Vocational Education Committees and which are legally non-denominational.[23] The remaining second-level students attend community schools that are legally regarded as Catholic, or comprehensive schools that are either Protestant or Catholic.[24] At that time there were no statutory provisions relating to official recognition of schools which received public funding. Draft head 26 of the Bill sought to make provision for such recognition by the relevant Education Board. The explanatory note stated that the purpose of recognition was to establish which schools should receive public funds. In addition, recognition was a means whereby the standards, educational, health and other operational requirements could be guaranteed.[25]

---

[22] *Irish Independent,* 22 April 1996.

[23] Department of Education, statistics provided at National Education Convention, October 1993.

[24] See, for example, ruling by Mr Justice Declan Costello, High Court, 17 January 1996.

[25] Draft Education Bill, p. 57.

The controversial issue of using state funds to compel schools to set up boards of management was also dealt with in the Bill. This issue has already been examined in chapter 1 but the references in the draft Bill and the explanatory notes are worth recording. Head 36 provided that schools in receipt of public funds would have a board of management as provided for in the Bill.[26] An explanatory note to Head 28, which also dealt with annual school funding, stated that the only effective mechanism which the state had for ensuring that this requirement for boards of management was complied with was through funding.

> In using funding to achieve the aim of having representative boards of management in each school the minister must act reasonably and in a way which is proportionate to the objective. Schools have a legitimate expectation that arrangements which they have made with the state as regards funding will by and large continue without such alterations as would seriously damage their interests. On the other hand the state, as the funding authority of schools, has certain rights and obligations with respect to accountability and the public interest. Any statutory provisions should seek a balance between these potentially conflicting rights. The course proposed in this Sub-Head (7) is intended to meet the requirements of reasonableness and legitimate expectation while at the same time providing an effective mechanism to encourage schools to apply the provisions relating to school governance. This enforcement provision is relevant only to schools which are already in receipt of public funds on the date of the passing of the Act. Schools recognised after that date will apply for and be granted recognition in full awareness of their obligations vis-à-vis boards of management so the issue of entitlement to funds on the grounds of legitimate expectation will not arise. The effect of the provisions would be that the public funding and staffing of a school would be frozen at the level obtaining at the time of the passing of the Act. Funding in this context does not mean the absolute amount of grants paid but an amount based upon the amount paid per pupil on that date.[27]

The intention clearly was that only schools that established boards in compliance with the legislation would receive incremental funding

---

[26] Ibid, pp. 83-84.
[27] Ibid, p. 82.

– those that refused to do so would have their annual state grants
'frozen' at the existing level. However, doubts about the legal right
of the state to legislate for such issues as the establishment and
composition of school boards of management were expressed by
a Trinity College Dublin law lecturer Gerry Whyte, who wrote that

> The current proposals require that schools who wish to receive
> public funding must establish a board of management in accordance
> with the proposed legislation. By implication while this model might
> pass constitutional muster in relation to second-level schools, the
> state has a prior constitutional obligation to provide for free primary
> education and, in the absence of an extensive network of state-
> owned primary schools, it may not be open to the state to impose
> such a condition on the funding of privately owned primary
> schools.[28]

School ethos

The importance to the Churches of maintaining a denominational
ethos should not be underestimated, because they have traditionally
seen the educational process as transcending beyond secular
instruction into the spiritual. For instance, Sr Eileen Randles, General
Secretary of the Catholic Primary School Managers' Association,
told a conference on Pluralism in Education that to 'seek to exclude
the religious formation of the pupil from his education would be to
truncate what the Church understands to be a true and full
education'. She went on to clarify that religion was not so much a
discipline as a vision.

> It cannot therefore be confined to a class period. One's faith should
> be the basis of one's outlook on all areas of life, areas which will
> be explored through the secular subjects. (The Catholic Church)
> seeks a synthesis of faith, life and culture, a synthesis which is
> facilitated through education in a Church-linked school.[29]

The assurances that the Churches wanted regarding school ethos
were contained in the draft legislation. Draft Head 35 stated that
'A Patron of a recognised school may require that a particular ethos,

---

[28] *Irish Independent,* 7 May 1996.
[29] Sr Eileen Randles, *Relationship of Church to Schools: its Nature and Value,*
Belfast, 23 February 1996.

as determined by that Patron, shall be promoted by that school; provided that such ethos does not conflict with the provisions of this Act or any law of the State'.[30] The explanatory note stated:

> It is accepted that preparing a statement of ethos can present difficulties for Patrons. There is first the difficulty in setting out in writing what is usually a fairly intangible concept. Secondly, ethos is not immutable – it inevitably changes with the change in mores and outlook in the community which subscribes to the particular set of beliefs and traditions from which it arises. In recognition of these difficulties it is proposed that Patrons should be allowed amend the statement of ethos as required. In granting this power it is again recognised that it could, at its worst, become a weapon of oppression on a board. Change in ethos statements might be made so as to achieve a particular result in the deliberations of a board. To safeguard against this it is proposed that during the term of office of a board instant changes cannot be made in the statement of ethos. If a board does not agree to a change, this can only become effective after the passage of six months. This is proposed as a balance between the right of the Patron to promote and protect the ethos of schools and the right of boards to manage without undue interference from the Patron.[31]

Deeds of Trust

Meanwhile discussions were taking place in another forum on the actual wording of the Deed of Trust (or Deed of Variation in the case of schools where an official lease already existed). This was the facilitation process referred to in chapter 4 whereby the educational partners could discuss and hopefully agree changes in the composition of boards of management. Until then the school owners or Patrons had nominated half of the membership of primary school boards, including the chairperson, who had a second or casting vote. The proposal under discussion was a 'core' board comprising two elected parents, two teachers and two nominees of the Patron. This core would then propose two extra members from the wider community, agreed unanimously among them, to

---

[30] Draft Education Bill, p. 79.
[31] Ibid, p. 82.

the Patron for appointment. The eight-member board would then be formally appointed as such by the Patron. In return for giving up majority control the Churches would be given legal guarantees for the continued ethos of their schools.

Towards the end of May *The Irish Times* disclosed the contents of a document which contained the wording of the draft deeds.[32] In the case of Roman Catholic schools the deed would include the following sentence: 'The school will be managed in accordance with the doctrine, practices and traditions of the Roman Catholic Church as stated by the Irish Episcopal Commission and interpreted by the Patron of the school'. In the case of Church of Ireland schools the deed would state that

> The school will be managed in accordance with the doctrine, moral teachings, traditions, practices and customs of the Church of Ireland, as defined by the General Synod from time to time, and in the event of any question or dispute arising as to the interpretation thereof, the same shall be determined by the Bishop of the Diocese in which the relevant school is situated on an interim basis but subject always to final determination by the General Synod.

In the case of Educate Together's multi-denominational schools the deed would read that 'the ethos reflects the ethos of the society in which many social, cultural and religious strands exist in harmony and mutual respect'.

The leaked document disclosed by *The Irish Times* contained a clause which stated that people nominated to the core board 'shall have a commitment to the ethos of the school and the community/ parish served by the school'. This was hardly surprising but what was somewhat unexpected was the statement that the two co-opted members of the board were also expected to have 'an understanding of, and commitment to, Catholic education', in the case of Catholic schools. In the case of Church of Ireland schools the two co-opted members would be vestrymen, elected members of the parish committee.[33]

The Irish Times carried an editorial on the day following its

[32] *The Irish Times*, 20 May 1996.
[33] Ibid.

disclosures stating that the effect of the proposed legislation was to 'copperfasten the denominational stranglehold on Irish education and fossilise church influence at its present level'.[34] However, the minister issued a statement saying that the document quoted was one of a number of drafts which the partners in education were considering under the facilitation process, which was independent of her department.[35] Significantly she added that 'if we are to see genuine sharing of power on the boards of management of primary schools, then the core boards, consisting of equal representation of owner nominees, parents, and teachers must be free to select the two additional members onto the board from the local community without any preconditions'.[36] It is known that the leak led to tensions among the education partners; by the end of the summer the talks were still not concluded. The document which eventually emerged from the talks, however, was broadly in line with what had been reported in the newspaper account.

Denominational and multi-denominational schools.

In her statement the minister had also denied that she was copper-fastening the denominational stranglehold on Irish education but, in effect, it appears that this would have been the outcome of the proposed legislation as originally drafted by her. Certainly this was not the intention of Mary O'Rourke who had initiated the whole process when she began preparing a Green Paper in 1990. O'Rourke has indicated that she wanted to provide for a situation in the future where religious numbers would dwindle and different social mores would require different types of schools. It is, of course, a matter of conjecture what O'Rourke would have done had she remained in office – would she have been able to convince the Churches to give up direct majority control of Church-linked school boards without at the same time giving them very strong legal guarantees for the future ethos and character of their schools?

---

[34] *The Irish Times,* 21 May 1996.
[35] Minister for Education, *Press Release,* 21 May 1996.
[36] Ibid.

Discussion and conclusions

The legal underpinning of the voluntary sector in the latter years of the twentieth century may have greater justification in a state where there is freedom of choice for parents and a system parallel to that of the predominantly Church-provided schools. However, there is relatively little choice for the majority of parents in Ireland. In 1999 there were only sixteen multi-denominational primary schools out of nearly 3,200, while at second level the non-denominational vocational schools have traditionally been accorded a lower social status than the majority, voluntary, denominational secondary schools. The lack of choice was adverted to in the report of the Constitution Review Group, which suggested that with an increasingly diverse and rights-conscious society, problems in relation to right of access to a suitable education would become more acute.[37]

It is not just those who wish a multi-denominational school for their children that face difficulties. The Review Group gave the theoretical example of members of the Islamic community moving into an area where the only school is Roman Catholic. The Islamic parents would be within their rights to withdraw their children from formal religious instruction but what would happen if they objected to the Roman Catholic ethos which permeated instruction in other subjects and which was also reflected in religious pictures and religious feast days. The Review Group asked: 'Must a school which is in receipt of public moneys accede to these objections, or may it give preference to the wishes of the majority of parents who wish the school to retain its Catholic ethos?'

The Review Group also noted that the constitutional guarantee that one could attend a school which is in receipt of public money without attending religious instruction at that school was undermined in 1971 by the introduction of an integrated curriculum, albeit unintentionally and for what were deemed to be excellent educational reasons. Curricular integration meant that the constitutional requirement of separate religious and secular instruction was no longer strictly observed. There has been talk for some years of a

---

[37] *Report of the Constitution Review Group,* Dublin, Stationery Office, June 1996, pp. 368-388.

legal challenge to the integrated curriculum by the Campaign to Separate Church and State. However, the group chose to concentrate its very limited financial resources instead on a High Court challenge to the payment of chaplains in community schools, which was unsuccessful. This has left the still very sensitive issue of the integrated curriculum on the 'back burner', so to speak. In her original draft Green Paper Mary O'Rourke agreed that the integrated curriculum would appear to be in conflict with Article 44.2.4 of the constitution, which safeguards the right of children not to attend religious instruction in schools in receipt of public money.[38] This was watered down slightly in the Green Paper published by Séamus Brennan in June 1992:

> Provision is made in the curriculum and the school timetable for religious instruction. Various changes made to the Rules for National Schools over time, and embodied in the Rules published in 1965, could be seen to have the effect of weakening the protections that existed for children of religious beliefs different to those of the majority in the schools. The general review of the Rules for National Schools, recommended by the Primary Education Review Body, will seek to ensure that all aspects of the Rules fully reflect the relevant articles of the Constitution. Furthermore, the 1971 Teachers' Handbook for the Primary School, as part of its promotion of an integrated curriculum, also sought to integrate religious and secular instruction. The Handbook will be reviewed to ensure that the constitutional rights of children are fully safeguarded.[39]

The issue was also dealt with at the National Education Convention in Dublin Castle in October 1993. A representative of the Campaign to Separate Church and State fully accepted the rights of the majority in denominational education but pointed out the conscientious dilemmas which existed for non-believing parents who had no choice but to attend religious-run schools.[40] The NEC report recommended the setting up of a working party to draw up 'good practice guidelines' and recommended that such a working party

---

[38] *The Irish Times,* 25 February 1992.
[39] Department of Education, *Education for a Changing World,* Green Paper, Dublin, Stationery Office, June 1992, p. 69.
[40] John Coolahan (Ed.), *Report on the National Education Convention,* Dublin, Stationery Office, 1994, p. 33.

might also explore legal and, perhaps, constitutional issues which may be involved.[41]

The White Paper published in mid-1995 promised that such a working party would be convened 'in the near future' and also agreed that the Rules for National Schools and the Teachers' Handbook would be reviewed to ensure that the constitutional rights of children were fully safeguarded.[42] It could be argued that these issues should have been dealt with before, if not in tandem with, the preparation of legislation which directly affected constitutional rights. However, a year after the White Paper was published there was still no sign of either the working party or the review promised. Instead, Niamh Bhreathnach, who went to great lengths to progress the White Paper and its implementation, concentrated on winning changes in the composition of school boards from the main Churches. But in so doing she was, initially at any rate, prepared to make concessions which amounted to a hefty price to pay for convincing the Churches to give up direct – but not indirect – majority control over primary school boards of management. As we will see in the next chapter the draft Education Bill underwent a certain metamorphosis before it got to the final stage of publication. Nevertheless, it is ironic that the first Labour Party Minister for Education in the state was, initially at any rate, prepared to concede so much to the Churches in return for a greater measure of democracy in Irish schools.

---

[41] Ibid.

[42] Department of Education, *Charting our Education Future*, White Paper on Educational Development, Dublin, Stationery Office, 1995, pp. 23-24.

CHAPTER 7

Legislation and Conclusions

The process of consultation and change that has taken place over the past few years has had a very significant impact on Irish education and will have for decades to come. Some of the results may have been disappointing in not realising earlier expectations but they set in train the beginnings of profound change in the administration of the education system, in the professional attitude of teachers, in the acceptance of the roles and responsibilities of parents and teachers, and, it is to be hoped, in the quality of the service provided to students.

We have seen how the Green Paper was followed by an intense period of consultations through the National Education Convention, position papers and round-table discussions in Dublin Castle, culminating in the White Paper in the summer of 1995. There was a confidence and an expectation that decisions would be taken on the basis of consensus among the education partners.

Managing the transition from discussions and consultation to implementing decisions was always going to be difficult and would take time. This final chapter will look at some of the main changes that flowed from the process of consultation, focusing in particular on legislation, but touching first on a number of other developments that help give a flavour of the background against which political and policy factors came into play.

Productivity talks under the Programme for Competitiveness and Work

The first attempt to implement a section of the White Paper proved unfortunate. It arose during the summer holidays in 1995 when a circular was issued dealing with the length of the school year.[1] This

---

[1] Department of Education, *Time in School*, Circular M 29/95, August 1995.

issue had been raised in the Green and White Papers, both of which had noted the erosion of the school year at primary and post-primary levels through factors such as early closures, special closures and days when only part of the student body was present in school.[2] The circular sought to address these issues and tighten up on early closures in particular but it soured relations between the department and teachers at a time when union support was necessary for the many changes that were proposed in the White Paper.

The circular also made it more difficult to secure agreement in discussions on a pay, pensions and productivity deal that was being negotiated under the Programme for Competitiveness and Work. The talks had concluded in February 1996 with a £66.7m offer and Minister Bhreathnach expressed the hope that all parties would find it acceptable.[3] It was a very complex package involving increased allowances, a shortening of the incremental pay scale, an early retirement scheme for 300 teachers, and an agreement that all teachers could retire at fifty-five with thirty-five years service. Additional promotional posts were offered with defined tasks; teachers were asked to accept non-teaching duties as part of their professional role; and fifteen hours were to be specified for such duties each year outside of teaching time.

The offer signalled the end of seniority as the main determining factor in deciding who obtained middle management posts in secondary schools. If this was accepted it could have had a major impact on middle management in a system that was rapidly moving from one dominated at the top by religious owners of schools to one where lay teachers were emerging in the majority of promotional posts. Appointing people on seniority had been written into an agreement made between the school owners and the ASTI in 1979. That 1979 agreement stated: 'In the case of lay teachers, there should be automatic promotion, on a seniority basis, from Grade B to Grade A posts, i.e. the senior Grade B post-holder having applied moves to a Grade A post when one becomes available for a lay teacher'.

---

[2] White Paper 1995, p. 61.
[3] Department of Education, *Press Release*, 27 February 1996.

The 1979 agreement may have avoided tensions over promotions but it resulted in a weak middle management in many secondary schools and therefore a relatively poor pool of applicants from which to draw when competition was held for open principalships. The weakness had long been recognised by the managers who complained to a government appointed Review Body on Teachers' Pay in 1980 that they were unable to select the candidates best suited to discharge the range of duties necessary to meet the needs of the schools.[4] Their submission stated that the level of restrictions imposed by the ASTI led to a position where many areas of responsibility were neither accepted nor discharged. It stated that the automatic promotion from a B post to an A post was unprecedented in any other employment and it criticised the fact that managers were precluded from specifying the duties attached to a post when advertising a vacancy. The submission went on to argue that the interpretation of capability and suitability by the Appeals Board set up as a result of the agreed memorandum

> made it extremely difficult for schools not to appoint the next (teacher) in order of seniority to the post of vice-principal when such a vacancy arises in a school. Managers who have departed from the order of seniority have almost invariably had to justify and defend their appointments to the Appeals Board. Such appeals, irrespective of their result, have caused great tension and division in staffs.[5]

Unfortunately from the managers and the government's point of view the £66.7m package negotiated under the Programme for Competitiveness and Work was rejected by the ASTI, partly because it signalled the end of seniority. It was also rejected by the TUI for a variety of reasons including the fact that the original expectation of a general scheme of early retirement was not realised.[6] But it was accepted by the INTO which stood to gain most through the creation of additional promotional posts, which would have meant that for the first time more than 50 per cent of primary teachers were in promoted posts.[7]

---

[4] Joint Managerial Body, *Final Submission to The Review Body on Teachers' Pay*, 30 July 1980.
[5] Ibid, Section 2.
[6] *Irish Independent*, 29 March 1996.
[7] INTO, *Tuarascail*, Issue No 2, March 1996.

Following the rejection by the two post-primary unions a facilitator – Sean Healy, Director of Advisory Services at the Labour Relations Commission – was appointed to try to break the deadlock in April 1996.[8] The language in the final PCW document, which was issued in December, was more conciliatory than in the first.[9] It acknowledged the extra-curricular work done on a voluntary basis by teachers and it reduced the demand for fifteen hours stipulated per year for non-teaching duties to an unspecified amount which the unions interpreted as a maximum of six. It also increased the number of places available for early retirement and the package was accepted by both the TUI and ASTI.

The revised package, however, retained seniority as the main factor for middle management posts in secondary schools. The TUI used the opportunity to demand an element of seniority for promotion in vocational schools. Mr Sean Healy was again appointed as facilitator, this time in discussions between the TUI and the Irish Vocational Education Association, and in a report to the minister he basically recommended concession of the teachers' demands.[10]

The organisations representing the management of both the vocational and secondary school sectors wrote a joint letter to the minister describing seniority as an outmoded and ineffective indication of suitability to undertake managerial tasks.

> Our members are committed, as we hope is the department, to establishing effective and efficient structures within each of our sectors, which can only be effected through an appropriate middle management system. The original PCW proposals offered the hope of that framework being put in place. We therefore reiterate that we cannot agree to the current PCW proposals.[11]

The minister conceded the TUI demands for a 30 per cent weighting for seniority in promotional posts and for a revised selection board and a new appeals system. The changes would reduce from four to two the number of VEC nominees on selection boards. The concessions were made, significantly, the day before a special TUI

---

[8] Department of Education, *Press Release*, 23 April 1996.
[9] *Revised Teachers' PCW Proposals,* December 1996.
[10] *TUI News*, Vol. 19, No 4, February 1997.
[11] Irish Vocational Education Association/Secretariat of Secondary Schools, *Letter to Minister for Education,* 4 February 1997, unpublished.

congress called to discuss the revised PCW package.[12] They helped sway the delegates who voted against an amendment urging rejection of the package.[13]

The managers were still smarting over the package and inserted advertisements in the newspapers during the annual teachers' conferences headed 'Better Schools, A Lost Opportunity' in which they reiterated their concerns.[14] This infuriated the ASTI leadership which promptly issued a threat of action, including strike action, if the managers did not implement the deal in full.[15] In the event the managers had little option but to accept the deal given the pressure from the unions and from the minister who did not want a row with the teachers in the run-up to the examinations or to the general election.

The package averted industrial unrest in schools. The teachers had secured a relatively good early retirement scheme (even if not many were to avail of it subsequently), a shortening of the incremental pay scale, additional promotional posts and increased allowances. The department argued that it had gained from the revised offer in that, for the first time, it stitched into teachers' contracts a stipulation that their duties extended beyond classroom teaching. As far as the managers were concerned this was relatively small comfort from a package which cost the taxpayer at least £70m. Nevertheless, it was a significant step towards building a more effective middle management system, especially in voluntary secondary schools.

The teaching of history in the Junior Certificate

An unexpected furore also developed over the place of the teaching of history in the Junior Certificate. The White Paper specified a core curriculum of Irish, English, Maths and a science or technological subject, together with at least three further subjects for certificate purposes. It stressed that a 'combination of full and short courses could meet the curricular principles of breath and balance'

---

[12] TUI sources, 16 February 1997.
[13] *Irish Independent,* 17 February 1997.
[14] *The Irish Times* and *Irish Independent,* 3 April 1997.
[15] *Irish Independent* and *The Irish Times,* 4 April 1997.

and added that modules and short courses on a variety of subjects would be developed.[16]

No reference was made directly to history and this led to charges from several sources that history was being 'written out' of the curriculum as a compulsory subject. The History Teachers' Association of Ireland wrote to various individuals and organisations seeking support for 'the reinstatement of history in the core curriculum, seeing it as intrinsic to the rounded development of the individual and a crucial part of the bedrock of preparation for citizenship in an Irish and European context'.[17]

Department sources acknowledged that the subject had been overlooked in the preparation of the White Paper but they also pointed out that making it compulsory for all could create difficulties. Traditionally it had been mandatory for students of the old Intermediate Certificate but not for students taking the Group Certificate. The Junior Certificate brought together the two separate programmes.

There was considerable pressure on the minister to include history as a mandatory subject and she responded by asking the National Council for Curriculum and Assessment to deal with the issue of core subjects at Junior Certificate level. She stated that the NCCA, which represented all the educational partners, could best advise on how a balanced and broad curriculum – including history and geography and other curricular activities – could be offered to all students at Junior Certificate level. She specifically denied that any decision had been taken in relation to the study of history or geography.[18] Her successor, Micheál Martin, a graduate in political history, supported the retention of both history and geography on a number of occasions. Towards the end of 1998, the NCCA Junior Cycle Review Committee compiled its *Progress Report: Issues and Options for Development* in which it put forward a compromise proposal on this matter. It suggested that history and geography or environmental and social studies (ESS) be part of a required course

---

[16] White Paper 1995, p. 49.

[17] History Teachers' Association of Ireland, *Statement re. History in the Junior Certificate*, November 1995.

[18] Minister for Education, *Press Release re. History and Geography*, 23 April 1996.

for the junior cycle, except in the schools that were not already offering these subjects.[19]

Whole School Inspection

Proposals for Whole School Inspection (WSI) were put forward by the Department of Education at a conference in Killiney, Co. Dublin, on 13 March 1996. The media were not invited. The conference was attended by the education partners and the papers were subsequently disseminated to schools. Details were subsequently reported in the media.[20]

The discussion document circulated to participants stated that the inspection process would evaluate and monitor the school plan and individual teacher planning. It would evaluate student achievement; pupil-teacher interaction; the deployment of staff; the quality of school buildings; the extent to which educational guidelines were being followed; the provision for meeting individual needs in students; and the manner in which all the resources of the school – human, physical and financial – were being used.[21] The conference was also told that a Whole School Inspection Committee within the department had looked at scales for measuring performance indicators in schools and had proposed the following.

Evaluation rating: very good Major strengths – a very good performance (this would be the optimum level of performance)
Evaluation rating: good Strengths outweigh any weaknesses – some improvement desirable
Evaluation rating: fair The minimum acceptable level of performance – significant improvement possible
Evaluation rating: weak Major weaknesses – an unsatisfactory performance

[19] *Irish Independent,* 5 January 1999.
[20] *Irish Independent,* 8 May 1996.
[21] Department of Education, *Whole School Inspection – Discussion Document,* 13 March 1996, unpublished.

The obvious question that arises is why there was no provision for an average rating. According to department sources the rationale was that the temptation would be to go for the average in many cases whereas ratings of good or fair would require a lot more thought. The Chief Inspector, Sean Mac Gleannain, told the conference that WSI would be piloted in a small number of schools as part of the development process, after which further consultation would take place.[22]

However, the proposals were not well received by the teachers' unions. The ASTI expressed great concern that the mechanisms for the assessment of school performance would be counterproductive.[23] It said that the assessment of the performance of schools should be conducted by professionals who were aware of all the difficulties with which a school had to contend, who would assess the facilities and resources available to a school and who would help to create a climate in which the onus would be on government to provide such facilities and resources. Tony Deffely, President of the Teachers' Union of Ireland, said his union rejected the concept of evaluation-rating scales for schools or for aspects of school performance.[24] Joe O'Toole of the INTO said that teachers regarded with amazement the simplicity of those 'bean counters' in the less enlightened sectors of the social partnership who believed that all education could be reduced to the accumulation of 'measurable things' which the pupil or student acquired during the learning process.[25] Little progress was made for a further two years when revised proposals for Whole School Evaluation were put forward which were more acceptable to the ASTI and INTO, both of which agreed to pilot projects in the area. The TUI, however, held out against the proposals.

---

[22] *Address by Chief Inspector at the Consultation Seminar,* 13 March 1996, unpublished.
[23] See *ASTIR,* the journal of the ASTI, Vol. xxv, No 7, March 1996.
[24] Teachers' Union of Ireland, *Press Release re. Whole School Inspection,* 8 May 1996.
[25] Joe O'Toole, 'More Weights than Measures', in *Education Today,* Summer 1996, published by the INTO.

Legislative changes

In her last year of office Niamh Bhreathnach was determined to press ahead with her legislative programme as was confirmed in a department publication, implementing the Agenda for Change, which was ready towards the end of 1996 but which was not published until January 1997.[26] In addition to the Education Bill and the Universities' Bill the publication mentioned five other pieces of pending legislation. It promised appropriate legislation for TEASTAS and for a Further Education Authority. It noted that two other pieces of legislation were in the course of preparation. One of these was a Youth Service Bill which would provide a statutory basis for the provision of youth work services in Ireland: the Heads of the Bill had been approved by the government in mid 1996.[27] The Bill was subsequently published in March 1997 and defined the responsibilities of the department and of the proposed Education Boards regarding youth work.[28] The fifth piece of legislation was a School Attendance Bill. In 1995, a task force was established in the department to make recommendations for tackling the problem of truancy at first- and second-level schools. 'The task force has now made recommendations for new legislative provisions to deal with school attendance', the document reported.[29]

The minister later indicated that preparations were underway for yet a further piece of legislation for the establishment of a Teachers' Council, an issue that had been on the agenda for several years.[30] She subsequently announced the appointment of a committee, headed by Dr Séamus McGuinness from TCD, which would examine the legal, constitutional and operational issues associated with the establishment of such a Council.[31] Following completion of the work of the committee she would publish a draft legislative framework for the establishment of the Council.

---

[26] Department of Education, *Implementing the Agenda for Change*, 1996.
[27] Minister of State Bernard Allen, *Letter to Co. Dublin Local Voluntary Youth Council*, c/o Co. Dublin VEC, 5 July 1996.
[28] *Youth Work Bill 1997*, 5 March 1997.
[29] *Implementing the Agenda for Change*, 1996.
[30] Minister for Education, press briefing for education journalists, 3 February 1997.
[31] Minister for Education, *Press Release re. Teaching Council*, 26 March 1997.

For a department with a relatively poor record of legislation this roll call of seven Bills was impressive. The number of Bills proposed is a testimony to the work of successive Ministers for Education and to a department determined to have an appropriate legal framework for educational development.

The Education Bill 1997

The publication of the Education Bill 1997 was handled in a somewhat different manner to that of the Universities' Bill. The minister obviously wanted to avoid a repetition of the embarrassment of having to amend a second Bill in such a way as to strip it of many of its original provisions, which she had to do with the draft legislation for the universities. For this reason at least three organisations were consulted on a confidential basis about the penultimate draft. These were the INTO, the National Parents' Council (Primary) and the Conference of Religious of Ireland. It is known that they were cautioned by the department against allowing the document to leak out.[32]

The Catholic bishops were not given the same opportunity as CORI, which is ironic because previous administrations would have been very willing to consult the bishops in advance of major decisions about education. The chairman of the Episcopal Commission on Education, Bishop Thomas Flynn, has confirmed that the bishops did not receive a copy of the penultimate draft from the department.[33] It was also ironic that it was the new 'parents' constituency' which was among those consulted prior to publication. The minister may have found it necessary to consult selected groups in this manner at the last minute but the fact that she did so undermined to some extent her claims of transparency and openness throughout the consultation process.

The main provisions of the Bill were as follows:

- the establishment, composition, operation and function of Ten Education Boards

---

[32] Off-the-record sources.

[33] Bishop Thomas Flynn, press conference to launch *Statement of Irish Bishops' Conference,* Maynooth, 12 March 1997.

- the recognition of schools for the purposes of funding by public funds
- the establishment of the Inspectorate on a statutory basis
- the establishment, composition and function of boards of management of schools
- the establishment and role of parents' associations
- appeals by students or their parents
- the making of regulations by the minister.[34]

However, if the minister was hoping for a relatively easier passage for the Education Bill than for the Universities' Bill she was greatly mistaken. Reaction to the Bill was relatively slow in coming and this was mainly because legal representatives for the various organisations needed time to look at its provisions in detail. The reactions from the Churches were not made available to the media initially but public representatives were furnished with copies in the hope that they would lobby for changes in the Bill.

The response of the Episcopal Commission of the Catholic bishops was presented to the Department of Education in mid-February. This claimed that the Bill did not appear to recognise the rights of Patrons as owners of Catholic secondary schools and that it had eroded the rights of Patrons as owners of primary schools. It alleged that the Bill made inroads into the internal management of schools which received state aid but were privately owned and privately managed.[35] The concerns of the Catholic Church were also conveyed to the then Taoiseach, John Bruton. This was confirmed by Bishop Flynn who told the author that the four archbishops had raised the issue with the Taoiseach at a meeting called mainly to discuss the North. He himself had raised it at a function during which he sat beside the Taoiseach.[36]

The minister responded to the bishops' concerns by welcoming their commitment to continued dialogue – a commitment which she shared. She said the intention behind the Bill was not in any

---

[34] Department of Education, *Education Bill 1997, Explanatory and Financial Memorandum.*
[35] *Education Commission of the Episcopal Commission Response to the Education Bill,* 19 February 1997, unpublished.
[36] Bishop Thomas Flynn, interview with author, 12 March 1997.

sense to bring about a state 'takeover' of Irish education but to achieve a balance between the rights and responsibilities of all the partners in a pluralistic system.[37] The fact that the minister felt forced to officially deny any suggestion of a state takeover was a reflection of how far and how fast she had lost the consensus in the debate about governance and management of schools.

The Association of Management of Catholic Secondary Schools drew up a lengthy series of amendments that would have had the effect of curtailing the minister's powers in relation to Education Boards and boards of management. The amendments would have restored powers to the Patrons – the AMCSS also felt the Patrons were being sidelined by the Bill.[38]

The Church of Ireland Board of Education argued that the Bill was short on principle but provided quite considerable discretionary powers to the Minister for Education. It objected to what it regarded as the 'statutory takeover' of a school by a board of management, because it was clear that the Patron could not veto or otherwise interfere with a decision of the board. Its language was unusually emotive:

> We take the view that the minister has failed to honour the several assurances given concerning the future security of Church schools and especially those of the minority community. The provisions of the Bill in which the mandate of a board of management is derived from the legislation rather than from the Patron is contrary to the word and spirit of the White Paper and represents a breach of faith.[39]

Legal opinions

A battery of legal experts entered the fray over the following few weeks and many insisted that the Bill was unconstitutional in parts. The first person to raise doubts about the constitutionality of the Bill was Michael McDowell SC – a TD with the Progressive

[37] Minister for Education, *Press Release re. Education Bill,* 12 March 1997.
[38] Association of Management of Catholic Secondary Schools, *Education Bill 1997 – A Response,* February 1997.
[39] Church of Ireland Board of Education, *Education Bill 1997 – Submission to the Minister for Education,* March 1997, unpublished.

Democrats – in an article in the *Irish Independent* the day after the
Education Bill was published.[40] This prompted a reply from the
minister which was not published due to an editorial decision that
it was not suitable for publication because it did not add anything
new to the debate.[41] The reply basically argued that the minister
had the necessary powers to prescribe a core curriculum as well as
to freeze funds to schools that refused to establish boards of
management, and it denied that what was proposed amounted to
state control of education. The minister wrote as follows:

> The interpretation of the constitution is a matter for the higher
> courts so I do not intend to engage in debate on what are highly
> speculative views. They are all the more speculative as the relevant
> constitutional provisions have been subject to relatively little
> interpretation by the High and Supreme Courts.

Apart from the fact that the Bill had been drawn up with the
assistance of the department's own legal adviser it is known that
the Bill was cleared by the Attorney General's office before
publication as is the case in all government Bills.[42] This did not
prevent the various groups from seeking opinions elsewhere. One
of those whose opinion was sought was the respected lecturer at
TCD and member of the Constitution Review Group, Gerard Hogan.
The querist in this case was Padraig O'Shea, principal and owner
of St Joseph's College, Borrisoleigh, Co. Tipperary. Hogan advised
that it was difficult to see how key sections of the Bill could survive
constitutional challenge. Practically every managerial decision was
to be vested in the board of management which could, in theory,
dismiss an owner/principal of a school such as St Joseph's. The
state was constitutionally required to ensure that all children received
a certain minimum education advised Hogan who added:

> While views may differ about the desirability of boards of
> management, it is difficult to see how even their most ardent
> supporters would contend that the existence of such boards is
> objectively necessary to ensure that proper educational standards

---

[40] *Irish Independent,* 8 January 1997.
[41] Minister for Education, *Draft Reply to Article by Michael McDowell SC,* January 1997, unpublished.
[42] Department of Education sources.

are maintained. Querist's school – and dozens of other schools – have functioned perfectly well without the benefit of a board of management. Accordingly, it is difficult to see how such a far-reaching interference with Querist's property rights could be justified in the circumstances by the need to maintain and preserve educational standards.[43]

The opinion obtained by the Catholic bishops also suggested that the threat to freeze funding to schools that refused to establish boards was unconstitutional. The opinion furnished by George Brady SC further suggested that even the constitutionality of the section dealing with the right of the minister to prescribe a core curriculum must be in question.

> In Section 42 (c) of the Bill there is a provision that a school shall provide 'social, personal and health education for students'. If that were to mean, or to include, sex education – having regard to the economic realities of present day life, and the options which parents have in relation to the schooling of their children, it appears to me that provision could also be contrary to the provisions of Article 42 of the Constitution.[44]

Changes in the draft Bill

So what had gone wrong? Was the much vaunted consensus so fragile that it could splinter at the first real difficulty? More importantly, what had changed from the earlier draft which, as we have seen, was very favourably disposed towards the denominational schools?

By this stage the Catholic Church had been unofficially furnished with a copy of the earlier draft and it was obvious to the Church representatives that the Bill had undergone a metamorphosis.[45] From the Church's point of view the legal provision initially afforded to protect the ethos of its schools through its veto on teacher appointments was removed entirely and transferred to the Employment Equality Bill. A campaign was underway to oppose sections of that Equality Bill (see below) and this worried the Churches. They were

---

[43] Gerard Hogan, *Education Bill 1997 – Opinion of Counsel*, 4 March 1997, unpublished.
[44] George Brady, *Opinion re. Education Bill*, 27 January 1997, unpublished.
[45] Off-the-record information.

also concerned at what they saw as the excessive degree of control proposed for the minister and for the Education Boards.

In March 1997 all of the main Protestant and Catholic Church groups met to publicly denounce the Bill and were photographed with the head of the Muslim community, Mr Yahha Al-Hussein, in the grounds of the Church of Ireland college of education in Dublin.[46] *The Irish Times* rightly referred to the meeting as an unprecedented coalition of religious interests against the Education Bill. Two days later the Catholic bishops, following their Spring meeting in Maynooth, issued a statement saying that if the Bill became law it would result in the creation of a system of education which was not consistent with the religious and cultural values of the vast majority of Irish people.[47] The leader of the Progressive Democrats, Mary Harney, issued a statement the same day claiming that the minister was 'hell-bent on wrecking the education system'.[48]

The following month the annual education conferences at Easter 1997 saw strong criticism of the Bill, particularly at the ASTI convention. The criticism was summed up in one *Irish Times* heading 'Delegates queue up to vent their anger at Bill'.[49] The criticism was not quite so trenchant at the other union conferences but the Bill was warmly welcomed by the National Parents' Council (Primary) conference held that same weekend.[50] The chairperson, Brian Foy, welcomed in particular the section promising a complaints procedure whereby parents and students aged sixteen and upwards could appeal against decisions that materially affected the education of the students. This had caused some concern to teachers, especially secondary teachers. An indication of the tensions generated by the Bill came in the reaction of the INTO delegate at the top table on the opening night of the parents' conference; the delegate had to be dissuaded privately from walking out in protest against the chairperson's comments.[51] The chairperson had spoken at some length on the issue of trust between the partners in education and said, *inter alia,*

---

[46] *Irish Independent* and *The Irish Times,* 11 March 1997.
[47] *Irish Independent* and *The Irish Times,* 13 March 1997.
[48] Ibid.
[49] *The Irish Times,* 3 April 1997.
[50] *Irish Independent,* 5 April 1997.
[51] Off-the-record information given to author at the conference, 4 April 1997.

> We parents rightly place enormous trust in our teachers – they have earned that trust and they will continue to enjoy our trust. I wish, though, that their leadership would show equal trust in parents. I refer to their reactions to the establishment of a complaints procedure. It is ungracious to claim that parents will clog the system with nuisance complaints.[52]

Fortunately, an embarrassing protest was averted but this author was left in no doubt about the feelings of the INTO representative. A walk-out would have added to the difficulties facing the minister who was present and who had spent all week vigorously defending her Bill at the teachers' conferences. Interestingly, she choose the venue of the parents' conference to announce the first of a series of amendments to the Education Bill, namely the inclusion of the National Council for Curriculum and Assessment in the Bill, giving it a formal advisory role – its absence from the Bill had been remarked on by several critics.

By that time her officials had prepared other amendments designed to take the heat out of the controversy surrounding her Bill. One in particular would have strengthened the role of the Patrons as owners of the schools.[53] Her amendments were announced the following month, some sixty in all.[54] The age at which pupils could appeal school decisions was to be raised to eighteen in the amendments, which also proposed to strengthen and make more explicit the powers of the Patrons of schools. Boards of management would be accountable to the Patron for upholding a school's 'characteristic spirit'. A further amendment stated that the composition of school boards of management must be agreed between the Patrons or owners, national parents' bodies, teacher unions and the minister. School boards were to be given the sole power to suspend or dismiss a teacher in accordance with procedures agreed with the minister, the Patron and the recognised trade union. There would be no role in this regard for the Education Boards. The Catholic Primary School Managers' Association welcomed the amendments which made the role of the Patrons

[52] *Irish Independent*, 5 April 1997.
[53] Off-the-record discussions with Department of Education officials.
[54] *The Irish Times*, 23 April 1997.

more explicit.[55] But it was becoming obvious at this stage that time was running out for the Bill in view of the imminence of the, as yet undeclared, general election.

School governance

By that stage the minister's timetable was hopelessly out of kilter. Even the hoped-for changes in primary school boards had not yet materialised despite the fact that the minister had hailed an 'historic agreement' on the composition of boards in November 1996.[56] That agreement was the result of two years of negotiations and discussion among the education partners under the facilitation of Dr Tom McCarthy from TCD. Instead of an inbuilt voting majority for the owners of schools it allowed for equal representation for parents, teachers, owners and the wider community. The change was in return for the statements guaranteeing the ethos of schools, which have been examined in the chapter on school governance. The INTO raised doubts about aspects of the agreement which seemed to empower the Church of Ireland to refuse access to pupils of other religions or none.

The impression had been given by the minister that all was well with the governance document but three weeks later she announced that as part of the process of consideration she had referred the agreement to the office of the Attorney General for advice on its 'format, constitutionality and general legality, prior to submitting an agreement to government for approval'.[57] This, of course, caused some confusion and led to further delays in establishing boards of management in primary schools. Inevitably, it took longer than expected to get the advice from the over-worked office of the Attorney General and in the meantime the political clock was ticking away. By the time the word came through from the Attorney General's office that the agreement was generally in order it was too late for the minister to make much political capital from it and

---

[55] *Irish Independent,* 23 April 1997.
[56] Minister for Education, *Press Release re. A New and Stronger Partnership in the Running of Our Schools,* 28 November 1996.
[57] Minister for Education, *Press Release re. Governance of Primary Schools,* 11 December 1996.

she indicated that she was recommending that the new elections for the school boards be held in the Autumn. She also indicated that the matter would not be going back to cabinet until the Supreme Court had ruled on the Equal Status Bill. This was because of fears that the court might rule it unconstitutional as it had done with parts of the Employment Equality Bill.[58]

Employment Equality Bill

The Churches, as we have seen, were very concerned at the campaign of opposition to parts of the Employment Equality Bill which was circulated in July 1996.[59] The Bill basically sought to outlaw discrimination at work but religious, educational and medical institutions run by religious bodies would be allowed to discriminate where this was 'essential for the maintenance of the religious ethos or is reasonable to avoid offending the religious sensitivities of its members or clients'.

The teachers' unions waged a concerted campaign to have this section deleted on the grounds that it was a charter for schools to interfere in the private lives of teachers. The Catholic and Protestant Churches were very concerned about this campaign and the Secretary of the Church of Ireland Board of Education, David Meredith, warned that amending or withdrawing Section 37 (1) from the Bill would undermine the governance of primary schools and would begin to unravel years of work. 'It would also test our patience significantly', he wrote.[60]

The government, however, agreed to amend the Bill at the end of January following consultations between Minister Mervyn Taylor and other ministers and the Attorney General.[61] The new provision stated that

> a religious, educational or medical institution which is under the direction or control of a body established for religious purposes or whose objectives include the provision of services in an environment which promotes certain religious values shall not be taken to

[58] Briefing with Minister for Education, 18 May 1997.
[59] *The Irish Times,* 4 July 1996.
[60] *The Irish Catholic,* 5 December 1996.
[61] Department of Equality and Law Reform, *Press Release,* 29 January 1997.

discriminate against a person for the purpose of this Part of Part 11 if, (a) it gives more favourable treatment, on the religion ground, to an employee or a prospective employee over that person where it is reasonable to do so in order to maintain the religious ethos of the institution; or (b) it takes action which is reasonably necessary to prevent an employee or a prospective employee from under-mining the ethos of the institution.

The minister said that this brought out expressly the possibility, reflecting existing broadly accepted practices, of institutions giving preference to their co-religionists. He said, however, that the new version was drafted to make clear that schools and other denomi-national bodies were included in the Bill and that claims could be brought and would be decided on by an independent Director of Equality Investigations. The ethos provision was therefore not a bar to the making of a claim, but rather a reply to a claim which would be raised by an institution in proceedings before the Director of Equality Investigations.[62]

Both the INTO and the TUI described the revisions as unaccep-table[63] but the Bill was passed in the Dáil in early February with the support of Fianna Fáil and the Progressive Democrats. Helen Keogh, the PD spokesperson on education, told the House that it was reasonable to expect that religious ethos be maintained. 'I have a great deal of sympathy with the minister. You would want the wisdom of Solomon to be correct on this one'.[64]

The following day a ginger group called Teachers for Pluralism in Education held a press conference to denounce the Bill and to pledge continued opposition.[65] It was attended by a former teacher, Eileen Flynn, whose dismissal from a Co. Wexford secondary school in 1982 was a *cause célèbre* at the time. Ms Flynn, who had had a relationship with a married man and who had become pregnant, was sacked because her lifestyle was not in keeping with the ethos and mores of the school that she had worked in. Her dismissal was upheld three years later in the High Court by Mr Justice Declan Costello.[66] There was rich irony in her decision to appear at the

---

[62] Ibid.

[63] TUI and INTO, *Press Releases*, 29 January 1997.

[64] *The Irish Times*, 6 February 1997.

[65] *Irish Independent*, 7 February 1997.

[66] *The Irish Times*, 9 February 1985.

press conference, given that the Bill would copperfasten in an Act employment practices which had led to her dismissal a decade and a half earlier. She told the media that she was amazed that fifteen years after she was dismissed 'the bishops are still the power players on the chess board'.[67]

The amended Bill got through both houses of the Oireachtas with the support of the main opposition parties but, somewhat unexpectedly, President Robinson decided to refer it to the Supreme Court to test its constitutionality. The decision was taken following a meeting with the Council of State, whose views she had sought.[68] It was subsequently deemed by the Supreme Court to be unconstitutional, not on the basis of the provisions for schools but on the basis of other provisions in the Bill.[69] This added to the nervousness of the Churches in the run up to the general election and added to the uncertainty over the deal on the governance of schools.

New government – new minister, new Bill

Niamh Bhreathanch was one of the many high-profile Labour Party TDs who lost their seats in the June 1997 election. A combination of good vote management by Fianna Fáil and the general public reaction against the Labour Party cost the minister her seat in the Dun Laoghaire constituency where, ironically, the Progressive Democrats spokesperson on education Helen Keogh also failed to retain her seat. The free fees, as they were called, seemed not to have benefited the Labour Party which lost almost half of its seats in the election.

Breathnach commented afterwards that there were lessons to be drawn from what happened 'once you put your head above the parapet'.[70] She had sought to introduce a very wide range of reforms which, at times, annoyed some of the major stakeholders in education – the teachers and managers. Apart from aspects of her Education Bill, some people were also critical of the manner in

---

[67] *Irish Independent*, 6 February 1997.
[68] *The Irish Times* and *Irish Independent*, 5 April 1997.
[69] *The Irish Times*, 16 May 1997.
[70] Niamh Bhreathnach, interview with author, 8 June 1997.

which she promoted the introduction of Relationships and Sexuality Education in schools. Yet the RSE programme, expensive and extensive though the teacher in-service was, warranted special mention in an OECD report on teacher professional development. The report commented that teachers in general needed to learn to take on new roles, with respect to student wellbeing, that were not only not familiar to them, but also not yet fully legitimised in the eyes of society.[71] Schools had benefited considerably from increased resources over the previous few years. Many of the Dun Laoghaire constituents had also gained from the introduction of free third-level education, but none of these benefits were sufficient to save her seat. A senior Labour Party figure was heard to comment afterwards 'she spent a billion pounds on education in four years – what do you have to do to be elected in this country?' Shortly afterwards, to add insult to injury her own party did not even choose her as one of its nominees for the Seanad elections.

Fergus Finlay, who worked with three governments as adviser to the Labour Party leader Dick Spring, predicted in his book *Snakes and Ladders* that history would record Breathnach as one of the two or three best Ministers for Education the country has ever seen. 'She was swept from her job in a tide of indifference, in a constituency where she had made a profound difference to thousands of families', he wrote.[72]

The place in the history books of the Labour Party's first Education minister would certainly have been more secure had she succeeded in getting her Education Bill on to the statute books. Although she had talked of introducing eight Bills, only two of them – the Universities' Bill and the Youth Work Bill – were enacted by the time Niamh Bhreathnach left office. The Youth Act was effectively inoperable because it was predicated on the introduction of Regional Boards. The Universities' Act, while very important, is not exactly one that will be remembered by the general public – Niamh Bhreathnach must regret that she did not seek to enact her Education Bill first. Had she done so the course of Irish educational

[71] OECD/CERI, *Staying Ahead: In-service Training and Teacher Professional Development,* OECD, Paris, 1998, p. 26.
[72] Fergus Finlay, *Snakes and Ladders,* Dublin, New Island Books, 1998, p. 320.

development could have been much different.

The June 1997 general election saw the return to power of a Fianna Fáil/Progressive Democrat minority government. The new Taoiseach, Bertie Ahern, went against tradition by appointing front bench spokespersons to the portfolios that they had 'shadowed' in opposition. Thus, Micheál Martin was given the education ministry, which he renamed the Department of Education and Science. He proved to be an energetic minister and performed much better in office than he had in opposition where he tended to be somewhat unfocused, at least in some of his earlier encounters with Niamh Bhreathnach.

He was fortunate in coming to office at a time when the public coffers were full and there was a growing acceptance of the importance of preparing people for computer literacy and of education's role in combating exclusion. Thus, one of his earliest achievements was a £250m Education Technology Investment Fund, a three year programme to fund new facilities at institutions around the county. *Schools IT 2000* represented a £55m programme aimed at connecting every primary and second-level school to the internet and providing training in information technologies for most teachers. Specific funding for research and development at third level was also provided by his department for the first time.[73] The three measures were very welcome. They were also essential because multinational companies based in Ireland were beginning to express concern over possible shortages of skilled people for the rapidly expanding electronics and IT sector generally.

The correlation between educational disadvantage and poor performance in the labour market had been demonstrated in a succession of studies at home and abroad and Martin took a number of initiatives including measures to assist those at risk of dropping out early; a £57m disadvantage package; a £6.5m boost for school libraries; a National Educational Psychological service; an increase in intake to colleges of education in order to reduce primary school classes; an offer to purchase all school sites in future in order to reduce the cost on local communities; and the abolition of exam

---

[73] Department of Education and Science, *Press Release on first year of Government*, 26 June 1998.

fees for all families holding a medical card.[74] Such was the hectic pace set by the minister that it was putting strains on the department to deliver on all the announcements he made. This was shown in the response of the unions representing administrative and professional staff in the department's Planning and Building Unit to the announcement in regard to school sites. In January 1999 they pointed out that the capital allocation for first and second-level building projects had almost doubled over the previous four years. This had led to a vastly increased workload and inevitable delays in bringing projects to a conclusion, according to the unions, who claimed that the department had largely ignored requests for staffing levels to be addressed.[75]

In any discussion on educational disadvantage, it is recognised, of course, that early interventions are needed if a person's life chances are to be boosted. This issue was addressed in a Forum on Early Childhood Education which was held in March 1998 along the same lines as the National Education Convention, with contributions by interested parties and questions from an independent secretariat. A report on the Forum was published later that year.[76] The year 1998 also saw the publication of a Green Paper on adult education by Minister of State Willie O'Dea.[77] Adult education has been marginalised to some extent in Ireland by the concentration on the schooling of young people. But it will become increasingly important in the context of lifelong learning, as the European Commission has pointed out, and as a means of combating social exclusion.[78] This latter role for adult education was recognised by the OECD which prepared a report on the role of adult learning in helping to promote inclusion.[79]

---

[74] Ibid.

[75] Public Services Executive Union, *Press Release,* 15 January 1999.

[76] *Report on the National Forum for Early Childhood Education*, Dublin, Stationery Office, 1998.

[77] Department of Education and Science, *Adult Learning in an Era of Lifelong Learning*, Green Paper on Adult Education, Dublin, Stationery Office, 1998.

[78] *European Commission Strategy for Lifelong Learning*, Brussels/Luxembourg, European Commission, 1996.

[79] OECD/CERI, *Overcoming Exclusion: Adult Learning Initiatives that Make a Difference*, Paris, OECD, 1999.

As expected, Micheál Martin made major changes to the Bill that he inherited. We have seen already that the new minister dropped plans for regional education boards, instead opting for executive bodies which would perform functions relating to the provision of support services. This, he said, was in keeping with the spirit of the Public Service Management Act and the Strategic Management Initiative. He also removed the element of compulsion on school owners to set up boards of management; he said that if they failed to establish boards they would be obliged to demonstrate why they had found it impracticable to do so.

The main elements of the Bill as subsequently enacted are that

- it defines clearly the functions of the minister and places an obligation on him/her to ensure that there is available to each person, including every person with a disability or other special educational needs, support services and a level and quality of education appropriate to meet the needs and abilities of that person
- it makes provision for the recognition of schools and the establishment of boards of management in all schools in receipt of public funding. This will ensure that parents, teachers and patrons will have rights under law to be involved in the management of their schools
- it places the inspectorate of the Department of Education and Science on a statutory basis and defines its role and functions
- it sets out the function of school principals and teachers
- it makes provision for procedures for appeals and grievances
- it makes provision for the establishment of a statutory body to promote the teaching of Irish
- it makes provision for the establishment of a committee to advise the minister on strategies to combat educational disadvantage
- it provides a statutory basis for the education support centres and the National Council for Curriculum and Assessment
- it provides a statutory basis for the state examination system
- it contains provisions enabling the minister, with the concurrence of government, to establish statutory bodies to carry out functions in or in relation to the provision of support services.

Martin, somewhat unexpectedly, inserted a section dealing with regulations relating to the operation of state examinations. Penalties were proposed for such acts as leaking of papers or tampering with results. Another clause had the effect of banning the preparation of league tables of comparisons of examination results. There was very little discussion about the latter aspect of the Bill, even though league tables have been a feature of the UK education system for years.

The legislation set out the rights and responsibilities of the various stakeholders. For instance, in regard to students it stated that schools will be obliged to identify and provide for the educational needs of all students, including those with a disability or other special educational needs. It will also be a function of each school to promote equality of opportunity to both male and female students. Each school will publish its policy concerning admission to and participation in the school. The inspectorate may conduct assessments of the educational needs of students in recognised schools and advise the students, their parents and the schools as appropriate. Students aged eighteen and over will have a right of access to their own school records. They will also have the right to appeal to the board of management against a decision of a teacher or member of staff of the school and to the Secretary General of the department against certain actions taken by the board of management. They will not be obliged to attend instruction in any subject contrary to their conscience. The rights of students who are younger than eighteen will, in respect of these matters, be exercised by their parents. Each board of management will establish and maintain procedures for the purposes of informing students in a school of the activities of the school and, in the case of post-primary schools, boards will encourage and give all reasonable assistance to students in the formataion and running of student councils. Student councils will be entitled to receive copies of any reports on the operation and performance of the school produced by the board of management and students will be involved in the preparation of the school plan.

In respect of teachers the legislation states that their representatives will have a statutory right to participation in boards of management. Procedures for the appointment of principals and teachers must be agreed between the minister, the Patron, school management organisations and teacher unions or staff associations. Criteria and procedures for school inspection will be determined following consultation with the partners in education, including representatives of teachers, and inspectors will report to teachers, and the other local partners in education, in relation to the evaluation of schools. Provision will be made for a teacher who is affected by an inspection to request the Chief Inspector to review the inspection. Schools must identify and provide for staff development needs, including the needs of staff involved in the management of the school. Procedures for grievances and appeals procedures will be determined in consultation with teacher representatives. Teachers will be entitled to receive copies of any reports on the operation and performance of the school produced by the board of management and will have access to the school accounts on the same basis as the minister. They will be involved in the preparation of the school plan, copies of which will also be circulated to them.

The Bill provided an obligation on the minister to consult the partners, a provision that was warmly welcomed by the ASTI which said this would copperfasten the place that teachers occupied in regulating education in a way which teachers in other countries could only envy.[80]

In respect of parents the legislation gave statutory recognition to the National Parents' Council. Parents have a statutory right to establish parents' associations in schools and the parents' representatives have a statutory right to participate in boards of management. Parents are entitled to receive copies of any reports on the operation and performance of the school produced by the board of management and have access to the school accounts on the same basis as the minister. Parents will be involved in the preparation of the school plan, copies of which will also be circulated to them. Parents have a right of access to their children's school records. Parents will be consulted in relation to the assessment of the psychological needs of their children and will be advised by the psychologists concerned in relation to the education and psychological development of the children. Parents have the right to appeal to the board of management against a decision of a teacher or member of staff of the school and to the Secretary General of the Department of Education and Science against certain actions taken by the board of management.

---

[80] ASTI, *ASTIR*, Vol. xxx, No 5, January 1999.

In respect of Patrons/owners the legislation gives statutory recognition to the role of Patrons as owners of schools. It states that boards of management will be established by Patrons in a spirit of partnership and the composition of these boards will be subject to agreement by all parties. Each board of management will be required to uphold the characteristic spirit of the school and to consult with and keep the Patron informed of decisions and proposals of the board. Subject to the consent of the minister, a Patron will be entitled either to remove a member of the board of management, for stated reasons, or to dissolve the board, if satisfied that the functions of the board are not being efficiently discharged. Procedures for the appointment of principals and teachers must be agreed between the minister, the Patron, school management organisations and teacher unions or staff associations. Patrons will be involved in the preparation of the school plan, copies of which will also be circulated to them.

In respect of students with disabilities and special educational needs the legislation provides that one of the objects of the Act will be to give practical effect to the constitutional rights of children, including children with a disabililty or other special educational needs. It requires the minister, wherever practicable, to consult with persons representing people with disabilities and other special educational needs. The minister will have to ensure that there is available to each person, including those with a disabililty or special educational needs, an appropriate level and quality of education and appropriate support services. The legislation provides that each school will have to ensure that the educational needs of all students, including those with a disability or other special educational needs, are identified and provided for. It provides that each board must publish the policy of the school concerning admission to and participation in the school by students with disabilities or other special educational needs. It provides that the inspectorate must include persons with expertise in the education of students with special educational needs; it also provides that members of the inspectorate will assess the implementation and effectiveness of any programmes of education which have been devised in respect of students with a disability or other special educational needs; finally, it provides that members of the inspectorate will advise recognised schools on policies and strategies for the education of children with special educational needs. The legislation also provides for the minister to make regulations regarding access to schools and centres for education by students with a disability or other special educational needs, including matters relating to reasonable accommodation and technical aid and equipment for such students.

In respect of educational disadvantage the legislation provides for the minister to set up a committee to advise him/her on policies and strategies to combat educational disadvantage. The minister will consult with the education partners prior to establishing the committee and the membership will be appointed from nominees of the relevant voluntary and other bodies. It defines educational disadvantage as meaning the impediments to education arising from social or economic disadvantage which prevent students from deriving appropriate benefit from education in schools.

Overall, it was a much less controversial Bill than the one the minister had inherited. It was seen as more teacher-friendly and perhaps less parent-friendly, but his supporters would argue that all he was doing was restoring the balance that was needed. The Bill took almost a year before it got through all stages of the Oireachtas. It received much less media attention than Niamh Bhreathnach's Bill partly, it must be said, because the revised version was much less controversial. Nevertheless, it remains the most significant piece of legislation enacted for the educational system, which was put on a statutory basis for the first time. The Education Bill was finally signed into law on 23 December 1998.

Conclusions

It is too early to assess the effects of the Education Act or indeed of the flurry of announcements made by Micheál Martin since coming to office. Critics argue that there are similarities between what was happening in the late nineties and the late eighties when there was a lot of activity on different fronts but no sense of overall direction. These critics argue that the earlier versions of the Education Bill would have allowed the department to divest itself of much day-to-day activity and give it over to Education Boards, thus allowing the centre to concentrate on mapping out strategic developments for the education system as a whole. Supporters of the Act accept that the department is overburdened but argue that once the executive agency idea is embedded into the system this will have the same effect of freeing up a revamped department to play such a role.

Getting the Bill onto the statute books was an achievement in itself. The length of time the process took – almost a decade – is an indication of just how difficult it is to bring about major reform in an education system. The process involved a succession of ministers who were directly involved – Mary O'Rourke, Noel Davern, Séamus Brennan, Niamh Bhreathnach and Micheál Martin. Much has been achieved in that time – the roles and responsibilities of the various stakeholders are clearer; there is a new system of middle management in secondary schools; there is acceptance of the need to target educational disadvantage; representative boards are accepted by the vast majority of school owners; in-career programmes are recognised as part of the professional development of teachers; different types of educational experiences have been introduced to cater for a wider range of abilities; classes have become smaller; the necessary investment has begun in the infrastructure of school buildings and in IT hardware.

For decades much of the debate about Irish education had been dominated by issues of structure, ownership and control of schools. Now, however, the principle of partnership has become firmly rooted in the educational landscape. The partners have been involved in the formulation of policies, beginning with early childhood education, stretching through the primary and post-primary sectors into further, higher and adult education. Now there are opportunities to dwell on issues that are assuming greater importance, issues such as quality of education, curriculum development, professionalism, equality and equity, accountability, democracy, pluralism, lifelong learning, and the impact of information technologies on teaching and learning. To successfully meet the challenge of change in the new millennium teachers need to become reflective practitioners and their schools need to become learning organisations. The beneficiaries of the reforms that are still taking place and the opportunities provided by those reforms should be the very people for whom the education system was created in the first place — the students.

Bibliography

Government and other official publications

Akenson, Donald Harman, *A Mirror to Kathleen's Face: Education in Independent Ireland 1922-1960*, Montreal and London, McGill-Queen's University Press, 1975.

Alvey, David, *The Case for Secular Reform*, Dublin and Belfast, Church and State Books in conjunction with Athol Books, 1991.

Atkinson Norman, *Irish Education, A History of Educational Institutions*, Dublin, Allen Figgis, 1969.

Bell, Robert and Grant, Nigel, *Patterns of Education in the British Isles*, London, Unwin Education Books, 1977.

Brown, Alice and Fairley, John, *Restructuring Education in Ireland: The Question of Sub-National Structures*, Commissioned by the Association of Chief Executive Officers of VECs, acting as a reference group for the Irish Vocational Education Association, published by the VECs for Cork city and county, Kerry and Tralee, 1992.

Bunreacht na hÉireann, Constitution of Ireland, Dublin, Stationery Office.

Clancy, Patrick, *Access to College: Patterns of Continuity and Change*, Dublin, Higher Education Authority, 1995.

Clancy, Patrick, *Participation in Higher Education*, Dublin, Higher Education Authority, 1982.

Clancy, Patrick, *Who Goes to College?* Dublin, Higher Education Authority, 1988.

Clancy, Patrick, Drudy, Sheelagh, Lynch, Kathleen and O'Dowd, Liam (Eds), *Irish Society: Sociological Perspectives*, Dublin, Institute of Public Administration in association with the Sociological Association of Ireland, 1995.

CMRS Education Commission, *Inequality in Schooling in Ireland: The Role of Selective Entry and Placement*, Dublin, CMRS, September 1989.

CMRS Education Commission, *Local Education Committees. A Case for their Establishment and a Tentative Proposal,* Dublin, CMRS, January 1993.

Commission on Adult Education, *Lifelong Learning,* Dublin, Stationery Office, 1984.

Commission on School Accommodation Needs, *Report of the Technical Working Group: Rationalisation of Vocational Education Committees,* June 1996.

Commission on the Points System, *Consultative Process – Background Document,* Dublin, Stationery Office, 1998.

Comptroller and Auditor General, *General Report: Education Sector, Matters Arising out of Audit of 1995 Accounts,* Dublin, Stationery Office, 1997.

Coolahan John, *Irish Education: History and Structure,* Dublin, Institute of Public Administration, 1981.

Coolahan, John (Ed.), *Issues and Strategies in the Implementation of Educational Policy,* Maynooth, Education Department, St Patrick's College, 1995.

Coolahan, John and McGuinness, Séamus (Eds), *Report on the Round-table Discussions in Dublin Castle on the Minister for Education's Position Paper 'Regional Education Councils',* June 1994.

Coolahan, John (Ed.), *Report on the National Education Convention,* Dublin, National Education Convention Secretariat, 1994.

Coolahan, John, *Background Paper for the National Education Convention, 11-21 October 1993,* NEC Secretariat.

CORI Education Commission, *Religious Congregations in Irish Education – A role for the future?* Dublin, CORI, November 1997.

CORI Education Commission, *The Future of Trusteeship: a Review of some Options for the Way Forward,* Dublin, CORI Education Commission, 1997.

Department of Education and Science, *Adult Learning in an Era of Lifelong Learning,* Green Paper on Adult Education, Dublin, Stationery Office, November 1998.

Department of Education and Science, *Memorandum for the Government – New Third-Level Institution at Blanchardstown,* 29 June 1998, released under the Freedom of Information Act.

Department of Education and Science, *Report of the Steering Committee on the Establishment of a Teachers' Council,* Dublin,

Stationery Office, 1998.

Department of Education, *Charting our Education Future*, White Paper on Education, Dublin, Stationery Office, 1995.

Department of Education, *Education Bill, 1997. Explanatory and Financial Memorandum*, 1997.

Department of Education, *Education for a Changing World*, Green Paper on Education, Dublin, Stationery Office, June 1992.

Department of Education, *Introduction to Green Paper*, 21 April 1992.

Department of Education, *Partners in Education: Serving Community Needs*, Green Paper, November 1985.

Department of Education, *Position Paper on Proposals for University Legislation*, November 1995.

Department of Education, *Position Paper on Regional Education Councils*, March 1994.

Department of Education, *Position Paper on the Governance of Schools*, July 1994.

Department of Education, *Report of the Review Body of the Primary Curriculum*, Dublin, Stationery Office, 1990.

Department of Education, *Rules for National Schools*, Dublin, Stationery Office, 1965.

Department of Education, *Statistical Report*, Dublin, Stationery Office, various years.

Department of Education, *The Restructured Curriculum for Second-Level Schools*, Department of Education, 1996.

Department of Education, *White Paper on Educational Development*, Dublin, Stationery Office, 1980.

Department of Enterprise and Employment, *Economic Status of School Leavers*, Dublin, Stationery Office, various years.

Drudy, Sheelagh and Lynch, Kathleen, *Schools and Society in Ireland*, Dublin, Gill and Macmillan, 1993.

European Commission, *Strategy for Lifelong Learning*, Brussels/Luxembourg, Office for Official Publications of the European Commission, 1996.

European Commission, *Teaching and Learning; Towards the Learning Society*, Brussels/Luxembourg, Office for Official Publications of the European Commission, 1995.

Farren, Sean, *The Politics of Irish Education 1920-65*, Belfast, the Queen's University of Belfast, Institute of Irish Studies, 1995.

Fianna Fáil and Labour, *Programme for a Partnership Government,* January 1993.

Fianna Fáil, *Education – A Fianna Fáil Position Paper,* Fianna Fáil, May 1997.

Fine Gael, *Action Programme for Education in the 80s,* November 1980.

Fine Gael, The Labour Party, Democratic Left, *A Government of Renewal,* December 1994.

Finlay, Fergus, *Snakes and Ladders,* Dublin, New Island Books, 1998.

Government of Ireland, *Ireland – National Development Plan 1994-1999,* Dublin, Stationery Office, 1993.

Government of Ireland, *Programme for Competitiveness and Work,* Dublin, Stationery Office, 1994.

Greaney, Vincent and Kellaghan, Tom, *Equality of Opportunity in Irish Schools,* Dublin, Educational Company, 1984.

Hannan, Damian and Boyle, Maura, *Schooling Decisions: The Origins and Consequences of Selection and Streaming in Irish Post-Primary Schools,* Dublin, ESRI, General Series, Paper No 136, November 1987.

Hannan, Damian, et al. *Schooling and Sex Roles: Sex Differences in Subject Process and Student Choice in Irish Post-Primary Schools,* Dublin, ESRI, General Series, Paper No 113, 1986.

Hannan, Damian, McCabe, Breda and McCoy, Selina, *Trading Qualifications for Jobs: Overeducation and the Irish Youth Labour Market,* Dublin, Oak Tree Press in association with the ESRI, 1998.

Healy, Seán and Reynolds, Brigid, *Social Policy in Ireland,* Dublin, Oak Tree Press, 1998.

Higher Education Authority, *Annual Report of First Destination of Award Recipients in Higher Education,* Dublin, Higher Education Authority, various years.

Hyland, Áine and Milne, Kenneth, *Irish Educational Documents,* Dublin, Church of Ireland College of Education, 1987 and 1992.

Investment in Education – annexes and appendices, Dublin, Stationery Office, 1966.

Investment in Education – Report of the Survey Team, Dublin, Stationery Office, 1966.

Kearney, Richard (Ed.), *Migrations: The Irish at Home and Abroad,*

Dublin, Wolfhound Press, 1990.

Labour Party, *Socialist Principles in Education: A Discussion Document*, February 1985.

Lee, Joe, *Ireland 1912-1985: Politics and Society*, Cambridge, Cambridge University Press, 1989.

Lynch, Kathleen and O'Riordan, Claire, *Social Class, Inequality and Higher Education: Barriers to Equality of Access and Participation among School Leavers*, Dublin, Equality Studies Centre, UCD, 1996.

Lynch, Kathleen, *The Hidden Curriculum*, London, The Falmer Press, 1989.

Mac Greíl, Micheál, *Educational Opportunity in Dublin*, Maynooth, Research and Development Unit, 1974.

Making Knowledge Work For Us, Report of the Science, Technology and Innovation Advisory Council, Dublin, Stationery Office, 1995.

McElligott, T. J., *Secondary Education in Ireland 1870-1921*, Dublin, Irish Academic Press, 1981.

McNamara, Gerry, Williams, Kevin, and Herron, Donald (Eds), *Achievement and Aspiration: Curricular Initiatives in Irish Post-Primary Education in the 1980s*, Dublin, Drumcondra Teachers' Centre, 1990.

Mulcahy, D.G., *Curriculum and Policy in Irish Post-Primary Education*, Dublin, Institute of Public Administration, 1981.

National Economic and Social Council, *A strategy for Competitiveness, Growth and Employment*, Dublin, NESC, Dublin Castle, November 1993.

National Economic and Social Council, *Education and Training Policies for Economic and Social Development*, Dublin, NESC, Dublin Castle, October 1993.

National Economic and Social Forum, *Early School Leaving and Youth Unemployment*, Dublin, National Economic and Social Forum, 1997.

National Planning Board, *Proposals for Plan 1984-8*, Dublin, Stationery Office,1984.

National Youth Policy Committee, *Final Report*, Dublin, Stationery Office, 1984.

Ó Buachalla, Séamas, *Education Policy in Twentieth-Century Ireland*, Dublin, Wolfhound Press, 1988.

O'Connor, Pat, *Emerging Voices – Women in Contemporary Irish*

Society, Dublin, Institute of Public Administration, 1998.

O'Connor, Sean, *A Troubled Sky: Reflections on the Irish Education Scene 1957-1968,* Dublin, Educational Research Centre, St Patrick's College, Drumcondra, 1986.

O'Flaherty, Louis, *Management and Control in Irish Education: the Post-Primary Experience,* Dublin, Drumcondra Teachers' Centre, 1992.

OECD, *Education at a Glance, OECD Indicators,* OECD, Paris, various years.

OECD, *Reviews of National Policies for Education Ireland,* Paris, OECD, 1991.

OECD/CERI, *Decision Making in 14 OECD Education Systems,* Paris, OECD, 1995.

OECD/CERI, *Overcoming Exclusion: Adult Learning Initiatives that make a Difference,* Paris, OECD, 1999.

OECD/CERI, *Parents as Partners in Education,* Paris, OECD, 1997.

OECD/CERI, *Staying Ahead; In-service Training and Teacher Professional Development,* OECD, Paris, 1998.

Osborne, R.D. and Fisher, N.A., *Recent Developments in Third-Level Education in the Republic of Ireland,* Research Paper No 4, Centre for Policy Research, Northern Ireland, June 1992.

Programme for Government, December 1982.

Programme for National Recovery, October 1987

Randles, Eileen, *Post-Primary Education in Ireland 1957-1970,* Dublin, Veritas Publications, 1975.

Report of the Advisory Committee on Third-Level Student Support, Dublin, Stationery Office, 1993.

Report of the CIRCA Group Europe, *A Comparative International Assessment of the Organisation, Management and Funding of University Research in Ireland and Europe,* Dublin, Higher Education Authority, December 1996.

Report of the Committee on In-service Education, Dublin, Stationery Office, 1984.

Report of the Comptroller and Auditor General, *Procurement in Universities,* Dublin, Stationery Office, 1996.

Report of the Constitution Review Group, Dublin, Stationery Office, 1996.

Report of the Expert Advisory Group on Relationships and Sexuality Education, 1994.

Report of the High-level Group to advise on the Technological Sector, May 1997.

Report of the International Review Group to the Higher Education Authority – review of the application by the Dublin Institute of Technology for establishment as a university under Section 9 of the Universities Act 1997, Dublin, Review Group, 1998.

Report of the Primary Education Review Body, Dublin, Stationery Office, 1990.

Report of the Special Education Review Committee, Special Education Review Committee, Dublin, Stationery Office, 1993.

Report of the Steering Committee on the Future Development of Higher Education, Dublin, Higher Education Authority, June 1995.

Report on The National Forum for Early Childhood Education, Dublin, Stationery Office, 1998.

Revised Teachers' PCW Proposals, December 1996. *Responding to Ireland's Growing Skills Needs: The First Report of the Expert Group on Future Skills Needs to the Tánaiste and the Minister for Education and Science,* 1998.

School Attendance/Truancy Report, Department of Education Working Group, Dublin, Department of Education, 1994.

Sexton, J.J. and O'Connell, P.J. (Eds), *Labour Market Studies: Ireland,* Brussels/Luxembourg, Office for Official Publications of the European Commission, 1997.

Study on Governance and Management Structures of Irish Universities, Report by Deloitte and Touche, Dublin, Higher Education Authority, September 1997.

TEASTAS – the Irish National Certification Authority, *First Report,* January 1997.

Technical Working Group, *Interim Report of the Steering Committee's Technical Working Group,* Dublin, Higher Education Authority, 1995.

The Report of the Industrial Policy Review Group, *A Time for Change, Industrial Policy for the 1990s,* Dublin, Stationery Office, 1992.

Titley, E. Brian, *Church, State and the Control of Schooling in Ireland 1900-1944,* Queen's University Press/ Gill and Macmillan, 1983.

Tussing, A. Dale, *Irish Educational Expenditure; Past, Present and Future,* Dublin, Economic and Social Research Institute, 1978.

Westmeath VEC, Report of the Inspector appointed Pursuant to

Bibliography 217

Section 11 of the Vocational Education Act 1930, Department of Education, September 1994.

Whyte, John, *Church and State in Modern Ireland, 1923-1980,* Dublin, Gill and Macmillan, 1981.

Unpublished source material

Brady, George SC, *Opinion re. Education Bill,* 27 January 1997.

Confidential Note for the Taoiseach on University Legislation, 31 October 1995.

Department of Education, Draft Green Paper, 25 October 1991.

Department of Education, Draft Green Paper, 29 January 1992.

Department of Education, Draft Green Paper, 8 June 1992.

Department of Education, *Draft heads of The Education (Education Boards and Boards of Management) Bill,* 1995.

Department of Education, *Education Green Paper 1992: List of Submissions,* 1993.

Department of Education, *Minutes of first Meeting of Committee on Regionalisation,* 19 October, 1973.

Department of Education, *Minutes of Meeting of Committee on Regionalisation,* 11 January 1974.

Department of Education, *Minutes of Meeting of Committee on Regionalisation,* 9 November 1973.

Department of Education, *Minutes of Meeting of Committee on Regionalisation,* 27 November 1973.

Department of Education, *Minutes of Meeting with Minister for Education,* 3 October 1973.

Department of Education, *Position Paper on University Legislation,* July 1995.

Department of Education, *Programme for Action in Education 1984-1987,* Dublin, Stationery Office, 1984.

Department of Education, *Regionalisation of the Education Sector, Analysis and Recommendations,* 1974.

Department of Education, *Summary of Main Issues – What the Partners are Saying,* 1993.

Department of Education, *Tuarscáil shealadach ón Choiste a cuireadh i mbun scrúdú a dhéanamh ar Oideachas Iarbhunscoile,* December 1962.

Department of Education, *Whole School Inspection Discussion*

Document, March 1996.

DIT, *Memorandum to all Staff,* issued by Declan Glynn, Director of External Affairs, 21 November 1996.

Dundalk Regional Technical College, *Study on Transfer and Output Rates,* 1997.

Episcopal Commission, *Education Commission – Response to the Education Bill,* 19 February 1997.

Gallagher, Paul SC, *Legal Opinion for UCD,* 21 October 1996.

Hogan, Gerard SC, *Education Bill, 1997 Opinion of Counsel,* 4 March 1997.

Irish Vocational Education Association/Secretariat of Secondary Schools, *Letter to Minister for Education,* 4 February 1997.

Minister for Education, *Memorandum to Government,* 31 March 1995.

National Council for Curriculum and Assessment, *The Junior Cycle Review Committee, Progress Report: Issues and Options for Development,* Draft Report, National Council for Curriculum and Assessment, 1998.

Presentation Provincialate, *Letter to Principals and Chairpersons of Boards of Management,* 15 February 1993.

Report of the Academic Council Group, UCC, October 1996.

Report of the Interim Review Group on the Cork Institute of Technology,

Report of the Interim Review Group on the Waterford Institute of Technology.

Report of the International Review Team, *Review of Quality Assurance Procedures in the Dublin Institute of Technology,* June 1996.

Rooney, Joe, *Confidential Letter to VECs,* Irish Vocational Education Association, 21 October 1994.

Secretariat of Catholic Secondary Schools, *Letter to Managerial Associations and other Church-linked School Organisations,* 23 November 1973.

Secretariat of Catholic Secondary Schools, *Minutes of Meeting of Church Management Bodies,* 12 October 1974.

Secretariat of Catholic Secondary Schools, *Report of Minister's Meeting on Regionalisation,* 3 October 1973.

Secretariat of Secondary Schools, *Newsletters,* various dates.

Working Party from the Episcopal Commission on Education, *Report*

on Regionalisation of our Education Structure, presented to the
Episcopal Conference, June 1982.

Working Party on the Future Role of the Religious in Education,
*The Future Involvement of Religious in Education: The 'FIRE'
Report,* February 1973.

Other material used

Annual reports for AMCSS, CPSMA, IVEA, NPC, teacher unions, etc.

Church of Ireland, *General Synod: Reports.*

Dáil and Seanad reports.

Department of Education estimates for proposed Education Boards
– laid in the Oireachtas Library in May 1998.

Internal newsletters from various organisations.

Legal opinions obtained by various organisations.

Press releases from unions, managerial and parental organisations,
NCEA, Church bodies, political parties and other organisations.

Responses to Green Paper and Education Bill by various organisations.

Speeches by ministers, managerial body representatives, parents'
representatives, teacher union leaders, university presidents, etc.

Submissions to National Education Convention, round-table
discussions on regionalisation and school governance, Review
Body on Teachers' Pay, etc.

Newspapers and periodicals

Administration
ASTIR
Decision Maker
Education Matters
Education Times
Education Today
Eolas
Irish Independent
Issues in Education
Oideas
Science
Solus

Studies in Education
Studies
Sunday Independent
The Argus
The European Journal of Education
The Examiner
The Irish Catholic
The Irish Journal of Education
The Irish News
The Irish Press
The Irish Times
The Secondary Teacher
The Sunday Tribune
The Times Educational Supplement
The Times Higher Education Supplement
Tuarascail

Legislation

Dublin City University Act, 1989
Dublin Institute of Technology Acts, 1992 and 1994
Education Act, 1998
Ministers and Secretaries Act, 1924
National Council for Educational Awards Act, 1979
National University of Ireland Act, 1908
Regional Technical Colleges Act, 1992 and 1994
School Attendance Act, 1926 to 1967
Universities' Act, 1997
University of Dublin Charter, 1591
University of Limerick Act, 1989
Vocational Education Acts, 1930 to 1994
Youth Work Act 1997.

Index